Roman, Runes and Ogham
Medieval Inscriptions in the Insular World
and on the Continent

ROMAN, RUNES AND OGHAM

MEDIEVAL INSCRIPTIONS
IN THE INSULAR WORLD
AND ON THE CONTINENT

Edited by

JOHN HIGGITT
KATHERINE FORSYTH
&
DAVID N. PARSONS

SHAUN TYAS
DONINGTON
2001

© Copyright, 2001, the authors

Typeset and designed by Shaun Tyas
from the discs of John Higgitt

Published by

SHAUN TYAS
(an imprint of 'Paul Watkins')
1 High Street
Donington
Lincolnshire
PE11 4TA

ISBN

1 900289 44 X

Printed and bound in the United Kingdom by the Alden Group, Oxford

CONTENTS

RUNES IN THE BRITISH ISLES, IN SCANDINAVIA AND BEYOND

THE INSULAR WORLD AND THE CONTINENT

EARLY MEDIEVAL ITALY

THE LATER MIDDLE AGES: MONUMENTS AND MASONS

LIST OF TABLES

LIST OF FIGURES

9 cm. (after R. Rachini in Lusuardi Siena, *Arte medievale* 2nd ser., 4.1 (1990), fig. 2), *page 167.*

43 (Mitchell). Inscriptions from painted tomb in S.Ambrogio, Milan (after Fiorio Tedone), *page 169.*

44 (Badham). Monumental brass commemorating Eel Buttry, *ob.* 1545, St Stephen, Norwich. The figure of the lady is a re-use of a plate produced in the London D workshop *c.*1410, combined with a Norwich 6 inscription of *c.*1545, *page 198.*

45 (Badham). Monumental brass commemorating William Twaytis, *ob.* 1499, Drinkstone, Suffolk. Typological analysis of the lettering style reveals that this inscription was produced *c.* 1525 in the Suffolk 2 workshop in Bury St Edmunds operational between *c.* 1515 and 1534, *page 199.*

46 (Badham). Lettering styles employed by the London marblers before the Black Death for brasses and incised slabs, *page 199.*

47 (Badham). Purbeck marble relief cross slab to John Havevile, *ob.* 1303–11, Clothall, Hertfordshire. The inscription on the top surface was inlaid with Main Group brass letters, while the inscription on the chamfer was incised in Ashford style script, *page 200.*

48 (Badham). Operational spans of medieval brass-engraving workshops in England, *page 200.*

49 (Badham). Monumental brass to Richard Howard, *ob.* 1499, and his wife Cecily, Aylsham, Norfolk, produced in the Norwich 3 workshop. The 'split letter' style of majuscules shown on this brass (see the O, H and C) is also found on contemporary Norwich-produced painted windows and screens, *page 201.*

50 (Alexander). Masons' marks (not to scale). (a.)-(d.) Lincoln Cathedral, Angel Choir, mid 13th century. (e.) Knossos, Bronze Age (after Sir Arthur Evans). (f.) Southwell Minster, choir, early 13th century. (g.) Peterborough Cathedral, *c.*1496-1509 (after Davis); Cambridge, King's College Chapel, *c.*1447-9; Lavenham, *c.*1523; Burford, mid fifteenth century (after Davis). (h.) Winchester College, *c.*1437; Ludlow, *c.*1471 (after Davis); Lincoln Cathedral, crossing tower, mid 13th century; Southwell Minster, choir, early 13th century, *page 213.*

51 (Alexander). Assembly marks on the underside of the arches of the bell tower of Saint-Jacques, Reims (after Deneux), *page 215.*

52 (Alexander). Number of strokes used for masons' marks in the choirs of Lincoln Cathedral and Southwell Minster, *page 220.*

LIST OF PLATES

ETERNAL/I | VEDOMALI Reversed As; horizontal Is; minuscule H; horizontal last stroke in R; F-I and L-I ligatures (Carlo Tedeschi).

13 (Tedeschi). Mathry, Pembrokeshire, Wales, Parish Church. [–] | C/VDICCL | FILIUS | C/ATIC|V/VS Greek letter sigma used instead of S for last letter (Carlo Tedeschi).

14 (Tedeschi). Henllan Amgoed, Carmarthenshire, Wales, Parc y Maen. QVENVENDANI | F/IL/I BARCVNI Minuscule Q; horizontal final Is; As with V-shaped cross-bar; B with separated loops; F-I and L-I ligatures (Carlo Tedeschi).

15 (Tedeschi). Lundy Island, Churchyard. – IGERNI | [–]TIGERNI 'Uncial' E (second line); 'half-uncial' Gs; horizontal final Is (Carlo Tedeschi).

16 (Tedeschi). Whitchurch, Flintshire, Wales, Parish Church. HIC IACI/T MVL/I|ER BONA NOBIL/I A with V-shaped cross-bar; trident-shaped M; L-I ligature (Carlo Tedeschi).

17 (Hamlin). Connor, Co. Antrim: inscribed stone now in Ulster Museum (copyright Ulster Museum).

18 (Hamlin). Kirkinriola, Co. Antrim: slab in St Patrick's Church, Ballymena (copyright Ann Hamlin).

19 (Hamlin). Clonca, Co. Donegal: damaged stone built into west wall of church (copyright Ann Hamlin).

20 (Hamlin). Movilla, Co. Down: slab set into wall of Augustinian abbey church (copyright Ann Hamlin).

21 (Hamlin). Aghavea, Co. Fermanagh: inscribed stone now in National Museum of Ireland, Dublin (copyright Ann Hamlin).

22 (Hamlin). Devenish, Co. Fermanagh: recently-recognized fragment (Crown Copyright).

23 (Hamlin). Inishmacsaint, Co. Fermanagh: broken slab with fragment of inscription (Crown Copyright)

24 (Hamlin). Kilcoo I, Co. Fermanagh: slab recently moved into Fermanagh County Museum (Crown Copyright).

25 (Hamlin). Kilcoo II, Co. Fermanagh: broken stone in National Museum of Ireland, Dublin (copyright Ann Hamlin).

26 (Hamlin). White Island, Co. Fermanagh: slab photographed when first found in 1958 (Crown Copyright).

27 (Hamlin). White Island, Co. Fermanagh: slab as set on site (Crown Copyright).

28 (Higgitt). The dedication inscription from Deerhurst, Gloucestershire. Ashmolean Museum, Oxford (copyright Ashmolean Museum, Oxford).

CONTRIBUTORS

Jennifer Alexander	University of Nottingham
Sally Badham	Leafield, Oxfordshire
Michael Barnes	University College London
Jerome Bertram	The Oratory, Oxford
Nick Everett	Clare Hall, Cambridge
Katherine Forsyth	University of Glasgow
Jost Gippert	Universität Frankfurt
Anne Haavaldsen	University of Bergen
Ann Hamlin	Belfast
Mark Handley	University College London
Anthony Harvey	Royal Irish Academy, Dublin
John Higgitt	University of Edinburgh
Katherine Holman	University of Hull
Jeremy Knight	Cardiff
Walter Koch	Universität München
Krzysztof Maciej Kowalski	University of Gdansk
John Mitchell	University of East Anglia
Elisabeth Okasha	University College Cork
Espen Ore	University of Bergen
Ray Page	Corpus Christi College, Cambridge
David Parsons	University of Nottingham
Terje Spurkland	University of Oslo
Carlo Tedeschi	Viterbo

ACKNOWLEDGEMENTS

This book grew out of the International Conference on Medieval Epigraphy: the Insular World and the Continent, which was held in St Hilda's College in Oxford in 1996, and the conference organizers, Katherine Forsyth and John Higgitt, are very grateful for generous financial support from the Humanities Research Board of the British Academy, from the Board of the Faculty of Modern Languages of the University of Oxford, from the Curators of the Taylor Institution (the Fiedler Memorial Trust) of the University of Oxford and from the Trustees of the Rhŷs Fund for the Promotion of Celtic Study and Research of the University of Oxford. These grants contributed greatly to the success of the conference. The conference organizers are also very grateful to many colleagues for their help and advice in setting up the conference, in particular Professor Charles Thomas and Professor Richard Sharpe.

The academic editors would like to thank Caroline Higgitt for her help in bringing order and uniformity both to the format and to the variety of software packages in which papers were submitted and to Rita Winter for sharp-eyed copy-editing. They would also like to thank the publisher, Shaun Tyas, for the sympathetic care with which he has designed the book.

John Higgitt
Katherine Forsyth
David Parsons

The printing of this book is made possible by a gift to the University of Cambridge in memory of Dorothea Coke, Skjaeret, 1951.

CONVENTIONS FOR EDITING INSCRIPTION TEXTS

The following conventions are used in the transcription and transliteration of inscriptions in this volume.

Roman and ogham:
ORATE   legible characters
T   damaged but legible character
[*B*]   character, the reading of which is uncertain because of damage
          or for some other reason

Norse runes:
loþbrok   legible characters
s   damaged but legible character
[*m*]   character, the reading of which is uncertain because of damage
          or for some other reason
∗   legible, but unidentified, character

Anglo-Saxon runes:
'aldred'   legible characters
'*b*'   damaged but legible character
[*c*]   character, the reading of which is uncertain because of damage
          or for some other reason

General:
—   uncertain number of characters lost at beginning or end of the text
[—]   uncertain number of characters lost within the text
[.]   lost (or illegible) character
[..]; [...] two or three characters lost (or illegible), one dot per character
:   punctuation mark of any sort
$\overset{\frown}{ae}$; $\overset{\frown}{TE}$ bind-runes, ligatures etc.
| line break
|| text interrupted by ornament or other feature

Edited texts from the transcriptions or transliterations (and linguistic interpretations) are in italics with expanded abbreviations and restorations in brackets. Translations are in roman and in inverted commas. Thus:

HEREBERICHT $\overline{\text{PRB}}$, *Herebericht pr(es)b(yter)*, 'Herebericht the priest'
ingibiorh:hinfahra:æhkia, *Ingibiǫrg, hin fagra ekkja*, 'Ingibjǫrg, the fair widow'

Introduction

JOHN HIGGITT

This book takes as its subject medieval uses of literacy outside the world of books and documents. During the medieval centuries Latin literacy and books were almost exclusively the province of the church, being employed principally in the education and edification of the clergy and in the performance of the liturgy. This clerical dominance was only seriously challenged in the later Middle Ages. Inscriptions, normally understood as written texts other than those in books and administrative documents and on supports other than vellum, parchment or paper, served a much wider range of functions.[1] When, as often, they were publicly displayed, they could be seen by a much wider section of society than would see the inside of a book. Some medieval inscriptions were products of ecclesiastical learning but the people who commissioned or spoke through inscribed monuments and objects, and the audiences whom the inscriptions addressed, were by no means limited to those trained in Latin literacy. Flourishing traditions of inscriptions in vernacular languages can be found both in the early and in the later Middle Ages. Similarly, in parts of northern Europe other alphabets, runes in some regions where Germanic languages were spoken and ogham in some Gaelic-speaking areas, were in use in the early centuries, and were later sometimes preferred to the Roman alphabet.

Medieval inscriptions have long been studied by those concerned with the past and are already drawn on as historical sources by such medieval historians as William of Malmesbury and, in post-medieval centuries, they have attracted the interest of national historians and antiquarians. Over the course of time the study of various types of medieval inscriptions has become more professional and, in some cases, highly specialized and has led to collection and scholarly publication. The linguistic and historical complexities involved in the interpretation of inscriptions in runic and ogham alphabets and in early medieval vernaculars have dictated that the study of, for example,

---

[1] Traditional definitions of 'inscriptions' stress the durability of the materials onto which the texts are inscribed. See, for example, the definition of 'epigraphy' in J. E. Sandys, *Latin Epigraphy: an Introduction to the Study of Latin Inscriptions* (London, 1927), 1. By convention (and for convenience) medieval epigraphy, the study of medieval inscriptions, normally leaves those on coins and seals (but not always seal matrices) to specialists in numismatics and sigillography.

Irish, Anglo-Saxon and Norse inscriptions has been developed as an offshoot of the study of the relevant languages. Inscriptions in Latin (and later medieval vernaculars) have been collected for ambitious and systematic national corpora, of which several are at present in progress.[2]

Particular skills and types of specialized knowledge are required to deal competently with the various classes of medieval inscriptions and scholars studying analogous material from different cultural backgrounds have often been ignorant of each others' work, or even existence. Epigraphy, the study of inscriptions, can, however, be looked at more broadly and very similar issues are raised by inscriptions in very different contexts. Epigraphic studies, like most fields of medieval studies, have been greatly stimulated in recent years by a new concern with the varied nature and role of medieval literacy and by a much greater awareness of the implications of literacy in very diverse social conditions through the medieval centuries and across Europe.[3]

The time seemed ripe in the mid 1990s to set up a conference somewhere in the British Isles for those interested in the study of medieval inscriptions. The principal aims of the conference were to bring together scholars working in different, and often entirely separate, fields of medieval epigraphic studies in the British Isles to look at new directions in epigraphy and to compare notes on approaches, identifying common ground as well as differences. Another, equally important, aim was to establish better links with scholars working on the Continent and the organizers were very pleased that the conference was able to attract speakers from Germany, Norway, Italy, Poland, Spain and the United States of America – as well as from England, Ireland, Scotland and Wales. The 'International Conference on Medieval Epigraphy: the Insular World and the Continent' took place in Oxford in March 1996 and the chapters of this book are based on papers delivered at the conference. The editors hope that, like the conference, this volume will help to encourage cross-cultural comparisons and an international perspective, as well as a greater awareness of the work that is being done by scholars in related fields of epigraphy in the British Isles and on the Continent.

[2]   For an up-to-date survey of the field see: R. Favreau, *Épigraphie médiévale*, L'Atelier du médiéviste, 5 (Turnhout, 1997). His Introduction provides a concise review of epigraphic publications. The literature of medieval epigraphy is surveyed and evaluated in two very useful volumes: W. Koch (ed.), *Literaturbericht zur mittelalterlichen und neuzeitlichen Epigraphik (1976–1984)*, Monumenta Germaniae Historica, Hilfsmittel, 11 (Munich, 1987); W. Koch (ed.), *Literaturbericht zur mittelalterlichen und neuzeitlichen Epigraphik (1985–1991)*, Monumenta Germaniae Historica, Hilfsmittel, 14 (Munich, 1994).

[3]   For the British Isles, see in particular: M. T. Clanchy, *From Memory to Written Record: England 1066–1307*, 2nd end (Cambridge, 1993); R. McKitterick (ed.), *The Uses of Literacy in Early Medieval Europe* (Cambridge, 1990).

The individual chapters examine a wide range of inscriptions and classes of inscriptions from the earliest Middle Ages to the sixteenth century. Chapters are grouped according to cultural type, geographical area, or period. We start with the Insular[4] world and first with three chapters on the Latin inscriptions of the British West that illustrate three different perspectives on these inscriptions. Jeremy Knight investigates the broader archaeological contexts of early inscribed memorials, noting associations in some cases with prominent sitings and with funerary monuments of much earlier cultures. Carlo Tedeschi's approach is that of the palaeographer analysing the letter-forms of the early medieval inscriptions of Wales and south-west England. In the face of recent scepticism over Nash-Williams's chronological groupings of letter-forms, he presents the case for a consistent evolution of forms and 'typological continuity'. A series of recent studies by Charles Thomas of early medieval inscriptions in British Latin have argued that their texts are much more sophisticated and complex than has hitherto been suspected.[5] Approaching this question from a different angle, Mark Handley examines the vocabulary and structure of the inscription from Llanllyr and argues that it demonstrates an ambitious use of Latin drawing on a knowledge of 'Hisperic' style and the work of Isidore of Seville.

The three papers on Irish inscriptions are equally varied in approach. Anthony Harvey draws on new developments in the study of Irish ogham inscriptions to assess the problematic linguistic and contextual evidence for dating the invention of the ogham script. He argues that the origins of ogham should perhaps be placed earlier than normally allowed and he makes a plea for scholars to keep an open mind on the question in the present state of knowledge. Ann Hamlin surveys surviving early medieval Roman-letter inscriptions in Northern Ireland. The number of inscriptions that remains is surprisingly small compared with the rest of Ireland but seems to reflect a poorer rate of survival rather than a lower level of literacy. Computers have already contributed greatly to epigraphic studies and Jost Gippert describes the development, from pioneering beginnings, of a computer-based corpus of ogham inscriptions. He describes the possibilities that such a corpus opens up

[4]   The word 'Insular' is used in this volume as a neutral adjective relating to the British Isles and embracing both 'British' and 'Irish'. See the discussion in R. M. Spearman and J. Higgitt (ed.), *The Age of Migrating Ideas: Early Medieval Art in Britain and Ireland*, Proceedings of the Second International Conference on Insular Art ... (Edinburgh and Stroud, 1993), 1–2.

[5]   Charles Thomas gave a paper at the Oxford conference on the 'Idnert' inscription at Llandewi-Brefi in which he presented his interpretation of the text as an example of 'biblical style' containing encoded messages in addition to the literal meaning. He has published his paper separately as 'The Llandewi-Brefi "Idnert" Stone', *Peritia* 10 (1996), 136–83. He gives a general introduction to his approach in C. Thomas, *Christian Celts: Messages and Images* (Stroud, 1998).

but concludes that the judgement of the epigrapher remains crucial in the assessment of the evidence.

The publication of her *Hand-List* of Anglo-Saxon non-runic inscriptions allows Elisabeth Okasha to analyse the contents of these inscriptions. Her chapter shows their potential as a source for social history by surveying those inscriptions that include the names of women, thus throwing light on their roles as commissioners, makers, owners and the commemoratees on memorials and in other contexts. My own paper examines a single late Anglo-Saxon inscription, the well known dedication stone from Deerhurst. I argue that that the physical layout of this skilfully executed inscription was deliberately devised in order to highlight the powerful secular founder of the chapel, his secular overlord the king, and especially his deceased brother, for the benefit of whose soul the chapel was built.

Six papers tackle runic topics and again the approaches and material are diverse. Ray Page draws attention to the value, and dangers, of archival material and serendipity for runic studies. He introduces to non-runologists the important, and much more widely applicable, distinction between the *feltrunolog* and the *skrivebordsrunolog* (the field runologist and the desk runologist). Michael Barnes provides an update and a supplement to his list of Scandinavian runic inscriptions in the British Isles. In addition, he draws some conclusions about the nature of Scandinavian runic activity in the British Isles, pointing to contexts that range from 'stable rune-using communities' such as Man, where the inscriptions 'address a local audience', to passing visitors. Katherine Holman's focus is on the Scandinavian runic inscriptions of the Northern Isles. The inscriptions are somewhat disparate but an interesting contrast emerges between Shetland, where the inscriptions come mainly from ecclesiastical sites, and Orkney, where the finds have tended to be on high-status secular sites. Terje Spurkland takes the texts on Norwegian rune-sticks as his point of departure for his investigation of the relationship between runic and Roman literacy in Scandinavia in the central and later Middle Ages. He contrasts the roles of the two scripts and the mentalities behind them in this two-script culture. Espen Ore and Anne Haavaldsen describe a computer-based project that is experimenting with ways of recording rune forms and of devising a graphic typology that could be used as the basis for a scheme of transliteration that is dependent on the graphic form of the runes and not on their presumed phonetic value. In spite of the rarity of runologists (they estimate about 100 throughout the world!), their web-site is much visited. Runic (and other epigraphic studies) have been strongly influenced by the nationalisms of the last two centuries. Krzysztof Kowalski explores a fascinating scholarly will-of-wisp, the conviction of some Polish scholars of the nineteenth and early twentieth centuries that there was a class of 'Slavonic runes'. This theory led some scholars to fantastic hypotheses and others to forgery but, as he demonstrates, it must be understood against the background of Romanticism and Poland's loss of independence.

Three papers examine issues relating to early medieval inscriptions on the Continent, particularly in Francia, Bavaria and the areas of Langobardic rule. Walter Koch investigates the question of Insular influence on Continental inscriptions. Although the Irish and Anglo-Saxon missions leave clear traces in the script and decoration of manuscripts, he shows that the Insular contribution to inscriptions, while traceable in certain symptoms and letter-forms, is much harder to pin down. The only unambiguous example seems to be the well known tombstone of Aldualuhus from Worms, an interesting example of epigraphic lettering that is closely related to manuscript display script. John Mitchell presents a group of memorials from the wealth of inscriptions found on the monastic site of San Vincenzo al Volturno in the south of Italy. These carry inscriptions arranged around the powerful symbol of the cross, a type that also appears in northern Italy and the Insular world, illustrating the international currency of Latin epigraphy in the early Middle Ages. The next chapter takes us to the Langobards of northern Italy in the eighth century, where Nick Everett demonstrates the deliberate use of inscriptions by King Liutprand and other members of Langobard élites to bolster their authority in an impressively worded and finely lettered series of monuments.

The last three chapters deal with later medieval topics, of which the first two are complementary aspects of English brasses and incised slabs. Jerome Bertram examines the texts on memorials in Oxford and Sussex, showing, amongst other things, how their characteristic formulae distinguish them from epigraphic traditions on the Continent. The most individual aspect of many of these texts are their echoes of liturgical and devotional texts, especially the Office of the Dead. Sally Badham is concerned with the lettering of these monuments and surveys the careful and fruitful work of classification that has been carried out since the 1970s, assisting in the identification of workshops and the dating of inscriptions and monuments. The chapter by Jennifer Alexander approaches 'masons' marks' as a specialized 'form of non-phonetic writing that stands outside literacy' and surveys their probable functions. Most of the marks are geometric forms with no obvious meaning but a number are based on letter forms and suggest contacts with letter-cutting masons.

The editors hope that this volume conveys something of the wealth of epigraphic material that is being explored at the moment and that remains to be explored. The individual chapters take a variety of interpretative approaches to text, form and function and illustrate the contributions that epigraphy can offer to wider historical debates. Inscriptions remain a comparatively neglected source for the understanding of medieval literate culture.

It is no accident that the majority of chapters in this book deal with the inscriptions of the earlier Middle Ages. This reflects scholarly activity in the British Isles where epigraphic studies have, for many years, been mainly concerned with early medieval inscriptions. As a result, there exist published corpora that include most of the early medieval inscriptions of Britain and Ireland and there are projects under way to fill the gaps and to revise the existing corpora.[6] This activity is, in part at least, a product of the interest in national origins and identities. The central and later Middle Ages are not so well served in these countries. There are no national corpora of medieval inscriptions from periods later than the cut-off points around the eleventh or twelfth centuries that have been adopted for collections of Irish, Welsh, Anglo-Saxon, Insular runic inscriptions and so on. Inscriptions of the central or later Middle Ages, if they have been noticed at all, have, until recently, normally been the province of antiquarian rather than critical epigraphic study. The principal exception has been the very interesting work on the lettering of memorials on brasses and incised slabs in England that has been undertaken over the last two or three decades.[7] The lack of national corpora was made all the more apparent at the conference by the presence of a number of scholars who are working on the very successful German corpus, *Die Deutschen Inschriften*.[8] Two participants at the conference, Jerome Bertram and I, later agreed that there is a pressing need for such collections in the British Isles. Unrecorded or inadequately recorded medieval inscriptions are at risk of damage or destruction from weathering, vandalism, theft and similar causes. With such a corpus in mind Jerome Bertram has written and circulated two sample fascicules, based on inscriptions in Oxford and Dorchester, for a

---

[6] The principal twentieth-century corpora are: R. A. S. Macalister, *Corpus Inscriptionum Insularum Celticarum*, 2 vols (Dublin, 1945 and 1949 (reprint of vol. I; Dublin and Portland, Or., 1996)); V. Nash-Williams, *Early Christian Monuments of Wales* (Cardiff, 1950); E. Okasha, *Hand-List of Anglo-Saxon Non-runic Inscriptions* (Cambridge, 1971); E. Okasha, 'A Supplement to *Hand-List of Anglo-Saxon Non-runic Inscriptions*', *Anglo-Saxon England* 11 (1983), 83–118; E. Okasha, 'A Second Supplement to *Hand-List of Anglo-Saxon Non-runic Inscriptions*', *Anglo-Saxon England* 21 (1992), 37–85; E. Okasha, *Corpus of Early Christian Inscribed Stones of South-West Britain* (London and New York, 1993). A new edition of Nash-Williams's volume is being prepared under the editorship of Nancy Edwards. The Celtic Inscribed Stones Project, which is based in the Department of History in University College London, is collecting data on early medieval inscriptions from Ireland, Celtic areas of Britain and Brittany. A database of ogham inscriptions is described in the chapter by Jost Gippert (see below, pp. 66–78).

[7] Surveyed in the chapter in this volume by Sally Badham (see below, pp. 202–10).

[8] The first volume of *Die Deutschen Inschriften* appeared in 1942. The volumes are conveniently listed in Favreau, *Épigraphie médiévale*, 10–13.

corpus of medieval inscriptions in England (from 1066 onwards).[9] Decisions will need to be taken on what is to be included, on conventions and on terminology ('Lombardic' or 'Gothic capitals'; 'black letter' or 'Gothic minuscule'?). Because of the scale of the task, such a corpus must be a co-operative undertaking. It will need funding and a base for its archive of information and photographs. Without such corpora much material of immense value for the understanding of medieval literacy, beliefs and society will remain unavailable to scholars and will gradually disappear.

---

[9] J. Bertram, *Mediæval Inscriptions and Sepulchral Slabs in the City and University of Oxford anterior to the Year 1350* (privately printed, Oxford, 1998); idem, *A Catalogue of Medieval Inscriptions in the Abbey Church of Dorchester, Oxfordshire* (Oxford, forthcoming).

Basilicas and Barrows:
The Latin Memorial Stones of Wales and Their Archaeological Contexts

JEREMY KNIGHT

It is no criticism of Victor Nash-Williams's book *The Early Christian Monuments of Wales* (1950), or of its author, to point out that this definitive work is essentially a museum catalogue (in the sense that individual items are presented with little attention to their physical context). The bibliography for individual stones was published earlier and separately, and though there is mention of the find-spots of individual stones within the catalogue entries, there is no detailed discussion of these. For details of the sites from which the stones came, it is necessary to work through such sources as J. O. Westwood's *Lapidarium Walliae* (1876–9), the inventories for individual counties published by the Royal Commission on the Ancient and Historical Monuments in Wales, or accounts of individual stones in *Archaeologia Cambrensis* by such people as Sir John Rhŷs (the first Jesus Professor of Celtic in the University of Oxford) between 1873 and 1913, or by Cyril and Aileen Fox in the 1930s. However, little of this material on the original contexts of the stones has ever been brought together in one place.

Many stones have quite complex histories of removals and resitings, often poorly recorded. The Carausius stone from Penmachno in Gwynedd was first recorded 'lying on a heap of stones in the churchyard'.[1] The church here has produced at least two other Latin memorial stones, and it has usually been assumed that this was also the original location of the Carausius stone. It has even been suggested that the '*congeries lapidum*' referred to in the inscription was this same heap of stones, which might even have been some sort of mound grave or *memoria* within the churchyard. However, Dr Nancy Edwards tells me that a local Welsh language source makes it clear that the stone was actually found some two miles up the valley in 1819–20, and a correlation of other sources suggests that the stone only arrived at the church

---

[1] J. O. Westwood, 'Early Inscribed Stones of Wales', *Archaeologia Cambrensis*, 3rd ser., 9 (1863), 257. For a fuller study of the Penmachno stones see J. K. Knight, 'Penmachno Revisited: The Consular Inscription and its Context', *Cambrian Medieval Celtic Studies* 29 (Summer 1995), 1–10.

some time after 1850, and that the 'heap of stones' may have simply been a heap of rubble from the then recent restoration of the church.

The famous (and rather later) Welsh language inscription from Towyn in Merionethshire,[2] the earliest written Welsh, save for a few brief manuscript entries, has a similar, but even more complex history. At one stage it was 'Removed to decorate the grotto of a Gentleman', but it seems originally to have stood at a site called Croes Faen ('Stone cross'), a couple of miles from Towyn, where a very similar natural volcanic pillar still stands, with another lying in the hedge nearby.[3] It reached Towyn church about 1850. Significantly, both this and the Penmachno stone reached the churches where they now are in the decade after the foundation of the Cambrian Archaeological Association in 1846–7, for the Cambrians had a large membership among the clergy, and through its journal *Archaeologia Cambrensis* did (and still does) much to stimulate interest in the study of such stones.

These examples, and others like them, suggested that it would be worth assembling the available information on the original find-spots and subsequent histories of early Welsh inscriptions and sculpture and to see what patterns emerged. All too often, the find-spot is no more than 'built into a barn' or 're-used as the lintel of a beast house' and the mere existence of such a stone can sometimes lead to antiquarian traditions of an early chapel on the site. Only one stone, from Arfryn in Anglesey, has ever been found in an archaeological excavation, and that excavation remains unpublished.[4] A few others, including those from Penprys farm at Llannor in Caernarvonshire, are known to be from long cist cemeteries,[5] but we do not know what other types

---

[2]   V. Nash-Williams, *Early Christian Monuments of Wales* (Cardiff, 1950) (hereafter *ECMW*), no. 287. I. Williams 'The Towyn Stone', *Archaeologia Cambrensis* 100 (1949), 161–72.

[3]   In about 1761 it was 'removed from its place as a gatepost' (W. Camden, *Britannia,* ed. R. Gough (London, 1789), II, 541). By 1821 it was said to 'decorate the grotto of a gentleman' at Morfa Towyn (*Cambro-Briton* (1821), II, 121) and by 1850 it was 'lying on the floor of Towyn church', where it now is (J. O. Westwood, *Archaeologia Cambrensis* 5 (1850), 90). Westwood's location of it at Cros Faen 'in a field close to the road-side, about half a mile from Towyn, on road to Dollgellau' (*Lapidarium Walliae: The Early Inscribed Stones of Wales* (Oxford, 1876–9), 158, n. 1) probably records its original location, but the record as it stands is ambiguous, and fresh evidence is needed.

[4]   For an interim report see R. B. White, 'Excavations at Arfryn, Bodedern, Long Cist Cemeteries and the Origins of Christianity in Britain', *Transactions of the Anglesey Antiquarian Society and Field Club* (1971–2), 19–51.

[5]   The two stones in the Ashmolean Museum (*ECMW*, nos. 96–7) were found about 1833 in a field called Cae Maen Hir (i.e. 'Menhir field' or 'field of the tall stone') serving as the side stones of a north–south oriented long cist. The tenant farmer had noted similar stones nearby (*Archaeologia Cambrensis* 2 (1847), 201). *ECMW*

of burial were present, whether the cemeteries were enclosed, or what associated features, if any, they contained.

Cemeteries of the pre-Roman and native-Roman Iron Age are rare in Wales, but a recent survey suggests that they were mostly small family or kin group cemeteries associated with individual farms or small settlements, not centrally organized burial places.[6] There is no convincing example from Wales of an early medieval memorial stone associated with Iron Age or native-Roman burials and I have argued elsewhere that there is little continuity between Romano-British tombstones like those from Caerleon, and the post-Roman Insular series.[7] The latter, in some cases using fifth-century Gallic memorial formulae like *hic iacet*, *hic requiescit*, or *in pace* must have been introduced (save perhaps in south-west Wales with its ogham tradition) through the medium of the Christian church. I would suggest that the means of introduction were the churches, perhaps few in number, of a sub-Romano-British church, presumably of an episcopal and pre-monastic character, organized like the fifth-century Gallic diocesan churches (*ecclesiae diocesanae*) or the Anglo-Saxon minster churches which derived from these. Many of their clergy would have been married, as Gildas in an aside implies that most sixth-century British clergy were.[8]

Possible examples of such primary minster churches are not easy to find, but two candidates from the eastern borderlands of Wales deserve mention. Llanerfyl is a small Montgomeryshire church at the point where the Roman road running north from the auxiliary fort at Caersws reaches the Banwy valley, about thirty-five miles due west of the Roman *civitas* capital of Wroxeter, which has itself produced a fifth-century Latin memorial inscription. Llanerfyl has what is almost certainly the earliest of the Welsh memorial stones, the stone of Rosteece, very close to the Gallic prototypes, with punctuation, the age of the deceased, and a final *in pace*, all features which are quickly dropped from the remainder of the series.[9] Llanerfyl is

---

nos. 94 and 97, found re-used in a cottage and as a church gatepost may be strays from the same cemetery. For other examples from long-cist cemeteries see Dol Tre Beddau, Denbighshire (*ECMW* no. 183, *Cambro-Briton* 1 (1820) 360, 410; *Gentleman's Magazine* (1820) 443) or Arfryn, Anglesey (see n. 4 above).

6   K. Murphy, 'Plas Gogerddan, Dyfed: A Multi-period Burial and Ritual Site', *Archaeological Journal* 149 (1992), 1–38, at 30–5.

7   J. K. Knight, 'In Tempore Justini Consulis: Contacts between the British and Gaulish Churches before Augustine', in *Collectanea Historica: Essays in Memory of Stuart Rigold*, ed. A. Detsicas (Maidstone, 1981), 54–62.

8   Gildas *De Excidio* c.66. M. Winterbottom (ed.), *Gildas, The Ruin of Britain and Other Works* (London, 1978). For discussion and references see J. K. Knight 'Glamorgan 400–1100: Archaeology and History', in *Glamorgan County History*, ed. H. Savory (Cardiff, 1984), II, 340 and n. 108 on p. 362.

9   *ECMW* 294. For the Wroxeter inscription see R. P. Wright and K. H. Jackson, 'A Late Inscription from Wroxeter', *Antiquaries Journal* 48 (1968), 296–300.

dedicated to an obscure female saint, Erfyl, and the church still contains the remains of her wooden shrine and reliquary. It was later supplanted as the principal church of the cantref (equivalent to an English hundred) of Caereinion by Meifod, the traditional burial place of the princes of Powys. Bassaleg in Gwent lies outside the distributional range of Latin memorial stones, but has a number of features in common with Llanerfyl. It lies at the point where the Roman road from Caerleon westwards crosses the River Ebbw. It is the only example in Wales of the place name *Basilica*, used both in Merovingian Gaul and in early Ireland for a church of early foundation containing important relics.[10] In this case they were the bones of St Gwladys, like Erfyl an obscure female saint, and the *Eglwys Y Bedd* or grave chapel of St Gwladys survived until the nineteenth century. Just as Llanerfyl was supplanted by Meifod, so Bassaleg was eclipsed by the church of St Gwynllyw, two miles away, the present Newport cathedral. St Gwynllyw was the eponym of the cantref of Gwynlliog. His church was itself an early foundation, already ancient in the twelfth century, when a community of canons under a dean served the grave of their patron. The mother church of Gwynlliog, however, was not the eponymous St Gwynllyw's but Bassaleg, which had a series of tributary chapels, later parish churches, in the uplands of the cantref. Though it is going beyond the available evidence, Bassaleg and Llanerfyl could have been parts of sub-Roman diocesan structures within the *civitates* of the Silures of Caerwent and the Cornovii of Wroxeter.

Among the 'Group I' Latin or ogham memorial stones,[11] the most obvious distinction is between those which stand, or once stood, in the graveyard of a Christian church and those sited in open country, at times on high moorland where there clearly never has been a church. It is difficult to arrive at exact figures, since many of the stones, as I have mentioned, are known only from secondary contexts. Preliminary analysis suggests a great deal of regional variation, which may tell us more than a single pan-Wales figure. Thus in Caernarvonshire two-thirds of the Group 1 stones are associated with known church sites (66 per cent). In Anglesey and Merioneth the figure is 50 per cent and in Clwyd (north-east Wales) 25 per cent. The

---

[10] C. Doherty, 'The Basilica in Early Ireland', *Peritia* 3 (1984), 303–15. Gregory of Tours has an exact vocabulary for churches, and uses *basilica* for a major church housing important relics or the body of a saint. On Bassaleg as basilica see Tomos Roberts, 'Welsh Ecclesiastical Place-names and Archaeology', in *The Early Church in Wales and the West*, ed. N. Edwards and A. Lane, Oxbow Monograph 16 (Oxford 1992), 41–2. A good watercolour drawing of the Bassaleg *Eglwys Y Bedd*, of *c.* 1847, has now come to light in the library of the Society of Antiquaries of London (*Gwentia: Ecclesiastical Antiquities*, vol.1, no. 10). I hope to publish this fully elsewhere.

[11] For 'Group I' see Nash-Williams in *ECMW*, 2 and 3–16.

overall numbers are, however, too small for reliable statistical analysis, though the figures would merit closer scrutiny.

Both the use of Latin literacy, and the Christian memorial formulae imply that the memorial stones were introduced through the medium of the Christian church and that they were first erected in the churchyards of Christian churches. In saying this, we should not overlook the fact that our Insular inscriptions differ in important respects from their Gallic prototypes. The latter are on horizontal slabs set in the floor of a church or the surface of a graveyard. The insular stones are standing monoliths, resembling nothing so much as a Roman milestone and, apart from Charles Thomas's early 'extended Latinate' group, the inscriptions are usually set vertically rather than horizontally on the stone. The stones standing in churchyards present few problems of context, though they do raise questions about what sort of church they were orginally associated with, and we cannot overlook the distinct possibility that they may have originally stood in a family or kin group cemetery before the building of a church there (in Charles Thomas's phraseology in an 'undeveloped cemetery'). It is, however, the stones sited away from any church which need further scrutiny.[12]

In the 1930s Cyril and Aileen Fox drew attention to a number of inscribed stones in upland Glamorgan which were 'crest sited'.[13] These stand on high moorland. When approached from uphill, or along the contour, they are inconspicuous to the point of being almost hidden, but when approached uphill from one particular angle, they stand out boldly on the skyline. The Foxs showed that the stones had been erected in relation to a settlement site, usually represented by a modern farm, lying at a lower, sheltered, elevation. Apart from the important implications for settlement archaeology, this model implies that such stones were erected by the owners of these upland farms to commemorate their descent and perhaps to emphasize their own property rights to that land. A variation on this theme appears with a group of stones in the upper Taf valley between Merthyr Tydfil and Brecon. Here the stones were sited where a side stream joined the main valley, in optimum locations to exploit the various environmental resources of valley-bottom meadow, hillside grazing, wood and moorland that the valley offered.[14] Most of these

[12]   For 'extended Latinate' inscriptions: C. Thomas, *And Shall These Mute Stones Speak? Post-Roman Inscriptions in Western Britain* (Cardiff, 1994), 68, 200–5. For 'undeveloped' cemeteries: C. Thomas, *The Early Christian Archaeology of North Britain* (London, 1971), 51.

[13]   A. Fox, 'The Siting of some Inscribed Stones of the Dark Ages in Glamorgan and Breconshire', *Archaeologia Cambrensis* 94 (1939), 30–41. A. and C. Fox, 'Forts and Farms on Margam Mountain, Glamorgan', *Antiquity* 8 (1934), 395–413.

[14]   J. K. Knight, 'Early Christian Origins and Society in South Wales', *Merthyr Historian* 2 (1970), 105–10.

ecological 'windows of opportunity' had also been occupied by post-medieval farms.

Discussion of such stones often assumes that they were Christian tombstones. However, unlike the lower-lying long cist cemeteries, no burials have been found associated with these upland stones, though this is hardly surprising in this highly acid soil. It could be argued that these were cenotaphs of people who had received (Christian?) burial elsewhere, or that there is little formal proof that the persons commemorated were Christian, despite the use of the Christian *hic iacet* formula. The Llannor long cist burial was oriented north–south in the long-standing traditions of the pre-Roman and Roman Iron Age. In my view, neither of these hypotheses is necessary. The stones were clearly erected after initial contact with Christianity and Christian literacy, but before the Church had established a network of rural churches, with the clergy and resources to staff them. Such a transition period, often lengthy, has been noted both in northern Gaul and in seventh-century Anglo-Saxon England.[15] The Anglo-Saxon 'late phase' cemeteries, orientated east–west, but still with grave-goods, sometimes jewellery with specifically Christian motifs, have long been recognized as belonging to this phase. These memorial stones from upland areas of Wales, where pastoral care may well have come late, may be similar.

One aspect of the siting of these memorial stones requires particular comment. Seven of them, from two areas of Wales, were associated with Bronze Age barrows. This has sometimes been seen as evidence for a continuance, or even a continuity, of prehistoric traditions, yet no case of pre-Roman or Roman Iron Age burials associated with a memorial stone is known in Wales. Other cases are known where early medieval burials or cemeteries are associated with prehistoric barrows and other monuments, as at Tandderwen near Denbigh in Clwyd,[16] one of the areas incidentally which has memorial stones from barrows. For present purposes, however, discussion can be limited to barrows specifically associated with memorial stones. It has sometimes been suggested that some of the associated barrows might have been early medieval *memoriae*, contemporary with the stones, but when the large cairn associated with the two inscribed stones from Abercar on the Glamorgan-Brecon border was cleared away, it produced a cremation with a Bronze Age collared urn and pygmy cup.[17] Similarly, the Bodvoc stone, now

[15] I hope to consider the evidence from north Gaulish cemeteries elsewhere. For the Anglo-Saxon late phase cemeteries see S. C. Hawkes and A. L. Meaney, *Two Anglo-Saxon Cemeteries at Winall, Winchester, Hampshire*, Society for Medieval Archaeology Monograph Series 4 (London, 1970), 45–55.

[16] K. S. Brassil, W. G. Owen and W. J. Britnell, 'Prehistoric and Early Medieval Cemeteries at Tandderwen, near Denbigh, Clwyd', *Archaeological Journal* 148 (1991), 46– 97.

[17] *ECMW*, nos. 40–1. J. O. Westwood, *Archaeologia Cambrensis*, 3rd ser., 4 (1858),

in Margam museum, originally stood on one of an alignment of four undoubted Bronze Age barrows on Margam mountain,[18] whilst the ruined remains of the cairns associated with the Gelligaer Mountain and the Banwen Pyrddin ('Seven Sisters') stones, with the centres robbed out for drystone wall building or the like, are all too typical of the majority of cairns in upland Glamorgan.[19] Of the two stones from Clwyd in north-east Wales, that from Cae'r Orsedd at Caerwys in Flintshire was removed by David Pennant (son of Thomas Pennant) from the site of a still well-preserved round barrow in about 1790. It is now in Whitford church.[20] However, the most revealing example does not concern a prehistoric barrow at all.

The site at Bryn Y Beddau ('Hill of the Graves') at Clocaenog in Denbighshire is a classic example of Fox's 'crest siting'. From the farm in the hollow below, a track climbs up to a low ridge on which stand two natural mounds evidently mistaken for barrows in early medieval times and known as Bedd Emlyn, 'the grave of Emlyn' (a misreading of SIMILINI). Next to one of these there stood until about 1813 'Two stones at each end of a grave, 4 ft asunder'. One, inscribed SIMILINI TOVISACI in both Roman and ogham alphabets, is now in the National Museum of Wales. The other, uninscribed, still lies on the site.[21] Evidently those who erected the stones mistook the natural mounds for ancient burial places which held the graves of those who had once owned and worked the land, and whose heirs and successors they in some way saw themselves to be. Such fictive descent is not uncommon in cases where there has been a radical change in social structures and in élite composition. Snodgrass has described a very similar situation in Dark Age Greece, where late in the Geometric period, Mycenean cists and tholos tombs, already ancient monuments, were identified as the supposed residences or burial places of heroic figures like Agamemnon or the Seven Against Thebes,

---

162. On the Bronze Age pottery see *ibid.* 1939, 22–4. J. K. Knight, *Glamorgan County History*, Vol. 2: *Prehistory and Early History* (Cardiff, 1984), 338.

[18] *ECMW*, no. 229.

[19] *ECMW*, no. 197 (Gelligaer) is the only stone remaining *in situ*, the others having been removed to museums. For the siting of Banwen Pyrddin (*ECMW*, no. 269) see A. Fox, 'The Siting of some Inscribed Stones of the Dark Ages in Glamorgan and Breconshire', *Archaeologia Cambrensis* 94 (1939), 32–4, and W. Camden *Britannia* ..., ed. E. Gibson (London, 1695), 619. The name 'Seven Sisters' used in *ECMW* is from a nearby mining village and colliery named after the children of the nineteenth-century mine owner.

[20] *ECMW*, no. 184. Ellis Davies, *Prehistoric and Roman Remains of Flintshire* (Cardiff, 1949), 84–5.

[21] *ECMW*, no. 176. W. Camden, *Britannia* ..., ed. E. Gibson (London, 1695), 679. Lhwyd, letter of 1693 printed in *Archaeologia Cambrensis* 3 (1848), 310. See also I. Williams and V. E. Nash-Williams, 'Some Welsh pre-Norman Stones', *Archaeologia Cambrensis* 92 (1937), 1–4.

and became centres of cult and burial.[22] Similarly, Robert van der Noort has drawn attention to the use or re-use of barrows over much of western Europe in the period 550–650, a trend which he associates with a reassertion of traditional sources of power as against the rising influence and power of the Christian church.[23]

This was no more than a transitional phase, however. Already, in most parts of Wales, stones were being erected in the cemeteries of Christian churches. Some of these seem to have been territorial minsters (to borrow the albeit anachronistic English term); some may have been estate churches. Some had a specific funerary context, as evidenced by the placename *Merthyr* or by dedications to the Archangel St Michael, guardian of the soul in death. Interestingly, early memorial stones are rare in churches which later emerge in the record as specifically monastic. By the late seventh century, however, the Latin memorial stones, with their emphasis on ancestry and status had disappeared, replaced by uninscribed cross-slabs. The dead were no longer commemorated as members of an élite, but as anonymous Christians.

[22] A. M. Snodgrass, *The Dark Age of Greece: An Archaeological Survey of the Eleventh to the Eighth Centuries* (Edinburgh, 1971), 192–6.

[23] R. Van der Noort, 'The Context of Early Medieval Barrows in Western Europe', *Antiquity* 67 (1993), 66–73. See now J. K. Knight, *The End of Antiquity: Archaeology, Society and Religion AD 235–700* (Stroud, 1999).

Some Observations on the Palaeography of Early Christian Inscriptions in Britain[1]

CARLO TEDESCHI

In Roman Britain, as in other provinces of the Empire, there developed alongside the inscriptions that, on the basis of functional and formal characteristics, can be defined as 'official', two other epigraphic currents: one funerary and private, the other military. These non-official inscriptions reveal strong 'provincial' or 'popular' tendencies.[2] From the point of view of form, these minor monuments are characterized by the use of local stone; by a coarseness in the shaping of the stone, or even a complete lack of working; by a general lack of decoration; and by the disordered layout of the text, with wavering lines of differing length and irregular spacing of letters and lines. From a palaeographical point of view, these 'popular' inscriptions are characterized by letter-forms which represent the result of a progressive translation into vernacular patterns of lapidary capitals. Letters, though preserving the general shape of capitals, are carved less accurately, with U-shaped instead of V-shaped sections. The traditional proportions between the height and width of letters are no longer observed, and the general sense of symmetry and the upright alignment of letters are often lost. Little by little, letters and ligatures unknown to the tradition of lapidary capital script, but derived instead from cursive and minuscule are introduced.[3]

From these preliminary conditions it is possible to trace during the third and, more clearly, during the fourth century, the gradual creation in Britain of a humble lapidary style which, while on the one hand sharing some of its features with the epigraphic corpora of the other provinces of the Empire, on

[1] The ideas presented here are treated more fully in my 'Osservazioni sulla paleografia delle iscrizioni britanniche paleocristiane (V–VII sec.). Contributo allo studio dell'origine delle scritture insulari', *Scrittura e Civiltà* 19 (1995), 67–121.

[2] The corpus of British Roman epigraphy has been published in R. G. Collingwood and R. P. Wright (eds), *The Roman Inscriptions of Britain* (Oxford, 1965; new ed. Stroud, 1995) (= *RIB*).

[3] J. Mallon, *Paléographie romaine*, Monumenta et Studia III (Madrid, 1952), the second chapter of which is a palaeographical approach to Roman epigraphy. For the relationship between monumental and everyday writing in particular, see pp. 58–60.

the other generated forms which were more specifically 'British'. Both components, the 'Provincial' (in the wider sense) and the local, were destined to be the primary basis of a new national script. Some of the main letter-forms which the late Roman inscriptions in Britain share with those of the other provinces are: (1) A with sloping or V-shaped bar; (2) B with separated loops; (3) minuscule B; (4) uncial E; (5) cursive F; (6) 'sickle-shaped' G; (7) M with the outer strokes wide apart and the inner strokes meeting level with the line; (8) R with the loop separated from the stroke, or with open loop.[4] The features which can be considered specifically British are: (1) reversed A, D, E, I, S and X (pl. 1);[5] (2) ligatures of C with I, V, A, E and T;[6] (3) ligatures of M and N with A and V[7] and a high number of ligatures in general;[8] and (4) the lack of space between letters on the same line.

The lettering of Early Christian inscriptions in Britain follows this kind of provincial, or popular, tradition.[9] Perpetuating and emphasizing to a greater and greater extent the tendency to deformation and to incoherence expressed by Late Roman inscriptions, the Early Christian tradition of Britain elaborated its own type of script which, after further developments, was eventually to be transferred to manuscripts, in the form of the so-called 'Insular decorative capitals'.[10]

Although one cannot recognize a strict stylistic uniformity in script, it is nevertheless possible to follow a consistent evolutionary line in which some recurrent features stand out and enable us to identify a distinct style of lettering. At one extreme we find those inscriptions which display a script still strongly dependent on the models represented by the third- and fourth-century British epigraphy (for instance the *Carausius* stone at

---

[4] These characters can be found, for instance, in *RIB*, nos. 256, 345, 508, 628, 631, 721, 1009, 1329, 1575, 1803, 1810, 1817, 1844, 1976, 2011, 2198, 2274, 2275, 2300 and 2310.

[5] *RIB*, nos. 2263, 221 and 1009.

[6] *RIB*, no. 191.

[7] *RIB*, nos. 1846, 1911 and 1919. It is possible to find the same ligatures sporadically in Continental epigraphy, too, but in Britain the phenomenon becomes common.

[8] *RIB*, nos. 590, 369 and 116.

[9] The standard edition of British and Irish Early Christian inscriptions is R. A. S. Macalister's *Corpus Inscriptionum Insularum Celticarum*, 2 vols (Dublin, 1945 and 1949) (= *CIIC*). For the Welsh inscriptions see also V. E. Nash Williams, *Early Christian Monuments of Wales* (Cardiff, 1950) (= *ECMW*); for the south-western inscriptions see also E. Okasha, *Corpus of Early Christian Inscribed Stones of South-West Britain* (London, 1993) (= *CECISSWB*).

[10] For a discussion of 'Insular decorative capitals', see J. Higgitt, 'The Pictish Latin Inscription at Tarbat in Ross-shire', *Proceedings of the Society of Antiquaries of Scotland* 112 (1982), 300–21; 'The Display Script of the Book of Kells and the Tradition of Insular Decorative Capitals', in *The Book of Kells*, ed. Felicity O'Mahony (Aldershot, 1994), 209–33.

Penmachno,[11] the *Rustece* stone at Llanerfyl,[12] the *Culidor* stone at Llangefni (pls 2, 3, 4),[13] the *Latinus* stone at Whithorn,[14] and the *Cunaide* stone at Hayle[15]), where the use of letter-forms close to those of Late Roman epigraphic capitals is often associated with a classically inspired horizontal layout of the text. At the other extreme are letter-forms or ligatures which are either already perfectly 'Insular' or recognizable as immediate antecedents of Insular forms. In particular, I refer to the Welsh inscriptions of Llangadwaladr, Llanfihangel-Cwmdw and Capel-Llanilterne;[16] also to the *Catgug* stone, Wareham,[17] and the Madron II stone,[18] both from south-west Britain; and to the Breton inscriptions of Lanrivoaré and Plouagat-Châtelaudren[19] (pls 5, 6, 7, 8). The majority of the inscriptions in question are found between these two poles, some closer to the capital model, others nearer the Insular one. All, however, exhibit characteristics that enable us to identify a typological continuity from one extreme to the other.

Some forms of this Early Christian lapidary style in Britain derive directly from the British Late Roman epigraphic tradition: in particular, the general and widespread taste for ligatures (sometimes extremely crabbed) and for reversed and inverted letters. In the case of the former, ligatures of C with I, E, A, V, T (pl. 9) and of Ms and Ns with A and V (pl. 10) are quite common.[20] As for the latter (pls 11, 12), the use of reversed and inverted letters becomes a sort of distinguishing mark of Early Christian epigraphy in Britain[21] in contrast to contemporary Continental epigraphy.[22] The letters

11 *ECMW*, no. 101.
12 *ECMW*, no. 294.
13 *ECMW*, no. 26.
14 *CIIC*, no. 520.
15 *CECISSWB*, no. 16.
16 *ECMW*, nos. 13, 54 and 214.
17 *CIIC*, no. 1061.
18 *CECISSWB*, no. 32.
19 G. Bernier, *Les Chrétientés bretonnes continentales depuis les origines jusqu'au XIème siècle*, Dossiers du Centre Archéologique d'Alet E-1982 (Rennes, 1982), 166 and 169–70. *The Inscriptions of Early Medieval Brittany. Les inscriptions de la Bretagne du Haut Moyen Âge*, ed. W. Davies et al. (Celtic Studies Publications, Andover and Aberystwyth, 2000). It seems clear that, both from the palaeographical and formulaic points of view, the few surviving Breton inscriptions can be considered as a branch of the Early Christian epigraphic tradition of the British Isles.
20 Representative examples of inscriptions rich in ligatures are, for instance, *ECMW*, nos. 78 and 289.
21 Although the phenomenon is quite common, some inscriptions are particularly rich in reversed letters, for example *ECMW*, nos. 73 and 229, and *CECISSWB*, no. 66.
22 Contemporary inscriptions on the Continent show an almost complete absence of this phenomenon. The only examples I know of reversed As appear on two German inscriptions: W. Boppert, *Die frühchristlichen Inschriften des*

involved in the phenomenon of reversing, or turning, are: I (so-called 'horizontal-I', 45 examples), N (13 examples), D (10 examples), A and S (5 examples of each), M and V (4 examples each), L and T (just one example each).

Other distinctive features of the Late Roman epigraphic tradition conserved in Early Christian inscriptions are: As with sloping or angular bar; Bs with separated, sometimes open loops; uncial Es; cursive Fs; 'sickle-shaped' and other distinctive forms of G; Ls with sloping cross-stroke; Ms with the outer strokes wide apart and the inner strokes meeting on the line; Rs with an open loop; and the Greek letter *sigma* used instead of S (pl. 13).[23] This last feature is particularly interesting, because the use of Greek letters was destined to continue in the so-called 'Insular decorative capitals'.

Some palaeographical features of the Early Christian inscriptions of Britain cannot, however, be related to the earlier Roman epigraphic tradition, but must instead be traced back to minuscule and cursive tendencies: the widespread ligatures F-I and L-I (pls 6, 11, 12, 14); half-uncial G, already known in minuscule cursive (pls 5, 6, 7, 11, 15); trident-shaped M, derived from a minuscule model (pl. 16); N with the first stroke descending under the line, used sometimes in minuscule cursive; and minuscule D, H, L, Q, R, S, T and V (pls 5, 6, 7, 8, 12, 14). These new forms are commonly believed to derive from book models, in particular from manuscripts written in uncial and especially half-uncial in Italy and Gaul and supposedly taken to Britain by missionaries.[24] It has also been suggested that new forms could derive from Insular or 'Hiberno-Saxon' manuscripts.[25] If all this is accepted, in the same inscription we might find side by side letters inspired by Continental half-uncial models and others by Insular ones, assuming therefore that the writer had a clear idea of the half-uncial and of the Insular scripts and could choose or mix freely between one or the other model.

As is well known, the earliest manuscript witnesses of half-uncial date back to the end of the fifth or the beginning of the sixth century. It is hard to believe that manuscripts written in Italy or Gaul at the beginning of the sixth century (at the earliest) had within a few years reached Britain and circulated so widely as to deeply influence the common writing of every Welsh or Cornish Christian community. It is even more difficult to believe that the same people who possessed and appreciated such sophisticated and elegant books – as these uncial and half-uncial manuscripts are – could at the same

---

Mittelrheingebietes (Mainz-am-Rhein, 1971), 72–4; N. Gauthier, *Recueil des inscriptions chrétiennes de la Gaule antérieures à la Renaissance carolingienne*, I, *Première Belgique* (Paris, 1975), 517–18.

[23] *ECMW*, no. 346.

[24] This thesis was originally expressed by V. E. Nash Williams ('Some Dated Monuments of the "Dark Ages" in Wales', *Archaeologia Cambrensis* 93 (1938), 31–56); *ECMW*, 12.

[25] *ECMW*, 12.

time favour such a profoundly anti-classical kind of funerary monument. It can, moreover, be added that the supposed influence of uncial and half-uncial models on the Early Christian inscriptions of Britain can hardly explain the presence of letters like the trident-shaped M and the H-shaped N,[26] which are related to traditions of script (respectively, primitive minuscule and the lapidary capital) different from those of uncial and half-uncial.

In terms of palaeography the Continental, and especially the Italian, influence on Britain after the fall of the Roman Empire can be considered certain only from the age of Gregory the Great onwards. We have in fact indisputable testimony to this influence in the existence of an English uncial script used both for book and documentary purposes[27] and based on the imitation of the Roman uncial studied by Armando Petrucci.[28] But for the previous couple of centuries the only evidence is that of lapidary script. In explaining the 'new' letter-forms in the Early Christian inscriptions of Britain, it is reasonable to assume that though sometimes similar to the corresponding uncial and half-uncial letters, in fact these forms followed their own autonomous evolution, starting from the remains of the Roman writing tradition (capital, minuscule, cursive) in Britain. This assumption is valid not only for the minuscule forms, deriving from models which can be related to common and semi-professional scripts (for instance the so-called 'quarter-uncial') but also for the forms deriving from capital models. In fact, capital letters too develop and assume new shapes: see the X-shaped As with an angular or X-shaped bar; the angular Cs; H-shaped Ns; Rs with open loop and the last stroke completely horizontal; and figure-of-eight-shaped Ss.

All these forms, together with many others (minuscule Ds, uncial Es, minuscule Hs, trident-shaped Ms, minuscule Qs, Ss, Ts, Vs, the ligatures C-I, F-I and L-I, and Greek letter-forms) have clear and exact counterparts in Insular book script, although not so much in the so-called Insular 'half-uncial' or 'majuscule' (the common script), as in 'Insular decorative capitals' the solemn and sometimes imposing script used for *incipit* and decorated pages.

The common and almost universally accepted interpretation of these astonishing correspondences is that the book-script was imitated by those who chiselled the stones, but simple chronological considerations argue against this view. The very *earliest* extant examples of Insular book script (the *Codex*

---

[26] These forms are commonly believed to derive from 'half-uncial' or 'Gaulish' lapidary models, though no examples of them are known in half-uncial codices or in Gaulish epigraphy.

[27] E. A. Lowe, *English Uncial* (Oxford, 1960); D. H. Wright, 'Some Notes on English Uncial', *Traditio* 17 (1961), 441–56; A. Brückner and R. Marichal (eds), *Chartae Latinae Antiquiores, III, British Museum, London* (Olten and Lausanne, 1963).

[28] A. Petrucci, 'L'onciale romana. Origini, sviluppo e diffusione di una stilizzazione grafica altomedievale (sec. VI–IX)', *Studi medievali*, ser. III, 12 (1971), 75–134.

Usserianus Primus,[29] the *Cathach of St Columba*,[30] and the Springmount Bog Tablets[31]) date back to the end of the sixth or the first half of the seventh century, an age to which we can assign the *latest* examples of Early Christian inscriptions in Britain.

If there was contact between epigraphic and book script (as indeed there was), it must have moved from the former to the latter. The same phenomenon can be noticed in Visigothic and Caroline scripts, where the display script used for the openings of texts is clearly inspired by epigraphic models. Returning to the script of the Early Christian inscriptions of Britain it is possible to trace the evolution of some letters through all the phases from a debased capital to the Insular form. For instance, A with angular bar is found in Late Roman inscriptions in a simple form, then with an upper horizontal stroke or with an X-shape, and ultimately with an X-shaped bar, as in Insular manuscripts. A similar process can be traced for the capital R.

To assume the existence of a genetic relationship between the Early Christian lapidary script of Britain and the Insular decorative capital is to find a link connecting the Insular script to the roots of a local Romano-British tradition. In some of Julian Brown's writings,[32] the problem of the origins of the 'Insular system of scripts' has already been presented as strictly bound to the other problem, that of the Roman educational tradition in Britain. According to Brown, in fact, the fifth and sixth centuries had developed the forms inherited from Roman times and prepared the ground for the making of a new book script (Insular 'Phase I'), while the weight of Continental and

---

29   Dublin, Trinity College Library, Ms. 55; E. A. Lowe, *Codices Latini Antiquiores* (= *CLA*) II, 2nd edn (Oxford, 1972), no. 271.

30   Dublin, Royal Irish Academy, Ms. 12 R 33; *CLA*, II, no. 266. Pictures of this manuscript can also be found in C. Nordenfalk, 'Before the Book of Durrow', *Acta Archaeologica* 18 (1947), 151–9, pls 7, 8, 12, 14, 15, 17; and in H. L. Lawlor, 'The Cathach of St-Columba', *Proceedings of the Royal Irish Academy C*, 23 (1916), 241–443.

31   Dublin, National Museum S. A. 1914:2. See *CLA Supplement*, no. 1684; D. Wright, 'The Tablets from Springmount Bog, a Key to Early Irish Palaeography', *American Journal of Archaeology* 67 (1963), 219. M. McNamara, 'Psalter Text and Psalter Study in the Early Irish Church (A.D. 600–1200)', *Proceedings of the Royal Irish Academy C*, 73 (1973), 201–98, especially 206–7, 213–14, 277–80.

32   T. J. Brown, 'The Oldest Irish Manuscripts and their Late-Antique Background', in *Irland und Europa*, ed. P. Ní Chathain and M. Richter (Stuttgart, 1984), 311–27, now also in *A Palaeographer's View. The Selected Writings of Julian Brown*, ed. J. Bately, M. P. Brown, J. Roberts (London and Oxford, 1993), 221–41; T. J. Brown, 'The Irish Element in the Insular System of Scripts to circa A.D. 850', in *Iren und Europa im früheren Mittelalter*, ed. H. Loewe, 2 vols (Stuttgart, 1982), 101–19, now in *A Palaeographer's View*, 201–21; T. J. Brown, 'Tradition, Imitation and Invention in Insular Handwriting of the Seventh and Eighth Centuries', in *A Palaeographer's View*, 179–200.

in particular Mediterranean book scripts, such as uncial and half-uncial, only appears with 'Phase II' of Insular script, which opens with the celebrated Lindisfarne Gospels, dating back to the end of the seventh century. While E. A. Lowe described Insular script as 'singularly untouched by Roman cursive',[33] Julian Brown, on the contrary, suggested looking to New Roman Cursive, in order to explain some of its typical features, such as the triangular wedges,[34] some ligatures,[35] the E-T ligature[36] and the predominance of the minuscule N in Insular 'half-uncial'.[37] The semi-professional minuscule or 'literary cursive' (for example, so-called 'quarter-uncial'), used for books in Late Roman times all over the Roman Empire, also played, as Brown showed, an important rôle.[38] According to Brown, the typical Insular 'diminuendo' ought to be considered proof of the adoption into the 'Insular system of scripts' of elements directly connected with informal and unofficial writings of this kind.[39] Moreover, in my opinion, it may also be added that the origin of particular letter-forms can be traced back to the same source: for instance, the 'trident M', widely used both in Early Christian inscriptions in Britain and in Insular decorative capitals, seems to be the lapidary version of the minuscule M commonly used in semi-professional book scripts.

Continental influence on Insular script before the second half of the seventh century was, according to Julian Brown, basically limited to manuscript decoration, as attested by the *Cathach of St Columba*, for which, in any case, Brown suggests a date later than 631.[40] The real change came in the second half of the seventh century, when the efforts made by Gregory I and the new relationship of the Anglo-Saxon church with the Continent, and in particular with Rome, yielded permanent consequences. During the two centuries prior to this, from about the middle of the fifth to the middle of the seventh century, Latin writing in Britain survived as part of the Late Roman inheritance. Up to the middle of the seventh century, developments happened only within this inheritance and there are no traces of a contemporary Continental contribution. From this perspective the principal and irreplaceable value of the Early Christian inscriptions in Britain is the fact that they are the only extant evidence for Latin script that we possess for the period between the beginning of the fifth and the second half of the seventh century. They witness for Britain the slow passage from the universalism in

[33]   *CLA*, II, p. xv.
[34]   *A Palaeographer's View*, 226–7, 206–7.
[35]   *Ibid.*, 188.
[36]   *Ibid.*, 230.
[37]   According to Brown, this is a sign of the influence of a documentary model, similar to those known in fifth-century Italy and Africa: *ibid.*, 189.
[38]   *Ibid.*, 232.
[39]   *Ibid.*, 192–3, 223.
[40]   *Ibid.*, 205.

writing typical of the Roman world to early medieval 'particularism'.[41]

So far, I have left the topic of the chronology of the Early Christian inscriptions in Britain untouched and have said only that they fall within a chronological space between the fifth century and the first half of the seventh century. I have avoided any chronological attribution, as I am aware it is necessary to discuss the topic with the highest degree of caution. Nevertheless, it is one of the main tasks of palaeographical research to attempt a solution to this problem.

I hope to have shown how the observation of the palaeographical aspects of the inscriptions can provide a logical evolutionary sequence of letter-forms. To be able to observe a stylistic evolution in the writing obviously means acknowledging a chronological and historical value in the lapidary script. Recently K. Dark repeated the assertion of Wright and Jackson that 'for dating the inscriptions the form of the letters gives little help, for they have been crudely fashioned with a pick'.[42] But it cannot be ignored that each letter, or at least most of the letters, presents particular forms which are not merely the result of chance, but are to be considered an expression of a particular cultural milieu and worthy of analysis as such.

The two main problems regarding the chronology of the inscriptions are, first, the chronological placing of the whole corpus; and, secondly, whether any criteria for an absolute dating of individual examples can be identified. As for the former problem, it has already been stated that the inscriptions can be dated between the fifth and the middle of the seventh century. Recently, objection has been made to taking the fifth and the middle seventh century as respectively *termini post* and *ante quem* for the series of the Early Christian inscriptions of Britain, and a much larger chronological space has been proposed instead: from the fifth to the eleventh or even the twelfth century.[43] The only chronological indicator accepted within this bracket is the presence of ogham inscriptions, which would give a date between the fifth and the eighth century. Nevertheless I would reassert that the first half of the seventh century can be taken as the *terminus ante quem* for the following reasons: (1) because one of the most evolved examples of Early Christian lapidary script in Britain – the *Catamanus* stone at Llangadwaladr – is dated on historical

---

[41]   The concept of 'particularism' in the history of Latin writing was originally expressed by G. Cencetti, 'Dall'unità al particolarismo grafico. Le scritture cancelleresche romane e quelle dell'alto medioevo', in *Il passaggio dall'Antichità al medioevo in Occidente*, Settimane di studio del Centro italiano di studi sull'alto medioevo IX (Spoleto, 1962), 237–64.

[42]   K. Dark, 'Epigraphic, Art-Historical and Historical Approaches to the Chronology of Class I Inscribed Stones', in *The Early Church in Wales and the West: Recent Work in Early Christian Archaeology, History and Place-Names*, ed. N. Edwards and A. Lane, Oxbow Monographs 16 (Oxford, 1992), 51–61, at 51.

[43]   *CECISSWB*, 53–5.

ground to the 620s; (2) because the tradition of Insular book script that, as I have tried to show, in the case of decorative capitals, is inspired by Early Christian epigraphic models, starts in the seventh century.

At the other end of the period, doubts have been expressed with regard to the fifth century as a *terminus post quem*, and the fourth century has been proposed instead.[44] I think this last hypothesis is scarcely convincing from the palaeographical point of view, basically because the British Early Christian inscriptions, though showing clear similarities with the epigraphy of the fourth century, represent a further step in the evolution of the writing.

Within these two formal and chronological limits – fifth to mid-seventh century – it is possible to identify different stylistic phases which indicate different chronological periods. Of course, it is not possible to aim at the precision we could expect if external dating evidence were available, and the dating of any kind of manufactured object, if based on stylistic observations, can often be distorted by phenomena of imitation or cultural backwardness. Nevertheless it is necessary to attempt to classify and recognize differences and give them a historical meaning, first of all through a chronological ordering.

Making use of quantitative (the number of features comparable to the Insular decorative capital) and qualitative observation (the degree of development of letter forms) within the chronological space of the fifth to mid-seventh century, four phases can be identified. In conclusion, then, these are:

(1) The first phase, within the fifth century, encompasses the inscriptions which present more or less the same letter-forms – even if exaggerated – as British Late Antique epigraphy (for instance, the *Vindicianus* stone, from Ravenscar[45]). These letter-forms are generally associated with a traditional layout in horizontal lines. The slanting stroke of R is often shorter than usual and it already tends to become horizontal. Horizontal Is are still unusual.

(2) In the following phase, which can be ascribed to the first half of the sixth century, alongside the characters inherited from the previous tradition, new ones appear: the ligatures F-I and L-I, uncial E, minuscule letters such as F, H, S and T. The first stroke of N starts to be longer than the second, descending below the line. The slanting stroke of R tends to be more and more horizontal and is sometimes at right angles to the first stroke. Horizontal Is are more and more common.

---

[44]   C. A. R. Radford, *The Early Christian Inscriptions of Dumnonia* (Redruth, 1975), 5; Dark, 'Epigraphic, Art-Historical and Historical Approaches', 54.
[45]   *RIB*, no. 721.

(3) The third phase, attributable to the second half of the sixth century, is characterized by the appearance of forms like the triangular A, Insular D and G, trident-shaped M, H-shaped N, or N with the first stroke descending below the line. The use of minuscule letters is more and more common: Q, V.

(4) In the fourth phase, placeable in the first half of the seventh century, all the elements so far scattered and occasionally attested, are standardized and definitively organized, as in the inscriptions of Llangadwaladr, Llanfihangel-Cwmdw and Capel Llanilterne.

Isidore of Seville and 'Hisperic Latin' in Early Medieval Wales: The Epigraphic Culture of Llanllyr and Llanddewi-Brefi

MARK A. HANDLEY

Given the paucity of contemporary documentary sources of all sorts, it is somewhat surprising that the corpus of Latin inscriptions from all over early medieval western Britain has been largely neglected as a source of cultural, rather than linguistic or historical information. This chapter attempts to begin to redress this imbalance by analysing a collection of inscriptions – one from Llanllyr, one from Tregaron and three from Llanddewi-brefi – from the former county of Cardiganshire in western Wales.[1]

The inscription from Llanllyr [fig. 1], which was read by Nash-Williams as, TESQUITUS DITOC MADOMNUAC OCCON FILIUS ASAITGEN DEDIT,[2] is the best place to start, containing, as it does, the only known example of the Latin word *tesquitus*. One searches in vain through CD-Roms, indices and dictionaries for this word. The only, if somewhat remarkable, conclusion is that the Llanllyr inscription contains a word which is unique within the entire corpus of Latin literature and epigraphy. Although the readings in the new *Cardiganshire County History* and by Macalister differ from that of Nash-Williams, concerning *tesquitus* they are identical.[3] Citing Sir John Rhŷs, who saw *tesquitus* as a diminutive of the obscure *tesqua*,[4] (a word whose semantic range extends all the way from 'desert' or 'uninhabitable

---

[1]   These are V. E. Nash-Williams, *The Early Christian Monuments of Wales* (Cardiff, 1950) (hereafter *ECMW*), nos. 124, 132, 115, 116 and 120 respectively.

[2]   *ECMW*, no. 124. The inscription is quite worn, yet upon visiting Llanllyr my reading agreed with that of Nash-Williams rather than those given in note 3.

[3]   The reading in W. G. Thomas, 'The Early Christian Monuments', in *Cardiganshire County History. I. From the Earliest Times to the Coming of the Normans*, ed. J. L. Davies and D. P. Kirby (Cardiff, 1994), 407–20, at 415–16, is TESQUITUS DITOC QUA DOMNUAC OCCON FILIUS ASAITGEN DEDIT. In R. A. S. Macalister, *Corpus Inscriptionum Insularum Celticarum* (Dublin, 1945, 1949), no. 993, it is TESQUITUS DITOC MADOMUACO UON FILIUS ASAITGEN DEDIT.

[4]   Sir J. Rhŷs, 'Epigraphic Notes', *Archaeologia Cambrensis* 13 (1896), 121–2.

Fig. 1: The Llanllyr 'Tesquitus' inscription (*ECMW*, no. 124) (after *ECMW*, fig. 98, by courtesy of the University of Wales Press).

Fig. 2: Llanddewi-brefi: Dallus Dumelus (*ECMW*, no. 115) (after *ECMW*, fig. 93, by courtesy of the University of Wales Press).

land' through to 'sanctuary', or 'temple'),[5] Nash-Williams translated this inscription as 'The small waste-plot of Ditoc which Occon son of Asaitgen gave to Madomnuac'. Before discussing the origins of *tesquitus*, and its suffix, we must first look at how the root word *tesqua*, itself extremely rare, found its way to seventh-century Wales.

Between the years 400 and 700 AD *tesqua* is only found in the works of two known writers. The first was Sidonius Apollinaris from fifth-century Gaul. He used this word three times, each time meaning 'desert', once in a panegyric of the emperor Majorian, once in a poem to the Briton Faustus of Riez, and a third time in a letter to Mamertus Claudianus, a deacon from Vienne.[6] Yet given that we have no examples of the works of Sidonius being

[5] C. T. Lewis and C. Short, *A Latin Dictionary* (Oxford, 1879), 1862, col. 2. For *tesqua* synonymous with *templum*, see *Oxford Latin Dictionary*, ed. P. G. W. Glare (Oxford, 1982), 1930, col. 3.

[6] *Sidonius: Poems and Letters*, 2 vols, ed. W. B. Anderson (London, 1936, 1965), *Carmina* V.91, *Carmina* XVI.91, and *Epistola* IV.iii.

used by an Insular writer of the fifth to seventh centuries,[7] and indeed that no manuscript of Sidonius survives from before the ninth century, it would perhaps be unwise, if there is an alternative, to see the works of Sidonius as the source of *tesqua* at Llanllyr.[8]

The other writer to use *tesqua* during our period was the Spanish bishop, Isidore of Seville (*c*.560–636). He used it once in Book XV of his *Etymologiae*, where he states that 'some people call it a hut and others a rough and wild place'.[9] Can we see this Isidorian usage as the model for the appearance of *tesqua* at Llanllyr? In Ireland knowledge of Isidore certainly pre-dated the year AD 658,[10] with at least twelve different seventh-century Irish writers using Isidorian texts.[11] Moreover, the earliest known manuscript of the *Etymologiae* was written under Irish influence,[12] and we have a further Irish manuscript of Isidore's *Etymologiae* perhaps dating to AD 655.[13] Given the extensive Irish, as well as Anglo-Saxon,[14] knowledge of Isidore, and the choice between Isidore and Sidonius for the origin of *tesqua*, I would argue that its appearance at Llanllyr was the result of familiarity with Isidore of Seville's *Etymologiae* in seventh-century Wales.

The debt to the *Etymologiae* has implications for the translation of the inscription, in that the meaning of *tesqua* may also have been borrowed from this text. The *Etymologiae* gives us the choice between 'a hut' and 'a rough and wild place' or desert.[15] I would argue that the meaning used here is that of

[7]   It used to be claimed that Aldhelm knew some of Sidonius' works; the most recent analysis has argued against this, see A. Orchard, *The Poetic Art of Aldhelm* (Cambridge, 1994), 215–16.

[8]   R. McKitterick, *The Carolingians and the Written Word* (Cambridge, 1989), 154.

[9]   W. M. Lindsay (ed.), *Isidori Hispalensis Episcopi Etymologiarum sive originum Libri XX* (Oxford, 1911), II, XV.12.3 ('Tescua quidam putant esse tuguria, quidam loca praerupta et aspera').

[10]   See, for example, *Cummian's Letter De Controversia Paschali together with a related Irish Computistical Tract, De Ratione Conputandi*, ed. M. Walsh and D. Ó Cróinín (Toronto, 1988), 130 n. 7.

[11]   See J. N. Hillgarth, 'Ireland and Spain in the Seventh Century', *Peritia* 3 (1984), 1–16.

[12]   B. Bischoff, 'Die europäische Verbreitung der Werke Isidors von Sevilla', in *Mittelalterliche Studien: Ausgewählte Aufsätze zur Schriftkunde und Literaturgeschichte* (Stuttgart, 1966), I, 171–94, at 180–7.

[13]   J. P. Carley and A. Dooley, 'An Early Irish Fragment of Isidore of Seville's *Etymologiae*', in *The Archaeology and History of Glastonbury Abbey, Essays in Honour of the 90th Birthday of C. A. Ralegh Radford*, ed. L. Abrams and J. P. Carley (Woodbridge, 1991), 135–61. For the dating of this manuscript to AD 655 see D. Ó Cróinín, *Early Medieval Ireland 400–1200* (London and New York, 1995), 214 n. 95.

[14]   See, for example, A. Orchard, *The Poetic Art of Aldhelm*, 212–14.

[15]   It should be noted that this section of the *Etymologiae* is entitled *aedificiis rusticiis*; it is not from the section on church buildings.

'desert', not so much as a description of the land (hardly likely in a region where pollen analysis shows a thriving arable and pastoral agriculture at this time[16]), but rather using 'desert' to signify a monastery. The long-standing association between the desert and monasticism, as well as the fact that in early medieval Ireland the word *dísert*, borrowed from Latin *desertum*, was used to denote a monastery, or hermitage,[17] supports such a contention. It is a possibility, therefore, that *tesqua* was used in our inscription to signify a monastery or hermitage, with the meanings of 'hut' and 'desert' being combined to provide the word with an altogether new meaning. The phrase 'the small waste-plot' as a translation for the word *tesquitus* is therefore difficult to justify and I would propose that the 'hermitage' or 'monastery' may be closer to the mark.[18]

Whatever the translation, the appearance of this word in western Wales requires explanation. Carlo Tedeschi, in a recent paper, argues that *tesquitus* is an archaization of *tesqua* or *tesca* and thus symptomatic of a proposed archaizing tendency in British Latin.[19] Tedeschi here cites Jackson as his source, yet Jackson never argued that the vocabulary of British Latin was archaic, but rather that it may not have adopted some of the sound changes then taking place in contemporary Continental Latin.[20] Moreover, the whole question of whether or not British Latin was actually archaic has been seriously challenged,[21] leaving Tedeschi's explanation problematic.

Although our knowledge of seventh-century western British Latin culture is very limited, just across the Irish Sea some of the learned clerics of the time were indulging in what is known as 'Hisperic' Latin. One of the most significant aspects of 'Hisperic' latinity was the widespread use of highly obscure and invented vocabulary. Within the A-Text of the *Hisperica Famina* there are almost thirty neologisms, all of which seem to have been used by the

---

[16] J. Turner, 'The Anthropogenic Factor in Vegetational History. I Tregaron and Whixall Mosses', *New Phytologist* 63 (1964), 73–90, at 73–84.

[17] D. Flanagan, 'The Christian Impact on Early Ireland: Place-names Evidence', in *Irland und Europa: Die Kirche im Frühmittelalter*, ed. P. Ní Chatháin and M. Richter (Stuttgart, 1984), 25–51, at 34–6, 48.

[18] There is a further problem with the received translation in that the Latin suffix *-itus* is adjectival rather than diminutive.

[19] C. Tedeschi, 'Osservazioni sui formulari delle iscrizioni britanniche dal V all'VIII secolo', *Romanobarbarica* 13 (1994), 1–13, at 13.

[20] K. H. Jackson, *Language and History in Early Britain: A Chronological Survey of the Brittonic Languages 1st to 12th centuries AD* (Edinburgh, 1953), 76–112.

[21] For varying views on this see A. S. Gratwick, '*Latinitas Britannica*: Was British Latin Archaic?', in *Latin and the Vernacular Languages in Early Medieval Britain*, ed. N. Brooks (Leicester, 1982), 1–79; D. McManus, '*Linguarum Diversitas*: Latin and the Vernaculars in Early Medieval Britain', *Peritia* 3 (1984), 151–88; and P. Russell, 'Recent Work in British Latin', *Cambridge Medieval Celtic Studies* 9 (Summer 1985), 19–29.

author as part of a conspicuous display of learning.[22] Another aspect of 'Hisperic' Latin is the use of a remarkable number of suffixes – including -itus[23] – which were added onto otherwise normal words in order to create both a new word and an impression of obscurity and learning. After analysing the use of suffixes in 'Hisperic' Latin Michael Herren concluded that although 'there are no suffixes that are peculiar to Hisperic ... what is Hisperic is the impulse to coin new words'.[24] In short one should not be surprised by the appearance of an otherwise unattested word in seventh-century Ireland. What is unexpected is that this should occur in Wales.

In attempting to define 'Hisperic' Latin Jane Stevenson has recently listed three characteristics, namely 'a particular kind of hyperbaton, a particular way of using words, which tends to reduce differently nuanced words to synonyms, and a characteristically recherché vocabulary, the last being the most important'.[25] The use of the word tesquitus would appear to fit all of these criteria. Not only is it a neologism created by the addition of a suffix, but it also appears to have been used in a sense which had little regard for the original meaning of its root word, a root word of irreproachably recherché credentials. Thus if these three defining marks can truly be taken as characteristic of 'Hisperic' Latin, then we can feel comfortable in assigning the title of 'Hisperic' to the word tesquitus and to the Llanllyr inscription.

How are we to explain knowledge of 'Hisperic' Latin and of the writings of Isidore of Seville on Welsh soil? It would seem that we have two possibilities: either they represent a borrowing from the literary culture of contemporary Ireland, or they provide evidence for an otherwise unknown 'Hisperic' strand in the indigenous Latin culture of Wales. If the influence came from Ireland then there are several possible historical explanations for how it might have reached Cardiganshire.

Western Wales had undoubtedly been the scene of much Irish settlement in the fifth and, perhaps, sixth centuries, as evidenced by the introduction of the ogham script, certain place-names and the use of Irish personal-names.[26] How long these settlements remained distinctly 'Irish' is not clear and the nature of their links with the 'mother country' into the seventh and eighth centuries is far from certain. In any case, such immigration seems an unlikely background to the transmission of learned Latin culture. As Isidore's works

---

[22] M. Herren, The Hisperica Famina: I. The A-Text. A new critical edition with English Translation and Philological Commentary (Toronto, 1974), 191–4.

[23] M. Herren, Hisperica Famina, 211.

[24] M. Herren, Hisperica Famina, 49.

[25] J. Stevenson, 'Bangor and the Hisperica Famina', Peritia 6–7 (1987–8), 202–16, at 206.

[26] For Irish settlement see C. Thomas, And Shall These Mute Stones Speak? Post-Roman Inscriptions in Western Britain (Cardiff, 1994), 51–66, 183–96.

date from the seventh century, a far more likely context would be the church of the seventh and eighth centuries

Some of those whose Irish names are preserved in the inscriptions of western Wales may be the descendants of early settlers there, but, given the well-known mobility of the personnel of the Insular church, it is possible they are Irish-born clerics working in Wales, as others did in eastern Scotland, independent of any previous secular settlement. Some such figures may be commemorated in our group of inscriptions: the *Dallus Dumelus* found on one of the Llanddewi-brefi inscriptions is an Irish name, and the *Occon, Asaitgen* and *Madomnuac* recorded on the Llanllyr inscription have also been identified as possibly Irish.[27] If, as seems certain, Llanllyr's *Madomnuac* and Llanddewi-brefi's *David* are the saints of those names brought down to us by tradition, then we have concrete evidence for a link between this area of western Wales and Ireland in the eighth century. The early ninth-century martyrology *Félire Óengusso* (The Martyrology of Óengus) commemorates St David on 1 March and Modomnoc on 13 February indicating that knowledge of these Welsh saints' cults had reached Ireland by around 800.[28] Even if a general link can be established it may not be sufficient to explain the specific transmission of 'Hisperic' learning to Cardiganshire. *Félire Óengusso* is associated with the monastery of Tallaght in Leinster, whereas the practice of 'Hisperic' Latin was associated with, and may have been restricted to, the monastery of Bangor in Ulster.[29]

An alternative explanation, of course, is that the Llanllyr text provides a glimpse of a Latin culture indigenous to Wales. The evidence for such a proposal is necessarily slim, given the lack of extant manuscripts, nonetheless most argue that the road towards 'Hisperic' Latin began with the *De excidio* of Gildas, a British writer of the early sixth century.[30] Moreover Michael Lapidge has argued that the *Hisperica Famina* was used in the production of the colloquy known as the *Colloquia Hisperica* and that this colloquy was a Welsh production of the ninth or tenth century which included an 'Hisperic' coinage;[31] that the *Hisperica Famina* may well have originated as a parody of the so-called 'Layer III colloquy' of the *De Raris Fabulis*, a colloquy of British

27   Thomas, *And Shall These Mute Stones Speak*, 110, n. 31. For *Dallus Dumelus* see *ECMW*, no. 115.
28   W. Stokes, *Félire Oengusso Céli Dé The Martyrology of Oengus the Culdee* (London, 1905), 60. See also P. Ó Riain, 'The Tallaght Martyrologies Redated', *Cambridge Medieval Celtic Studies* 20 (1990), 21–38, at 38, who argues for a date between 828 and 833.
29   J. Stevenson, 'Bangor and the *Hisperica Famina*', 202–16.
30   M. Herren, *Hisperica Famina*, 38–9.
31   M. Lapidge, 'Latin Learning in Dark Age Wales: Some Prolegomena', in *Proceedings of the Seventh International Congress of Celtic Studies*, ed. D. E. Evans *et al.* (Oxford, 1986), 91–107, at 97 and n. 59.

origin;[32] and that the lost exemplar of the A-Text of the *Hisperica Famina* may have been a Welsh manuscript.[33] Although such evidence derives from later than our inscriptions, nonetheless it strengthens the proposition that 'Hisperic' learning was known and used in Wales.

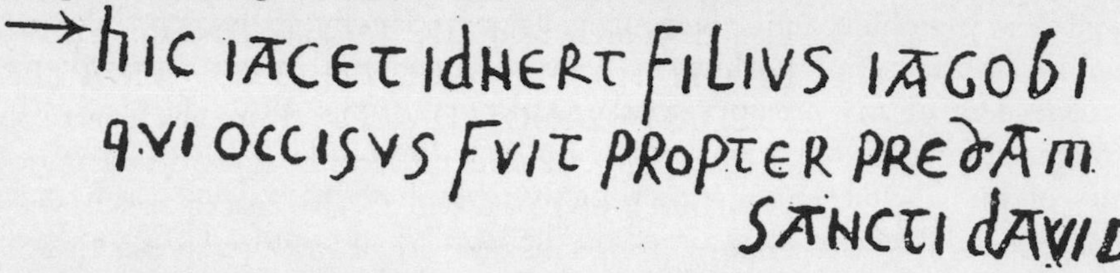

Fig. 3: Llanddewi-brefi: the 'Idnert' Memorial (*ECMW*, no. 116): drawing by Edward Lhuyd (after *Bulletin of the Board of Celtic Studies*, 19 (1960–2), fig. on p. 231, by courtesy of the University of Wales Press).

The inscriptions of Llanddewi-brefi and Llanllyr are, however, our best source of information for determining the nature and extent of the ecclesiastical culture of this region and it would now be appropriate to discuss their scripts and contents in greater detail. We can begin with an analysis of the palaeography of these inscriptions, starting with those from Llanddewi-brefi. Nash-Williams's no. 115 [fig. 2] has a cursive-looking AL ligature, two half-uncial Ss and what can best be described as an attempt at an uncial or cursive M. No. 116 [fig. 3] has four uncial Es, as well as one H, five Ts, 3 Ds, a B and a Q that are all half-uncial. The third inscription from Llanddewi-brefi [fig. 4] has half-uncial E, D, T and B, as well as two abbreviations. The first of these is $\overline{DS}$, this being the usual abbreviated form for *deus*, whilst $\overline{BT}$ has been interpreted as signifying *benedicat*.[34] Those responsible for the Llanddewi-brefi inscriptions clearly had an intimate knowledge of the letter-forms and abbreviation techniques used in manuscripts.

The inscription from Tregaron [fig. 5] has two uncial Es as well as a half-uncial T. Our *tesquitus* inscription from Llanllyr [fig. 1], on the other hand, has four half-uncial Ts, whilst the letters D, E, G, M, S and Q, are also half-uncial. It also has three different types of A; the open and closed varieties of Insular minuscule, and another that appears to be an attempt at the 'oc', or Insular half-uncial form of A. The inscriptions reveal that half-uncial, uncial, Insular minuscule, as well as *capitalis* scripts were all known in this region. We are in the presence of people who were perfectly familiar with a variety of manuscript-based scripts, and when these people were asked to lend their expertise towards the creation of public monuments they exploited this knowledge.

[32] M. Lapidge, 'Latin Learning', 94–7.
[33] M. Lapidge, 'Latin Learning', n. 58.
[34] *ECMW*, 99–100. I can find no other examples of this abbreviation.

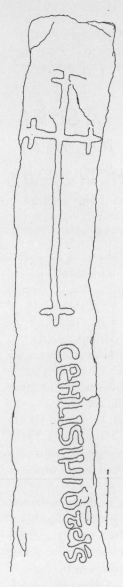

Fig. 4: Llanddewi-brefi: Cenlisini (*ECMW*, no. 120) (after *ECMW*, fig. 95, by courtesy of the University of Wales Press).

We must now look at what the inscriptions themselves say. The 'Idnert' inscription from Llanddewi-brefi read HIC IACET IDNERT FILIVS IACOBI | QVI OCCISVS FVIT PROPTER PREDAM | SANCTI DAVID.[35] 'Here lies Idnert son of Iacob, who was slain on account of the despoiling of (the church of) St David'.[36] This inscription is very important for a number of reasons; first its mention of St David not only provides us with our oldest record of the patron saint of Wales, but it would also seem to indicate that this was a monastery, in that the early sources for the life and career of David make him a monastic founder.[37] The inscription may also show a close relationship between the surrounding lay community and this monastery for not only has Idnert been associated with St David's after his death, but the inscription also talks of St David's as an establishment of some wealth, at least wealthy enough to be worthy of being despoiled, a situation only possible through the generosity of a local landowner, or landowners. Nor should we forget that Idnert's father was named Iacob, the only other person with a biblical name on a western British inscription outside of Wareham in Dorset. On the other hand Charles Thomas has recently argued that Iacob may have been the abbot of this monastery and Idnert his son, the intended heir to the monastery.[38] In either case, we are seeing here an aristocratic family's close connection to this monastery, either as abbots or as the principal benefactors. Indeed we need not perceive the two as mutually exclusive. Iacob having a son makes it

[35] *ECMW*, no. 116 (fig. 3b), also see G. Gruffydd and H. P. Owen, 'The Earliest Mention of St David?: An Addendum', *Bulletin of the Board of Celtic Studies* 19 (1960–2), 231–2 and figure on p. 231. The inscription is now only partly preserved. The reading of the full text is based on a late seventeenth-century drawing by Edward Lhuyd reproduced by Gruffydd and Owen (see fig. 3).

[36] The translation here used is that used by Charles Thomas in his paper to the International Conference on Medieval Epigraphy at St Hilda's College, Oxford in 1996, now published as 'The Llandewi-breffi "Idnert" Stone', *Peritia* 10 (1996), 136–83 (p. 140 for a translation in slightly different words). See also C. Thomas, *Christian Celts: Messages and Images* (Stroud, 1998), 26-31, 62, 79, 180.

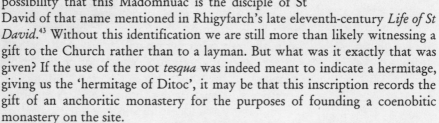

unlikely that he had spent his whole life as a monk. We can envisage a local family founding a monastery into which – once the familial succession had been secured – the head of the family could retire.

Another, although slightly later, inscription from this same churchyard reads CENLISINI $\overline{BT}$ $\overline{DS}$, *Cenlisini b(enedica)t D(eu)s*, further implying a Christian community.[39] The third inscription from Llanddewi-brefi contains simply an Irish name, this being DALLUS | DUMELUS.[40] The inscription from Tregaron is also just two words long, reading POTENINA | MULIIER.[41]

Our *tesquitus* inscription from Llanllyr provides us with a wealth of information. Whatever exactly the *tesquitus* of Ditoc is thought to be, it was given by Occon son of Asaitgen to Madomnuac, or perhaps, given the 'Celtic charter' tradition of using a founding saint's name as an eponym for a monastery or church, the *tesquitus* was given 'to Madomnuac's'.[42] It is a possibility that this Madomnuac is the disciple of St David of that name mentioned in Rhigyfarch's late eleventh-century *Life of St David*.[43] Without this identification we are still more than likely witnessing a gift to the Church rather than to a layman. But what was it exactly that was given? If the use of the root *tesqua* was indeed meant to indicate a hermitage, giving us the 'hermitage of Ditoc', it may be that this inscription records the gift of an anchoritic monastery for the purposes of founding a coenobitic monastery on the site.

Such a conclusion is supported by another aspect of this inscription which has so far been overlooked. The majority of the western British and Irish inscriptions from this time record the patronymic as part of the maintenance and provision of a familial title to land,[44] yet our Occon is here

---

[37]   A useful summary of the early sources for St David can be found in D. S. Evans, *The Welsh Life of St David* (Cardiff, 1988), xi–xix.

[38]   See n. 36.

[39]   *ECMW*, no. 120.

[40]   *ECMW*, no. 115.

[41]   *ECMW*, no. 132.

[42]   For the 'Celtic Charter' tradition and further examples, see W. Davies, 'The Latin Charter-tradition in Western Britain, Brittany and Ireland in the Early Mediaeval Period', in *Ireland in Early Medieval Europe. Studies in Memory of Kathleen Hughes*, ed. D. Whitelock *et al.* (Cambridge, 1982), 258–80.

[43]   J. W. James (ed.), *Rhigyfarch's Life of St David* (Cardiff, 1967), chs. 41, 43, 18–19.

recording that he was alienating land. The early Irish legal text *Córus Béscna* may explain why. It states that title to the offices and property of a monastery passed along the lineage of the founding Saint, which in this case was Madomnuac. It goes on to state, however, that if someone from the Saint's lineage could not be found, the office and property of the monastery passed to a descendant of the person who donated the land for the original foundation of the monastery – Occon.[45] It may be, therefore, that Occon commissioned this inscription with such a legal possibility in mind: he recorded his name and his father's name to ensure that his lineage would be known.[46] If this is the case, then not only can we argue that similar rules to those laid out in the *Córus Béscna* applied in Wales, but that the Llanllyr inscription may, in fact, record the foundation of a monastery.

The Cambro-Latin inscriptions of Llanllyr and Llanddewi-brefi are evidence, therefore, of a high level of cultural attainment within a significant group of monastic establishments in early medieval Wales. However, our picture of the Latin culture of these monasteries does not end there. If even half of the compositional complexity argued for by Charles Thomas on the 'Idnert' inscription from Llanddewi-brefi is correct,[47] then this may be further support for the argument that this area held centres of considerable cultural importance.

One last piece of evidence enables us, however, to posit an indigenous British Latin cultural context for Llanllyr and Llanddewi-brefi. During the early Middle Ages the Latin verse writers of Ireland employed a remarkable number of different metres. Not once, however, did they use a Classical quantitative metre.[48] According to work done by David Howlett, a number of the western British inscriptions do exhibit such quantitative verse metre. The 'Idnert' inscription from Llanddewi-brefi is one of these.[49] Given that metres

[44] See M. A. Handley, 'The Early Medieval Western British Inscriptions: Function and Sociology', in *The Community, the Family and the Saint: Patterns of Power in Early Medieval Europe*, ed. J. M. Hill and M. Swan (Turnhout, 1998), 339–61.

[45] See *The Ancient Laws of Ireland* (Dublin, 1865–1901), III, 3–79, and the discussions in P. Ó Riain, 'Conservation in the Vocabulary of the Early Irish Church', in *Sages, Saints and Storytellers: Celtic Studies in Honour of James Carney*, ed. D. Ó Corráin *et al.* (Maynooth, 1989), 358–66 at 358–61; and D. Ó Cróinín, *Early Medieval Ireland*, 162–4.

[46] Kilnasaggart in Armagh has a similar inscription, which has been translated as; 'This place did Ternoc son of Ciaran the Little bequeath under the protection of Peter the Apostle' (R. A. S. Macalister, *Corpus Inscriptionum Insularum Celticarum*, 2 vols (Dublin, 1945 and 1949), no. 946).

[47] See n. 36. I remain sceptical, however. See my forthcoming review in *Britannia* 31 (2000).

[48] D. Howlett, 'Aldhelm and Irish Learning', *Archivium Latinitatis Medii Aevi* 52 (1994), 37–75 at 64.

[49] I am grateful to David Howlett for this information in advance of publication of

of this kind were apparently unknown in Ireland at this time, we are justified in arguing that the composition of the 'Idnert' inscription at Llanddewi-brefi was the product of Cambro-Latin rather than Hiberno-Latin culture. Moreover if Llanddewi-brefi was a centre of Cambro-Latin learning, we can further posit that our Llanllyr inscription with its use of Isidore of Seville and its 'Hisperic' Latin construction was also the product of Cambro-Latin learning. The culture exhibited at Llanllyr and Llanddewi-brefi may well have shone bright within the constellation of Welsh monasteries, and thus what we find from them may not be truly representative of the whole. Nonetheless, it would, perhaps, be rash to dismiss them in this way; they may well have been perfectly representative, and if this were the case, we may have to alter radically our perception of the extent and nature of Latin culture in early medieval Wales and western Britain.

Acknowledgements
I would like to thank Charles Thomas, David Howlett, Rosamond McKitterick, Oliver Padel and Aedeen Cremin for their help with this chapter.

---

his 'Insular Latin Writers' Rhythms', *Peritia* 11 (1998), 53–116, at 80–1.

Problems in Dating the Origin of the Ogham Script

ANTHONY HARVEY

This chapter is about the difficulties inherent in attempting to date the origin of the strange, Morse-code-like script known as ogham, in which our earliest extant Gaelic-language texts are preserved [fig. 6].[1] The few hundred oldest surviving ogham inscriptions being on stones found across Ireland and southern Britain, it might be thought that archaeology would be the first discipline to which one would turn for assistance. However, it emerges in practice that historical linguistics have so far come closer to giving definite answers than has the other science; so that even archaeologists have, at least until very recently, tended to rely on linguistic arguments. For one thing, very few excavations have been conducted to place ogham stones in their archaeological context; the physical contexts often look likely to prove minimally informative (although scholars such as Peter Harbison, Fionnbarr Moore, Charles Thomas and Catherine Swift have recently been gleaning more from them than had previously been realized possible);[2] and in any case a large number of the prime examples are known to have been moved during their history.[3] Second, the straight lines and notches of ogham do not lend themselves to palaeographical or stylistic analysis. Third, the nature of the material taken in isolation is not conducive to dating by natural-scientific means: radiocarbon dating might tell us when a stone was erected in its current setting, but no more precisely than plus-or-minus half a century (and

---

[1] As well as being presented at the Oxford conference, this contribution was read with revisions at the Tionól of the School of Celtic Studies of the Dublin Institute for Advanced Studies in November 1996; I am grateful to those who participated in the subsequent discussion on each occasion.

[2] P. Harbison, *Pilgrimage in Ireland: The Monuments and the People* (London, 1991), 205–10; F. Moore 'Munster Ogham Stones: Siting, Context and Function', in *Early Medieval Munster: Archaeology, History and Society*, ed. M. A. Monk and J. Sheehan (Cork, 1998), 23–32; C. Thomas, *And Shall These Mute Stones Speak? Post-Roman Inscriptions in Western Britain* (Cardiff, 1994); C. Swift, *Ogam Stones and the Earliest Irish Christians*, Maynooth Monographs, ser. Minor 2 (Maynooth, 1997).

[3] D. McManus, *A Guide to Ogam*, Maynooth Monographs 4 (Maynooth, 1991), 47, 49.

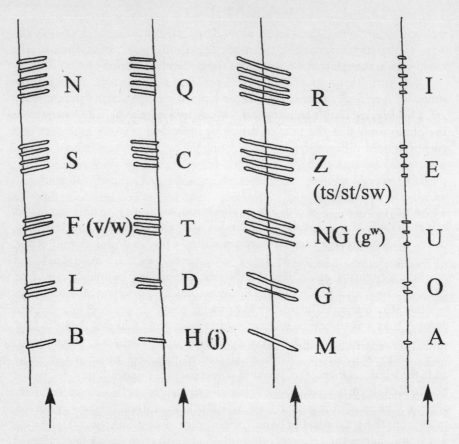

Fig. 6: The basic ogham alphabet with the traditional transcription of each symbol in capitals. Lower-case letters are phonetic ones, and indicate the earlier and, indeed, in some cases quite different values that particular symbols may have had to start with – these suggestions being due in recent years to Damian McManus (*Guide to Ogam*, 36–9) and Patrick Sims-Williams (*Trans. Philol. Soc.* 1993, referenced below, n. 21) (drawn by Caitlin Evans).

there would be no way of knowing whether or not this event was contemporary with the carving of the inscription). Indeed, the only scope that I am aware of for dating an ogham inscription taken by itself by such means would arise in a circumstance which, as far as I know, has not hitherto been mooted, so I do so very tentatively; it is where organic matter is found actually inside one of the notches. Furthermore, in the case of a lichen, its minimum age can in principle be determined from a knowledge of the (often very slow) growth-rate, and as some lichens apparently live for thousands of years,[4] there may be surviving datable organisms that are as old as the notches

---

[4]   V. A[hmadjian], 'Lichen', in *The New Encyclopaedia Britannica: Macropaedia*, 15th edn (London, 1943–74), X, 882–8, at 887.

where they are found. But I know of no actual attempts to date oghams in this way, and in any case such a technique could only give us a terminus ante quem (useful though that would be) for the particular inscription.

We turn, then, to the linguistic problems; but before raising those problems specifically, I need to make a couple of methodological points. They are, I believe, applicable to historical text corpora in general. They stem from the observation that the task of dating an individual text (or each text in a corpus) is quite different from that of dating the origin of the writing tradition represented by that text (or corpus). Although this may seem obvious, it is probably worth spelling out the implications. For example, we find that apparently opposed linguistic principles need to be applied depending on which of the two tasks we are attempting. Written standards tend to remain fixed, since texts survive from one generation to another and, as Daniel Jones put it, 'alphabetic traditions ... always grow up sooner or later'.[5] But a scribe or inscriber cannot anticipate linguistic changes that have not yet taken place. This gives rise to the first point that needs making: whenever a given alphabetic text displays mutually anachronistic forms of words, it follows that, at the time the text was executed, the language had reached at least the developmental stage reflected in the text's most advanced feature.[6] External influences apart, all other earlier-looking features must be examples of orthographic conservatism (and we come to the question of what that has to mean in a moment). Conversely, it was only very recently that linguists began to be able accurately to reconstruct past stages of languages by the comparative method and by internal reconstruction, independently of written tradition. Hence we have the second point: whereas any medieval text that displays mutually anachronistic forms must date from at least as late as the latest of them, the writing tradition to which the text belongs must have an origin at least as early as the earliest of them. All other forms in the text will reflect written conventions coined at stages through which the language passed during its development between these dates.

It is time to look at some specific ogham instances of the phenomenon under discussion. Let us take for example the inscription to which the number 145 is assigned in the first volume of R. A. S. Macalister's still-standard *Corpus Inscriptionum Insularum Celticarum:*[7] the stone is at Arraglen at the north-west end of Brandon Mountain in Co. Kerry, and in transliteration it reads QRIMITIR RON[A]NN MAQ COMOGANN.[8] It is one of the

5   D. Jones, *The Phoneme: Its Nature and Use*, 3rd edn (Cambridge, 1967), 253.

6   See A. Harvey, 'Retrieving the Pronunciation of Early Insular Celtic Scribes: The Case of Dorbbēne', *Celtica* 22 (1991), 48–63, at 51.

7   R. A. S. Macalister, *Corpus Inscriptionum Insularum Celticarum*, 2 vols (Dublin, 1945 and 1949), I.

8   Here and elsewhere Macalister's reading is controlled by reference to McManus's helpful Appendix 2 at *Guide*, 65–77.

best-known members of the whole corpus. On almost all ogham stones, the whole text is in the genitive case; one has to take as read an introductory phrase such as 'this is the stone of', and there seems no reason to regard this stone as any exception. What actually appears in most cases is a formula of the shape 'of N son of M', and that is what we have here;[9] the only thing unusual about text 145 is that it displays in addition a professional title (the word beginning with the Q symbol), which is derived via British Latin from Greek πρεσβύτερος:[10] the commemorand is a Christian priest. Now it is well known that, like the other Celtic languages, Irish at some stage lost the final syllables of its words and names in a so-called 'apocope'.[11] This had clearly happened by the time our stone was inscribed: it commemorates someone who would still in today's Irish be called Rónán and, as can be seen, there is no trace in the inscription of the original final vowel of the name (which, being in the genitive case, would once have been /rro:nagni:/). Thus it is no surprise to find the word for son (nowadays 'mic' in the genitive)[12] already rendered monosyllabically (the transliteration being MAQ) rather than as the earlier /maqqi:/; and Rónán's father's name similarly without the final front vowel. This is linguistically straightforward. But the same cannot be said of Macalister's no. 4, LUGADDON MAQI LUGUDEC. The two names beginning with L in this text are both consonantal stems (that is, they belong to an Irish declension corresponding to the Latin third); so, in the genitive case as here, they would each once have had a final syllable /-as/ (like the /-is/ in Latin 'legionis' from 'legio'). There is no trace of that in the ogham, showing that the language had already dropped its final syllables. How then to explain the word sandwiched between the two names and meaning 'of the son of'? It is clearly part of the same unitary text yet, coming out in transliteration as MAQI, it still displays the original final front-vowel (corresponding to the final /-i:/ of Latin second-declension genitives like 'domini'). If the Irish tongue had already dropped its final syllables by the time of this inscription, as we have just seen it must have done, then the 'son' word was already monosyllabic; and I am not aware of any suggestion that, at the time of our

---

[9] On the formulae customary in ogham inscriptions see McManus, *Guide*, 51–2.

[10] The stages in the derivation are given *ibid.*, 61.

[11] This statement seems satisfactory enough for present purposes, though if the ogham corpus contained the full range of parts of speech it would need refinements such as those indicated by K. McCone, 'Further to Absolute and Conjunct', *Ériu* 33 (1982), 1–29, at 24–5.

[12] My slightly non-standard notation is to distinguish spoken forms, which I write in normalized spelling and enclose in quotation marks as here, from specific Roman-letter written types, which I italicize in the usual way; on the advantages of making this distinction see A. Harvey, 'Suggestions for Improving the Notation Used for Celtic Historical Linguistics', in *Hispano-Gallo-Brittonica: Essays in Honour of Professor D. Ellis Evans on the Occasion of his Sixty-Fifth Birthday*, ed. J. F. Eska *et al.* (Cardiff, 1995), 52–7.

engraver, the linguistic skill was available to reconstruct a final syllable once it had disappeared. The only way our inscription can have come to display it, then, as it does, is by having been part of a living spelling tradition that was established at a time when the syllable in question would still have been pronounced. This is what the phrase 'orthographic conservatism' necessarily involves, and I feel we need to beware of a tendency to use it more loosely. Scholars sometimes refer vaguely to there having been in existence at particular times memories of earlier forms or even of earlier pronunciations, as if these could have been plucked from the air;[13] instead, the inscriber must have been conscious of a fairly definite injunction along the lines: 'for the monosyllabic word /mekʲ/, write the symbols for MAQI.' Such an injunction, whether mediated to him by the experience of having seen (and perhaps carved) many other inscriptions, or by having been taught it in some form of lesson, or by some other means, must nevertheless have reached him undistorted from as far back as necessary in the tradition. Hence we have indirect evidence of a fairly self-disciplined academy producing these inscriptions; its members knew more than merely the ogham alphabet and the individual sounds associated with each symbol.[14]

This point has an important methodological consequence. Consider ogham text Macalister no. 85, *GRILAGNI MAQI SCILAGNI*, which shows original final syllables still in place (albeit in poor condition in two of the instances, as McManus avers)[15] on each of its three genitive-case words (these all belonging to the o-stem declension, analogous to the Latin second). The temptation is to say that the inscription must date from before those syllables disappeared in pronunciation. But of course this is not necessarily so: we have just seen that, on occasion, inscribers must have been conscious of archaizing injunctions, so the same may have applied in this case. After all, it would not take a very complex injunction to have induced our man to inscribe an I-symbol at the end of each of the three genitives that he wished to write. Scholars from as long ago as Eoin MacNeill in 1931[16] have – sporadically, at least – shown that they were conscious of this conservative tendency, and Damian McManus has recently drawn full and systematic attention to it in his excellent *Guide*. But I feel that even McManus then falls victim to a subtler temptation when he uses the sound-changes revealed or not revealed in individual inscriptions as a basis for placing them in relative chronological

---

[13] On this syndrome see A. Harvey, 'Retrieving the Pronunciation of Early Insular Celtic Scribes: Towards a Methodology', *Celtica* 21 (1990), 178–90, at 188–9.

[14] For a discussion of what else they knew see A. Harvey, 'Early Literacy in Ireland: The Evidence from Ogam', *Cambridge Medieval Celtic Studies* 14 (Winter 1987), 1–15.

[15] McManus, *Guide*, 66.

[16] 'Archaisms in the Ogham Inscriptions', *Proceedings of the Royal Irish Academy* 39, C (1931), 33–53.

order.[17] In terms of the inscriptions we have looked at, this is the equivalent of saying that Macalister no. 85 is earlier than nos. 4 and 145. But in fact this, while certainly possible and perhaps likely, is not necessarily so; all that need be the case is that the carver of 85 was more familiar with the spelling conventions of the oghamist profession than were the individuals responsible for nos. 4 and 145, or that he simply applied the conventions more consistently. The inscriber of 85 may perfectly well have pronounced what he wrote as /gr^{j}ella:n^j μek^j sk^{j}ella:n^j/. It should be stressed that McManus's tabulation stands, and is very valuable, when it is viewed as a relative chronology of the different types of ogham word-forms, since clearly ones that show final vowels belong to a tradition that began before the tradition of not showing them; it is just that, annoyingly enough, it seems unsafe to declare that any given early-looking inscription necessarily pre-dates a later-looking one on those grounds alone.

Most of the work done in recent years in connection with the dating of ogham inscriptions has been directed towards dating the corpus of extant monuments, individually and collectively. This has proved very difficult. Ogham script consists of straight lines and notches, and that makes it particularly easy to carve on stone (and indeed indicates that it was probably designed for this or, as some early literary sources may suggest, for conveying messages on branches or twigs[18]); but, as pointed out above, it offers precious little scope for stylistic analysis that would give a clue as to dating from a strictly epigraphic point of view. It is true that we will have something more to go on if we are working with one of those stones in Britain that have Roman-letter equivalents or near-equivalents alongside their ogham texts or, as McManus pointed out, if our text can be shown to postdate a Christian cross on the same stone;[19] but in general we shall not have much to work from except the state of the Irish language as represented by our particular inscription. And as we have almost nothing but nouns (mostly names) in our corpus, there are no developments in verbs or syntax to analyse and date. Given the considerations that I have outlined so far, the situation might appear almost hopeless. Nevertheless, over forty years ago Professor Kenneth Jackson in his famous book *Language and History in Early Britain* tackled the whole question head-on, and brilliantly,[20] for the examples from Britain. Using the evidence from sound-changes and from the Roman-letter latinizations where available, he arrived at a rather precise relative chronology

---

[17] McManus, *Guide*, 93–6.
[18] McManus, *Guide*, 157–9; see, however, the associated discussion and McManus's conclusion (163) that the sources should perhaps be interpreted as simply referring to writing in general.
[19] McManus, *Guide*, 54.
[20] K. Jackson, *Language and History in Early Britain* (Edinburgh, 1953; reprinted Blackrock, 1994 with a new introduction by W. Gillies), hereafter *LHEB*, 149–93.

for his inscriptions. He also attempted to pin the whole structure down to absolute dates by reference not only to the epigraphy of the Roman-letter texts, but also to what was accepted to be knowledge of the floruit of an individual allegedly commemorated on stone no. 358 (which reads MEMORIA VOTEPORIGIS PROTICTORIS in Roman, and in ogham VOTECORIGAS), as well as to what were considered to be more or less absolute dates for various sound changes. The result was a picture of an oghamist phenomenon flourishing from the fifth to the seventh centuries, perhaps extending back to the fourth for some of the stones surviving in Ireland. Now I do not wish to imply that Jackson was unaware of the factor of orthographic conservatism when compiling his relative chronology, but the degree of precision he brought to the process does indicate that he tended to discount it. By using the supposed external reference points, his book ends up by assigning almost any particular stone to the early, middle or late period of an individual century. But a couple of considerations make this seem rather too precise even for the material from Britain. In the first place, as Patrick Sims-Williams has concluded, 'the absolute chronology of British Roman-letter inscriptions is [itself] necessarily vague since not a single inscription can be precisely dated'.[21] Second, there are actually problems in connection with the identification and date of the individual commemorated on the key stone no. 358. For one thing, there is a potentially crucial disparity between the ogham and corresponding Roman-letter versions of the name on the stone, on the one hand, and the name of the supposedly identical individual addressed by Gildas in his celebrated denunciation De excidio Britanniae,[22] on the other. Apart from any discrepancies there may be in the termination, neither of the forms on the stone indicates a resonant, /r/, after the first vowel symbol; whereas the manuscripts of Gildas, in giving us (vocative) forms varying from Vortipore to Vertepori, are nevertheless unanimous in presenting us with the letter r there before the t. This matters because the presence or absence of a resonant in that position makes all the difference between a prefix meaning Over- (or Super-) and one meaning Under- (or Sub-) respectively. This diametric opposition in meaning may well prompt us to hesitate in accepting Jackson's dismissal of the difference as trivial;[23] instead we should probably take seriously Sims-Williams's suggestion that we have perhaps to do with two members of the same dynasty.[24] For another thing, the king of Dyfed whom

21 P. Sims-Williams, 'Some Problems in Deciphering the Early Irish Ogam Alphabet', Transactions of the Philological Society 91:2 (1993), 133–80, at 135.
22 T. Mommsen (ed.), 'Gildae sapientis De excidio et conquestu Britanniae', in Chronica Minora III, Monumenta Germaniae Historica: Auctores Antiquissimi 13 (Berlin, 1898), 1–85, at 43.
23 Jackson, LHEB, 625, n. 1.
24 P. Sims-Williams, 'Dating the Transition to Neo-Brittonic: Phonology and History, 400–600', in Britain 400–600: Language and History, ed. A.

Gildas lambasts must (from the context) have been a contemporary of his; but there is now much uncertainty about the date of Gildas's work itself.[25] So we have to admit that we cannot be sure to within half a century of the dates of the recipient of Gildas's attacks; and that, even if we could be, stone 358 may well commemorate someone else. Jackson's anchor for his absolute dating-scheme seems therefore to be somewhat weakened; and when one finds Sims-Williams describing Jackson's epigraphically arrived-at starting point of circa 450 for the dual-script monuments in general as 'surely likely to be in about the right century',[26] the endorsement does not strike one as particularly ringing. McManus, for his part, preserves Jackson's general dating framework, apparently on the basis that revision thereof would, as he puts it, 'present as many difficulties as it would solve';[27] but in a 1992 review I described this as unsound because I felt that it would have been better to stress how uncertain the whole matter was.[28] Anyway, however we view the inscriptions from Britain, some of which at least have accompanying Latin, for the oghams in Ireland McManus points out that 'we do not have a single secure anchor point at an archaeological, palaeographical, historical or linguistic level. Absolute dating is beyond our reach as the identity of the people commemorated on the inscriptions is unknown'.[29] Having said that, it may be significant that Dr Catherine Swift has identified a close correlation between the occurrence in ogham inscriptions of the cryptic element spelled (in transliteration) KOI, on the one hand, and the retention of final syllables, on the other. In the course of a wide-ranging discussion, she argues for a syntactic correspondence amounting to functional equivalence between the element in question and the Latin formula HIC IACIT (or HIC IACET) as used on stones in south-west Britain.[30] This formula seems to have originated in fourth-century Italy. Since, as we have seen, the retention of final syllables in ogham inscriptions is something that on balance one would associate with early more than with late inscriptions, and since it is in this context that the element occurs, we may have here a buttress for the conventional view that the extant ogham corpus begins not before the fourth century. However, as Swift herself points out, it is clear from its shape that the symbol transliterated K in these inscriptions

---

Bammesberger and A. Wollmann, Anglistische Forschungen 205 (Heidelberg, 1990), 217–61, at 226.

[25] Sims-Williams remarks that 'we may have to reckon that Gildas may have written at any period between c. 500 and c. 560' (ibid., 223; to the relevant scholarship that he cites (ibid., n. 20) should be added M. W. Herren, 'Gildas and Early British Monasticism', ibid., 65–78).

[26] Ibid., 227.

[27] McManus, Guide, 99.

[28] A. Harvey, Éigse 26 (1992), 188–90, at 189.

[29] McManus, Guide, 78.

[30] Swift, Ogam Stones, 97–111.

'represents an addition to ... the original sequence of four groups of five symbols which make up the ogam alphabet', evidence that should perhaps be weighed against their morphological conservatism when considering whether the KOI texts really are earlier than those not featuring that element; while if they do indeed represent 'the earliest detectable phase of ogam inscriptions which we currently possess' then the presence of the K symbol on these stones, inasmuch as it represents a modification of the original alphabet, constitutes a further indication that 'ogam, as a writing system, must have developed at some point prior to the earliest stones which we now have.'[31]

The scholarship that I have mentioned so far has been directed, as I said, to dating the extant corpus of texts, and its members. There have, as I hope I have shown, been several false dawns; so one might expect that the situation would be even worse if we were to tackle the more theoretical question of when the tradition was first established; but, as I pointed out at the beginning, the methodology for this is different; it is simpler and, surprisingly enough, some of the problems seem to disappear. For example, we are no longer affected by the problem of orthographic conservatism. Even if none of the surviving inscriptions was actually carved at a time when Irish final syllables were still pronounced, the fact that such syllables are represented on some of the stones shows that they were still to be heard when the tradition began -- when the orthographic rules were set up, as it were. Otherwise the final syllables would have been irrecoverable. (The other logical possibility is that ogham borrowed the rules from some earlier tradition of writing the Irish language alphabetically; but, in the absence of any evidence for such, the principle of Occam's razor suggests that we should not pursue it.)

A further linguistic clue has to do with the question of lenition; that is, an earlier Irish sound change one of whose effects (to put it simply) was to transform stop consonants in certain environments into the corresponding spirants (thus /t/ became /θ/, /k/ became /χ/ and so on).[32] It has been a much argued question whether the ogham corpus as a whole reflects this change or not, given that it does not use the equivalent of what came to be the manuscript Roman-letter convention for indicating it. That convention – which I have argued was itself a Celtic coining, incidentally[33] – involves

---

[31]   *Ibid.*, 64–5.

[32]   For a fuller discussion see A. Harvey, 'Aspects of Lenition and Spirantization', *Cambridge Medieval Celtic Studies* 8 (Winter 1984), 87–100. Along lines since followed much further by Kim McCone (*Towards a Relative Chronology of Ancient and Medieval Celtic Sound Change*, Maynooth Studies in Celtic Linguistics 1 (Maynooth, 1996), 81–98), Sims-Williams has recently suggested that lenition took place in stages ('Dating the Transition', 230–6), in which case what I call lenition in what follows should where appropriate be understood as referring to voiceless consonants only.

[33]   A Harvey, 'Some Significant Points of Early Insular Celtic Orthography', in

adding the letter *h* to the relevant consonant symbol to indicate spirantization (*t* plus *h* representing /θ/, the spirantization of /t/; *c* plus *h* representing /χ/, the spirantization of /k/; and so on); and ogham does not have this. What it does have is a system by which double consonant symbols alternate with single ones; and a statistical analysis has shown that, within words, the doubling of symbols correlates significantly with non-lenitability (that is, with those environments where a stop rather than a spirant articulation can be shown to have continued beyond the time of lenition); while singularity of symbols goes with lenitability (that is, susceptibility to spirantization at that stage).[34] The great number of counter-examples in the corpus has led some scholars to discount the result, though in my view not convincingly.[35] However, the phonemic opposition between spirants and non-spirants was anyway, it would seem, already prefigured before the time of lenition by an opposition between short and long consonants respectively;[36] so in the case of any given ogham inscription, the presence of the convention to which I have been referring would make synchronic sense whether the sound-change had yet happened or not, and we should be none the wiser. But if what we are trying to do is date the origin of the tradition, the outlook seems somewhat brighter: original final consonants were in lenition position, and in this position we frequently find the S symbol. (We do, for example, on the consonantal-stem endings in the names in ogham nos. 358 and 66 discussed below). It seems unlikely that the original sibilant thus represented had progressed far, if at all, along the phonetic path to becoming its fully lenited counterpart [h] at the time ogham symbols began to be used, because once it had done so it is hard to see how the Irish could have retrieved the fact that the sound had once been [s]. Indeed, the only way they could have done so would be by means of being conscious of morphophonemic alternations between /s/ and /h/ at the beginnings of words and by extrapolating from there, which (*pace* some recent scholarship on this point) seems rather a tall order.[37] Instead, we can probably assert with reasonable confidence that,

---

[33]   A Harvey, 'Some Significant Points of Early Insular Celtic Orthography', in *Sages, Saints and Storytellers: Celtic Studies in Honour of Professor James Carney*, ed. D. Ó Corráin *et al.*, Maynooth Monographs 2 (Maynooth, 1989), 56–66.

[34]   A. Harvey, 'The Ogam Inscriptions and their Geminate Consonant Symbols', *Ériu* 38 (1987), 45–71.

[35]   McCone's perception of the (relatively elementary) mathematical techniques used as 'statistical prestidigitation' (*Relative Chronology*, 25) would seem indicative of the weight to be placed upon the specific objections as marshalled by him *ibid*.

[36]   Harvey, 'Aspects', 92–4.

[37]   McManus (*Guide*, 86–7) and McCone (*Relative Chronology*, 25–6) seem to argue for the morphophonemic explanation, apparently on the basis of the (perfectly valid) observation that 'a three-stage development -*s* > -*h* > 0 between the earliest Ogam inscriptions probably dating from around the beginning of the fifth century and some time before the apocope roughly at its end is more of a squeeze

whereas it is impossible to tell whether any given ogham inscriptions (such as no. 358, or no. 66) were carved before or after the time of lenition, the tradition of carving such inscriptions was established before that time.

One sound-change that may have already taken place when the ogham tradition began was that by which, in Gaelic as opposed to British Celtic, original clusters of nasal plus voiceless stop became long voiced stops; in other words, the change by which /nt/ and /nk/ became /dd/ and /gg/ respectively. In the present context we might call it denasalization, for convenience. To take an example, the name of the Welsh town of Deganwy probably reflects that of a local population group called the Decanti, and two entries for the ninth century in the A-text of the so-called *Annales Cambriae* still refer to them (in the Latin genitive plural) as *Decantorum* (that is, with *nt* preserved).[38] In contrast, Irish ogham inscription no. 66 reads, in transliteration, MAQI-DECCEDDAS AVI TURANIAS; and one can see the same element appearing as the second half of the initial compound name. Here one can see that the original /nt/ combination, occurring after the second syllable of this form, is already a unitary voiced stop (being spelt with a double D symbol). So the denasalizing change had already happened in Irish by the time of this inscription. Now there are, in fact, no ogham inscriptions where the earlier /nt/ sound is still represented;[39] the corpus shows no sign of being conscious that that sound had ever been there. There is also the fact that this phonological development can independently be shown to have happened before any of the other changes in respect of which the pre-shift sounds are found represented in some of the inscriptions.[40] It is these two considerations taken together that have led Celticists to conclude that this particular change had occurred by the time the ogham tradition itself was established. They cannot prove that it had; it might simply be that the convention of writing the NT and NC symbols did not last until the time of any of our extant

---

However, if one allows that the origin of the ogham tradition and its associated spelling conventions may pre-date the starting-point of the extant corpus of inscriptions (which is a distinction not drawn by McCone and McManus), then the half-century restriction disappears. That the morphophonemic argument should probably disappear with it is indicated by the fact that a largely analogous approach proposed by T. A. Watkins to explain early manuscript spelling features ('Points of Similarity between Old Welsh and Old Irish Orthography', *Bulletin of the Board of Celtic Studies* 21 (1964–6), 135–41, at 139–40) was decisively rejected by Jackson ('Some Questions in Dispute about Early Welsh Literature and Language', *Studia Celtica* 8/9 (1973–4), 1–32, at 23–6) in a manner implicitly endorsed by McCone (*Relative Chronology*, 31).

[38] E. Phillimore, 'The *Annales Cambriae* and the Old Welsh Genealogies from Harleian MS 3859', *Y Cymmrodor* 9 (1888), 141–83, sub annis 812 and 822; compare Jackson, *LHEB*, 39.

[39] McManus, *Guide*, 84.

[40] Jackson, *LHEB*, 138; McCone, *Relative Chronology*, 108.

stones, just as we earlier saw inscribers eventually losing track of the fact that one put an I-symbol on o-stem genitives. But, if we accept that this denasalizing change in the Irish language had taken place by the time ogham was invented, we seem to have managed to sandwich that invention chronologically between denasalization and lenition, since the former development has not, as it were, left any traces of its enactment within the corpus of stones, whereas the latter has.

This sounds promising; the question is how far it takes us, as it is not clear in absolute terms when the linguistic changes in question occurred. The Hill of Howth, which forms the north side of Dublin Bay, is known in Irish as 'Beinn Éadair', with a /d/ sound; and it is likely that this corresponds to a place-name *Andros*, which is referred to by Pliny the Elder and which still indicates the nasal element.[41] If so, Pliny's source of information is anterior to anything upon which the carvers of the extant oghams were drawing; but even if that means it is antecedent to the beginning of the ogham tradition, and even if it is contemporary with Pliny himself, the most we can say from this is that ogham originated some time after the first century AD. As for lenition as a cut-off point for the development, the date of that is highly contentious. Oddly enough, it is bound up with the matter of dating Ireland's national saint, St Patrick, since there occurs in the medieval Patrician dossier an obscure alternative name for him, 'Cothraige', which has long been argued to originate as a borrowing of Latin 'Patricius' into Irish before lenition turned the /t/ into /θ/ and the /k/ into /χ/. However, as I have pointed out in an article on 'The Significance of *Cothraige*',[42] this theory poses severe problems. Though later than denasalization, lenition was one of the earlier sound-changes in Irish.[43] If it had not yet happened in the fifth century, by St Patrick's time, then we have to see it and all the remaining changes in Irish as having occurred in an extremely short space of time in order for them to be in place by the time there come on stream our earliest extant manuscript sources of Irish, which show almost all of them completed. Even staunch defenders of the Cothraige-as-loanword theory, such as John Koch and Patrick Sims-Williams, seem to acknowledge the difficulty, the former by moving St Patrick back in time by anything up to eighty years,[44] the latter by saying that the name or title Patricius had already been borrowed into Irish by the time

[41]   C. Plinius Secundus, *Naturalis historia*, 4.103, on *PHI Latin CD ROM 5.3*, comp. the Packard Humanities Institute (Los Altos, 1991); compare R. Thurneysen, *A Grammar of Old Irish*, revised and enlarged edn (Dublin, 1946), 127.

[42]   *Ériu* 36 (1985), 1–9.

[43]   Jackson, *LHEB*, 142.

[44]   That is, placing his birth as early as 350 AD (J. T. Koch, '*Cothairche*, Esposito's Theory, and Neo-Celtic Lenition', in *Britain 400–600*, ed. Bammesberger and Wollmann, 179–202, at 187–97).

of the famous bishop.[45] Either way, Jackson's dating of lenition to the second half of the fifth century can hardly stand, but how much earlier it was is a moot point.

What linguistic principles taken alone seem to tell us, then, is that ogham was established at some point during a period perhaps four hundred years long, beginning when Pliny's ultimate informant sailed from Howth and ending when Irish lenited its consonants: that is, a period running from the first century (or earlier) to the fifth century (or earlier). Terribly vague though this sounds, it nevertheless appears more definite than does evidence so far interpreted to us by any other discipline. It does at least seem compatible with one other, independent consideration that I have deliberately not mentioned until now: the fact of the use of ogham for writing alphabetic inscriptions in the first place. Alphabets are hardly ever invented from nothing and, whereas attempts to connect ogham's symbol-sequence or design with specific Roman grammatical doctrines have all been disproved,[46] it remains one of the few uncontested points about ogham that, somehow, it was developed under the influence of Latin literacy.[47] Is it coincidence, then, that the Romans were firmly established across the narrow Irish Sea for hundreds of years at what we have concluded was just the right period in history? Probably not; and if not, then our linguistics have probably been on the right track. But the linguistics have suggested the first century and the fifth century as the latest dates for the beginning and end respectively of the period during which the origin of the ogham tradition is to be sought; both limits might have to be set considerably earlier. Historians and archaeologists, by contrast, have tended to prefer to place the invention (or 'the beginning of the use') of ogham towards the end, rather than the beginning, of the same stretch of time (namely, that corresponding to the Roman occupation of Britain).[48] I believe they have tended to do so because, other things being equal, the onus is felt to be on showing that the invention of ogham was early rather than late within the permissible period;[49] but this approach tends to equate saying that ogham must have been invented by the fourth century with saying that it was probably not invented until then, an equation that I feel needs further justification particularly considering that, if anything, the

---

45   Sims-Williams, 'Dating the Transition', 229.
46   See, for example, Sims-Williams's dissociation of the origin of ogham from any knowledge of Varro's *agma* (*ibid.*, 226).
47   Thomas, *Mute Stones*, 32; McCone, *Relative Chronology*, 22.
48   See, for example, N. Edwards, *The Archaeology of Early Medieval Ireland* (London, 1990), 103.
49   This perceived onus seems to be reflected in Thomas's carefully graded 'informed guess ... that the use of ogham was firmly established by the latter part of the fourth century, could well have been current in the earlier part, and could have been invented about AD 300 (or even before)' (*Mute Stones*, 33).

linguistic evidence strains towards the early end of the range.[50] Wider philological and contextual studies may be able to pin matters down for us more precisely; but in the meantime it seems appropriate to appeal to every scholar involved in these matters to keep an open mind.

[50]   While it is true that excavations have hitherto placed no oghams before the fourth century, I feel that we should be careful not to interpret this in an over-positivist manner: after all, the longer ago a particular artefact originated the less likely it is to have survived down to our time, and it only takes one discovery to breach perceived chronological limits for an entire class of objects.

Some Little-Known Ulster Inscriptions

ANN HAMLIN

My approach to this subject is not as an epigrapher or linguist, but rather as a historian and archaeologist. I also look after about 180 major historic monuments as part of my official work with the Environment and Heritage Service (Department of the Environment for Northern Ireland); these include a few inscribed stones, and occasionally our survey work produces new material. This chapter is unlikely to make any major contribution to epigraphic or linguistic studies, but I hope it will draw attention to a somewhat neglected body of inscribed stones, including a few recent finds.

The material remains of the early church in the north of Ireland are very sparse. My own research on the archaeology of early Christianity in Northern Ireland – six of the nine counties of historic Ulster – clearly demonstrated this.[1] The number of surviving pre-Romanesque stone churches in Northern Ireland, for example, is only six, and I am very conscious that the body of inscriptions which I am presenting here is small, and the stones are often damaged and sometimes fragmentary.

The totals of inscribed material in the second volume of R. A. S. Macalister's *Corpus Inscriptionum Insularum Celticarum* (Dublin, 1949) illustrate the uneven distribution of inscribed stones and artefacts across Ireland. Ulster (nine counties) had the lowest tally, with 27 inscriptions. Connaught came next, with 46, then Munster with 53, and Leinster had the huge total of 320 including, of course, the great collection at Clonmacnoise. Of Macalister's 27 Ulster inscriptions, 8 were on metalwork and 19 on stone.[2]

My review is confined to inscribed stones,[3] and I can add three 'new' discoveries, two of them fragments. I also look at two stones which Macalister

[1] A. E. Hamlin, 'The Archaeology of Early Christianity in the North of Ireland' (unpublished PhD thesis, Queen's University, Belfast, 1976).

[2] R. A. S. Macalister, *Corpus Inscriptionum Insularum Celticarum*, 2 vols (Dublin, 1945 and 1949) (hereafter *CIIC*), II, 111–27. In *CIIC*, I (1945), Macalister described and illustrated a possible inscribed stone on Station Island, Lough Derg in Co. Donegal (301–3, no. 314). This stone was 'desperately worn, ... the letters ... scarcely visible'. B. Lacy, *Archaeological Survey of County Donegal* (Lifford, 1983), 280–1, did not locate the stone and I have not been able to search for it so it is not included in my discussion.

[3] For inscriptions on metalwork shrines see P. E. Michelli, 'The Inscriptions on

did not include because they are not 'in the *Half-Uncial* character':[4] a doubtful 'runestone' and an inscription in Gothic lettering. What follows is a review of the Ulster material and a brief conclusion on its historical significance.

Despite my title, I want to mention two very well-known Ulster inscribed stones – I suspect they are the only two which *are* well known. They are an important element of the story, and they demonstrate that the battered fragments which will be described later are part of a bigger whole.

The Kilnasaggart pillar-stone stands in an early graveyard in south Armagh. The site is historically obscure but is in a very important location, on the great north-south 'main road', the *Slige Midlúachra*, through the mountains which separate Ulster from Leinster.[5] The stone is a very accomplished piece of craftsmanship – tall, carefully shaped, carved with many crosses of varying forms and with an unusually long inscription, datable to about 700. This records the granting of the place by Ternohc son of Ceran Bic under the protection of Peter the Apostle.[6] There are eight lines of majuscules, the top two lines larger than those below. This long inscription includes important elements which are emphasized many times in this volume: the donor (or author) and his family, the place and the function of the stone,[7] as well as the unusual and interesting reference to the Apostle Peter.

The second well-known and much studied Ulster inscribed stone is at Fahan Mura, far to the north-west in County Donegal. This tall, imposing slab has a finely detailed cross with interlaced decoration on each main face, and Macalister detected inscriptions on the two figures who flank the cross-shaft on the west side and offered readings.[8] Françoise Henry believed that the marks on the figures' clothing were decoration.[9] More recently Peter Harbison has accepted the inscriptions, but he concludes that 'they cannot be deciphered satisfactorily'.[10] Not in any doubt is the Greek inscription on the north narrow side, the only inscription in Greek on an Irish stone. It is in two

Pre-Norman Irish Reliquaries', *Proceedings of the Royal Irish Academy* 96, C (1996), 1–48.

[4]   *CIIC*, II, 'Introduction' (unpaginated).

[5]   C. Ó Lochlainn, 'Roadways in Ancient Ireland', in *Féil-Sgríbhinn Eóin Mhic Néill*, ed. J. Ryan (Dublin, 1940), 465–74, at 472 and map.

[6]   *CIIC*, II, 114–15, pl. XLVI; F. Henry, *Irish Art in the Early Christian Period to A.D. 800* (London, 1965), 118–20, pl. 49.

[7]   See also Michelli, 'The Inscriptions', 2–4.

[8]   R. A. S. Macalister, 'The Inscriptions on the Slab at Fahan Mura, Co. Donegal', *Journal of the Royal Society of Antiquaries of Ireland* 59 (1929), 90–1; also *CIIC*, II, 118–20, pl. XLVII.

[9]   Henry, *Irish Art to A.D. 800*, 125–6, pl. 54.

[10] P. Harbison, 'A Group of Early Christian Carved Stone Monuments in County Donegal', in *Early Medieval Sculpture in Britain and Ireland*, ed. J. Higgitt (Oxford, 1986), 49–85, at 59.

lines, reading from the top down: 'Glory and honour to the Father, the Son and the Holy Ghost', a form of the doxology sanctioned at the Council of Toledo in 633 but current in later times. The significance of this inscription and the dating of the stone have been much debated. Peter Harbison usefully reviews this discussion in a recent paper and favours a late eighth- or ninth-century date.[11]

REVIEW OF EARLY INSCRIPTIONS IN ULSTER (EXCLUDING OGHAMS)

ANTRIM

Connor (*CIIC*, II, 115, no. 947), pl. 17

Macalister strangely listed this stone as 'Locality Unknown ... believed to have come from somewhere in Co. Armagh',[12] yet sources which would have been available to him allow it to be located with some confidence to the important and well-documented ecclesiastical site of Connor. The stone was described by O'Laverty in 1884: it had been used in building a bridge to the Presbyterian manse at Connor and was then preserved in the grounds of the manse.[13] From here it entered Canon Grainger's collection and later passed to the Belfast (now Ulster) Museum. It is possible that this is the stone 'from the ruins of the Abbey of Connor ... with an inscription in the Irish language' exhibited in the Belfast Museum in 1852, though it is in Latin and not Irish.[14] If it is *not* the same stone, an inscribed stone from Connor (or Kells nearby) may remain to be found. By 1936, when a photo and note on the stone's complicated recent history were published in the Down and Connor History Society's *Journal*,[15] there was clearly doubt in the Belfast Museum over where the stone had come from, and this must explain Macalister's uncertainty.

As plate 17 shows, the inscription runs in a single line along the stone which is 3 feet (0.9 m.) long. The stone is battered and abraded, not surprisingly in view of its chequered history, and only the first four words are clear: in Latin, FRATRES ORENT P̄ NOBIS [—]. The chalking in plate 17 obscures some elements of the letters, like the cross-bar of E in ORENT and the upper element of B in NOBIS. Macalister read OGRECHU ET UNGEN as the second half of the inscription, but I could only detect a few letters, certainly not enough for a confident reading.

Two points are of particular interest. The use of Latin is strange, if this is an Early Christian period, rather than a medieval, inscription. The word

---

11   *Ibid.*, 59–61

12   *CIIC*, II, 115.

13   J. O'Laverty, *An Historical Account of the Diocese of Down and Connor, Ancient and Modern*, III (Dublin, 1884), 286.

14   *Ibid.*, 290.

15   *Journal of the Down and Connor History Society* 7 (1936), 73–4 (*anon.*).

FRATRES indicates a community of some kind, and the subjunctive form ORENT suggests the translation 'may the brothers pray for us'. There is much evidence, from written sources and archaeological material, that Connor was a sizeable, complex settlement in the Early Christian period, probably with monastic and secular elements coexisting.[16] There was no monastic establishment at Connor in the Middle Ages, though there was an Augustinian community at Kells nearby.[17] It is attractive to suggest that the inscribed stone is derived from an Early Christian period monastic context at Connor, but this cannot be absolutely certain.

Kirkinriola (*CIIC*, II, 112, no. 943, pl. XLV), pl. 18

This stone was found, according to different accounts, in 1827 or in 1868, either while levelling the earthen enclosure of the graveyard, or during grave digging. It was drawn by W. H. Patterson in 1869 and this drawing was published by Petrie in 1872.[18] As far as I am aware, no photograph of the stone has previously been published. The slab was taken for safety to St Patrick's Church of Ireland Church in nearby Ballymena, and in 1927 was set in its present position in the church porch. The cracks suggest that it was in two or three pieces when it was set in the porch.

The irregularly shaped basalt slab has a ringed cross potent, with the inscription arranged around the four quadrants outside the ring. It reads ORT |DO|DEG|EN (for *or(oi)t do Degen)*, in clear, pecked letters. This simple inscription means 'a prayer for Degen'. The E and G are ligatured in DEG and the last letter is the Roman form of N rather than the more familiar half-uncial form.[19]

Kirkinriola (formerly Kilconriola) is not documented in early written sources, but several strands of evidence suggest that it was an early church site. The place-name was originally a *cell* form (from Latin *cella*); a souterrain runs under the graveyard; and an early ecclesiastical bell from Cabragh may have come from the site. These factors and the inscribed slab all point to early activity at Kirkinriola. Lawlor claimed in 1938 that Degen could confidently be identified with Dagán who is mentioned in Bede's *Ecclesiastical History* (II.4), is commemorated on 13 September in the main text of the *Félire Óengusso*, and who died in 639.[20] Lawlor's confidence has not been shared:

[16] A. Hamlin, 'The Early Irish Church: Problems of Identification', in *The Early Church in Wales and the West*, ed. N. Edwards and A. Lane (Oxford, 1992), 138–44, at 143.
[17] A. Gwynn and R. N. Hadcock, *Medieval Religious Houses: Ireland* (London, 1970), 66 and 180–1.
[18] G. Petrie, *Christian Inscriptions in the Irish Language*, ed. M. Stokes, II (Dublin, 1878), 73, fig. 80, pl. XXXVIII.
[19] See T. O'Neill, *The Irish Hand* (Portlaoise, 1984), 61 on the inconsistent use of the two forms in manuscripts.

Dagán of *Inber Daele* was a Leinster saint from County Wicklow. Degen of Kirkinriola remains unidentified.

ARMAGH

Kilnasaggart (*CIIC*, II, 114–15, no. 946, pl. XLVI)
This pillar-stone is the only early inscribed stone in the county (see above, p. 52).

DONEGAL

Clonca (*CIIC*, II, 115–16, no. 948, pl. XLVI), pl. 19
This stone is built into the exterior west wall of the ruined church, near the south-west corner, at Clonca in Inishowen. There is much material attesting to the long ecclesiastical use of the site, from the Early Christian period to 1827.[21] The inscription is damaged and incomplete, probably because of the stone's re-use as a building block. In the earliest drawing I have come across the stone appears upside down,[22] while in 1915 it was loose in a hole in the west wall of the church, but no reading was attempted.[23] Macalister drew the inscription, of which parts of three lines survive, and read it as
– [*A*]N O DUBDAGAN DO RI [–] | [–][*OG*] SO DO DOMNALL O R [–] |
[*SUNN*]. I am not convinced of his reading in the damaged areas (at lower left and the third line at lower right). Macalister considered the work to be 'very rudely executed, and ... doubtless of late date'.[24] A medieval, rather than Early Christian, date is suggested by the carving of a mason's tools above the inscription – a hammer and chisel.

The stone is of interest in that it records a craftsman, O Dubdagan (Ó Dubhdhagán, modern O'Doogan), who was working for a patron, Domnall, though we do not know Domnall's family name or what work the mason was recording. References to craftsmen are not common in medieval Ireland, and we shall find the same family name on Devenish in County Fermanagh, again in a craft context (below, p. 59).

A second inscribed stone at Clonca (*CIIC*, II, 116–17, no. 949, pl. XLVIII) is in the tradition of the West Highland slabs of the fourteenth and fifteenth centuries. Though it is clearly a local Donegal product it will not be further discussed here.[25]

[20] H. C. Lawlor, 'Degen of Kilconriola', *Ulster Journal of Archaeology* 1 (1938), 32–5.

[21] B. Lacy, *Archaeological Survey of County Donegal* (Lifford, 1983), 254–6; M. R. Colhoun, *The Heritage of Inishowen: Its Archaeology, History and Folklore* (Coleraine, 1995), 45–7, including an excellent photograph on p. 46.

[22] R. S. Young, 'Archaeological Rambles in the Inisowen Mountains', *Ulster Journal of Archaeology* 4 (1897), 18–19.

[23] H. S. Crawford, 'The Crosses and Slabs of Inishowen', *Journal of the Royal Society of Antiquaries of Ireland* 45 (1915), 190.

[24] *CIIC*, II, 116.

Fahan Mura (*CIIC,* II, 118–20, no. 951, pl. XLVII)
This important slab was discussed above, pp. 52–3.

Finner (*CIIC,* II, 120, no. 952, pl. XLV)
This is one of Macalister's less confident readings: seven letters, LIATACH, but with much doubt about the first two letters and no complete assurance as to the other five. The stone is in the middle of a hilltop rath (earthwork of the Early Christian period), and is locally known as Flaherty's Stone. I have not managed to inspect it, but the surveyors of the archaeology of the county did not confirm Macalister's reading,[26] and it must be regarded as doubtful.

DOWN

Movilla (*CIIC,* II, 120–1, no. 953, pl. XLVI, as Moville), pl. 20
Movilla was one of Ulster's most important ecclesiastical sites, head church of the Dál Fiatach kings and clearly a large, complex settlement.[27] Much of the site is occupied by a graveyard, and the inscribed slab was dug up in about 1840 in this graveyard. It is now set with a group of Anglo-Norman coffin-lids into the north wall of the ruined Augustinian Abbey church at Movilla.[28]

The damaged, irregularly shaped rectangular slab of shale bears an incised ringed cross. The cross-head has a distinctive feature found on many free-standing crosses: the semicircular projections on the inner circumference of the ring. The only other Irish example I have noted on a slab is at Kilbrecan on Inishmore in the Aran Islands.[29] The very precise geometrical construction of the cross-head is also unusual, as is the placing of the inscription, from top to bottom, parallel to the stem of the cross. The letters decrease in height, from beginning to end, as in some manuscripts. The inscription is very clear, the letters pecked and reading $\overline{\text{ORDO}}$DERTREND, *or(oit) do Dertrend,* ('a prayer for Dertrend'), but the name cannot be identified and is difficult to make sense of etymologically. There are therefore many puzzling features about this stone and its inscription.

Nendrum

Another puzzling County Down stone comes from this island ecclesiastical site in Strangford Lough. One of the finds from H. C. Lawlor's excavations between 1922 and 1924 was a broken slab with part of an inscription and a

---

[25]   K. A. Steer and J. W. M. Bannerman, *Late Medieval Monumental Sculpture in the West Highlands* (Edinburgh, 1977), 43.

[26]   Lacy, *Donegal Survey,* 173–6, fig. 91.

[27]   A. Hamlin, 'The Early Church in County Down to the Twelfth Century', in *Down: History and Society,* ed. L. Proudfoot (Dublin, 1997), 47–70, at 49–50.

[28]   *An Archaeological Survey of County Down* (Belfast, 1966), 283–4, fig. 184.

[29]   *CIIC,* II, no. 539, pl. I.

design in a circle.[30] Macalister took this to be a runic inscription and attempted a reading: the Old Norse for 'of the chief abbot'.[31] There has always been doubt over this claim, and Professor Page has recently rejected the inscription as 'a doubtful example' of runes.[32] It would be interesting to know if any epigrapher would be prepared to attempt a reading of this puzzling stone.

Rubane (*CIIC*, II, 121, no. 954, as Rhubane)

This stone is unfortunately lost and I know of no illustration. It came to light in the 1870s, noted first by Patterson,[33] then described by O'Laverty: 'a stone ... on it is inscribed a cross formed by the intersection of two pair of parallel lines, and along the stem of the cross is inscribed in Irish letters *Deanlam*, the remainder of the inscription is gone'.[34] The stone had come from an extensive cemetery 'which had been entirely subjected to tillage' in the field nearly opposite the entrance to Echlinville demesne, and was at that time in Holywood Church. O'Laverty was Parish Priest of Holywood, so it is likely that he had taken the stone into safe-keeping.

Echlinville was formerly known as Rubane, and a saint called Tiu is associated with *Rubha* at 24 June in the twelfth-century Martyrology of Gorman, and a later gloss locates the place as in the Ards of Ulster. The rather complicated sources are usefully disentangled and discussed in Vol. 2 of the 'Place-Names of Northern Ireland' series.[35] The lost inscribed stone is the only material evidence recorded from what was clearly an early church site in this area.

Seaforde (*CIIC*, II, 121-2, no. 955)

This stone is also lost, or rather destroyed, and all later accounts are based on a description and rubbing published by Dubourdieu in 1802.[36] By then the stone was used for pounding whins (furze) and the inscription was already 'much defaced'. The stone had come from a destroyed souterrain ('cave') in a rath near Seaforde. His drawing, from a rubbing, shows rough letters which indicate an early formula but no further detail: OROIT AR E[..]AC -. It is

30   H. C. Lawlor, *The Monastery of Saint Mochaoi of Nendrum* (Belfast, 1925), 70-1, pl. II; *County Down Survey*, pl. 81.
31   Lawlor, *The Monastery of Saint Mochaoi of Nendrum*, 70-1.
32   M. P. Barnes, J. R. Hagland and R. I. Page, *The Runic Inscriptions of Viking Age Dublin*, Medieval Dublin Excavations 1962–81, ser. B, 5 (Dublin, 1997), 2.
33   W. H. Patterson, 'On some Ancient Sepulchral Slabs in the Counties of Down, Antrim and Donegal', *Proceedings of the Royal Irish Academy* 15 (1870-4), 274.
34   J. O'Laverty, *Diocese of Down and Connor*, I (1878), 425.
35   A. J. Hughes and R. J. Hannan, *Place-Names of Northern Ireland: County Down II, the Ards* (Belfast, 1992), 93–5 and 110.
36   J. Dubourdieu, *Statistical Survey of the County of Down* (Dublin, 1802), 277–8.

unusual to find an inscribed stone, as distinct from an ogham stone, re-used in a souterrain;[37] Warner points to only four examples of inscribed or cross-carved slabs, including Seaforde.[38] It is unlikely that a rath in which an inscribed slab had been re-used to build a souterrain was an ecclesiastical site. It is more likely that the stone was derived from elsewhere, though its original location cannot be suggested with any certainty.

FERMANAGH

Moving west to Fermanagh, we find a better rate of survival of all kinds of archaeological material than further east, including inscribed stones. Macalister listed nine stones, there are three new discoveries, and I add one late medieval inscription.

Aghavea (*CIIC*, II, 126, no. 965, pl. XLV, under 'Brookbrough'), pl. 21
This stone is in the National Museum in Dublin. The Revd Joseph Callwell, Rector of Aghavea, gave it to the Royal Irish Academy in 1857 and the Academy's *Proceedings* for that year record that it was 'found in an old wall near Brookborough [sic]'.[39] Brookeborough is in Aghavea parish, and there can be little doubt that the stone came from the Church of Ireland site in Aghavea townland.

Neither Petrie's nor Macalister's drawing does justice to this inscription and, as far as I know, no photograph of it has been published.[40] The inscription is carefully worked in two lines, with deep, V-sectioned letters. The script is minuscule, with a very clear minuscule A. O and R are ligatured and there are contraction marks. The inscription reads O̅R̅DODUNCHAD | P̅SPIT̅ BIC, *oroit do Dunchad p(re)spit(er) bic*, 'a prayer for Dunchad, the little priest' (not 'priest here', as sometimes claimed). The reference to Dunchad's position as priest is most unusual in an Irish inscription, and so is the epithet BIC, though it appears in the Kilnasaggart inscription. The use of P rather than B (*presbiter*) is quite common in Hiberno-Latin, but the use of the Latin word in an otherwise Irish inscription is not; *sacart* would be the usual Irish word for priest (as in the place-name Kilnasaggart).

Aghavea is associated with Lasair, commemorated at 13 November in the Martyrology of Gorman (glossed 'of *Achad Beithe*'). A late Life of the saint associates her with Aghavea and her bell was used for tax-collecting and holding water.[41] The church re-emerges in written sources as a late medieval

37   S. Ferguson, 'On Some Evidence Touching the Age of Rath-Caves', *Proceedings of the Royal Irish Academy* 15 (1870–4), 129–36.

38   R. Warner, 'The Irish Souterrains and their Background', in *Subterranean Britain*, ed. H. Crawford (London, 1979), 100–44, at 123–4.

39   *Proceedings of the Royal Irish Academy* 6 (1853–7), 512, in the record of the meeting on 25 May 1857.

40   Petrie, *Christian Inscriptions*, II (1878), 74; *CIIC*, II, pl. XLV.

parish church, and the medieval and modern churches occupied the ancient church site. The present topography, including traces of a large curvilinear enclosure, indicates early activity, and the inscribed stone must fit at some point in this long history, perhaps late in the Early Christian period.

Devenish, pl. 22

Devenish, in Lower Lough Erne, was Fermanagh's most important ecclesiastical site, in active use from the sixth to the seventeenth century.[42] In recent years, as part of the archaeological survey of the county, we have sorted a collection of hundreds of loose stones, mostly architectural fragments, and among them we located one small piece of an inscription. It is a tantalizing fragment of limestone with the start of the familiar formula: OR D[-], and traces of (probably) three letters in a second line below. While the recognition of an inscribed stone from this important site is very welcome, it is obviously disappointing that it is only a fragment.

The second Devenish stone was not included by Macalister in his *Corpus* because the inscription is in a Gothic script, but I think it is worth drawing attention to the stone. The Latin inscription records work by Matthew O Dubagan in the time of Bartholomew O Flanragan, prior of Devenish (*Daminys*), AD 1449. It is an unusual and precious survival, giving a date for the building of St Mary's Augustinian Priory and the name of a craftsman. This is the same family name as on the medieval stone with mason's tools at Clonca (above, p. 55): O Dubdagan at Clonca, O Dubagan at Devenish, modern O'Doogan. A celebrated scholarly member of this family, Seoán Mór Ó Dubhagáin of Ballydoogan in County Galway, died in 1372. He was chief historian to Ó Ceallaigh of Uí Mhaine.[43] Michelli has recently discussed the rôles of craftsmen and patrons in the late Early Christian period in Ireland,[44] and here we find a family associated with scholarship in Connaught in the fourteenth century and with stone-carving and building in north-west Ulster in the late Middle Ages.

Galloon (*CIIC*, II, 122, nos. 956-7, pl. XXXVI)

Galloon is an early ecclesiastical site marked by a graveyard on an island in Upper Lough Erne. It was little known until the building of a bridge to the island in the late 1920s, but in 1934 Lady Dorothy Lowry-Corry published an article describing the remains of at least three crosses in the graveyard.[45]

---

[41] L. Gwynn, *Ériu* 5 (1911), 81 and 101; J. F. Kenney, *The Sources for the Early History of Ireland: Ecclesiastical* (New York, 1929), 465-7.

[42] C. A. Ralegh Radford, 'Devenish', *Ulster Journal of Archaeology* 33 (1970), 55-62, provides a useful overview.

[43] F. J. Byrne, 'Introduction', in O'Neill, *The Irish Hand*, xxiv.

[44] Michelli, 'The Inscriptions', *passim*.

[45] D. Lowry-Corry, 'The Sculptured Crosses of Galloon', *Journal of the Royal Society*

Galloon was traditionally founded by Tigernach of Clones, and two saints are associated with it in calendars, Colmán and Comgall.

Macalister detected traces of inscriptions on the two surviving cross-shafts, in both cases at the bottom of the south side of the shaft (not a main face). On the upper (west) cross he tentatively read *DUBLITIR*, and on the lower (east) cross *MAELCHIARAIN*, with much reserve, pointing out that 'the decipherment can never be certain in either case'.[46] These possible inscriptions are not now visible. The site is very damp and there is active growth of lichen and moss, but in view of recent work on retrieving other inscriptions on crosses,[47] it is not out of the question that traces of these possible Galloon inscriptions may in future be recovered.

Inishmacsaint, pl. 23

Inismacsaint was an early church in Lower Lough Erne associated with St Ninnid, traditionally an active missionary saint. On the island site is a graveyard with the ruins of a multi-period church, a plain stone cross and once-extensive earthworks. An early ecclesiastical bell was also associated with Inishmacsaint.[48] During the clearing and sorting of a large collection of loose stones in the 1960s an inscribed fragment was recognized. The main feature is a cross of arcs in a circle, with a short 'stem' indicating the base. To the right of the circle three letters are visible in two lines: A above and LE below. This could be the remains of the formula *oroit* 'a prayer' (or *bennacht* 'a blessing') *ar* 'for' *Le—* (a name).[49] As with the Devenish stone, it is pleasing to record an inscription from what was a major site in Lower Lough Erne, but again it is frustrating that it is only a fragment.

Kilcoo (*CIIC*, II, 125, nos. 962–4, pls XLV and XLVII), pls 24–5

My next site in County Fermanagh was described by Wakeman in 1879 as 'one of the most curious, picturesque and archaeologically tantalizing and baffling spots in Ireland'.[50] It was 'tantalizing' because the site had been 'ruthlessly dismantled' already by the time he wrote and twelve or more inscribed stones had been removed, broken up and used for building drains

    of Antiquaries of Ireland 64 (1934), 165–76.

[46]   *CIIC*, II, 122.

[47]   For example, D. Ó Murchadha, 'Rubbings Taken of the Inscriptions on the Cross of the Scriptures, Clonmacnois', *Journal of the Royal Society of Antiquaries of Ireland* 110 (1980), 47–51; and L. de Paor, 'The High Crosses of *Tech Theille* (Tihilly), Kinnitty, and Related Sculpture', in *Figures from the Past*, ed. E. Rynne (Dun Laoghaire, 1987), 131–58.

[48]   J. E. McKenna, *Diocese of Clogher: Parochial Records* (Enniskillen, 1920), II, 436–9.

[49]   The medieval herenagh family in Inishmacsaint parish was Ó Leanáin (Lennon): P. Livingstone, *The Fermanagh Story* (Enniskillen, 1969), 41.

[50]   W. F. Wakeman, 'Kilcoo, County Fermanagh', *Journal of the Royal Society of Antiquaries of Ireland* 15 (1879), 34.

for an adjoining road.[51] The place was 'baffling' because the name, Kilcoo, cannot be identified with any documented church site, yet the material remains suggest a church of some importance. Two inscribed stones survive and one is lost.

The first, Macalister's no. 962, was on site, perhaps *in situ*, until recently when it was moved indoors, into Fermanagh County Museum in Enniskillen. It is an irregular slab with an outline Latin cross with a diamond-shaped expansion at the crossing and circular expansions at the ends of the arms, the expansions embellished with hollow relief circles. Along one side of this cross is the inscription: an initial cross is followed by ORTDU MAEL CLU|CHI (in two lines), *or(oit) du MaelCluchi*. Macalister read OR DU, but a more likely reading is ORT DU, with the T and D ligatured (the stone is very heavily weathered and not very clear at this end). The name Mael-Cluiche appears in Connaught in tenth-century annals;[52] it does not seem to be an Ulster name.

The second stone from Kilcoo is in the National Museum in Dublin (Macalister's no. 963). It is badly damaged and is broken across the inscription. A ringed cross potent is clearly pecked and not very carefully finished. The inscription is under the cross but inverted in relation to it. Wakeman and Macalister published quite different readings, and when I recorded the stone I could pick out little with certainty after the initial cross: perhaps MIC near the centre and E at the end.

The third inscribed stone is lost, but was described and drawn by Wakeman.[53] Again it was badly damaged, and all that was left of the inscription was the familiar formula $\overline{OR}$ D— to the right of a ringed cross with its arms and head expanded and sunken dots in the four quadrants defined by the ring. This damaged lost slab simply serves to underline the loss, before Wakeman wrote in 1879, of so many inscribed stones at this now remote but clearly once important site.

Killadeas (*CIIC*, II, 123, nos. 958–9, pl. XLVII)

The present Church of Ireland parish church in Rockfield townland occupies the site of an Early Christian period church, according to the place-name associated with the Culdees (and perhaps nearby Devenish). Neither of the two inscriptions published by Macalister can now be seen and one is doubtful. He suggested *Robarta(ch)* reading from bottom to top along the back of the delightful, energetic, walking cleric on the so-called 'Bishop Stone'.[54] He was

51 *Ibid.*, 26.
52 Annals of Ulster 913 and 923, *The Annals of Ulster (to A.D. 1131)*, ed. Seán Mac Airt and Gearóid Mac Niocaill (Dublin, 1983).
53 Wakeman, 'Kilcoo, County Fermanagh', 31, fig. 3.
54 D. Lowry-Corry, 'The Sculptured Stones of Killadeas', *Journal of the Royal Society of Antiquaries of Ireland* 65 (1935), 26–8, pl. VI.

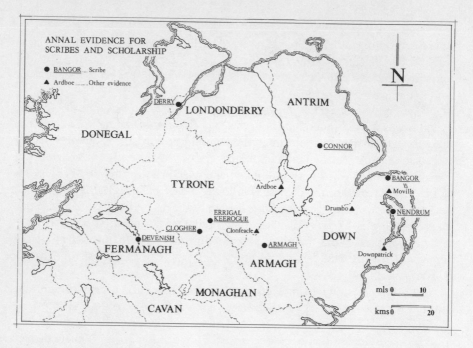

Within the map:

ANNAL EVIDENCE FOR
SCRIBES AND SCHOLARSHIP

● BANGOR ...Scribe
▲ Ardboe ....Other evidence

N

DONEGAL

DERRY
LONDONDERRY

ANTRIM

●CONNOR

TYRONE

Ardboe ▲

●BANGOR
▲Movilla

Drumbo ▲

ERRIGAL
KEEROGUE
CLOGHER
DEVENISH
FERMANAGH

Clonfeacle ▲

●NENDRUM

●ARMAGH

DOWN

Downpatrick

ARMAGH

MONAGHAN
CAVAN

mls 0   10
kms 0   20

Fig. 7: Annal evidence for scribes and scholarship in the six counties of Northern Ireland from the seventh to the twelfth century.

sure only about R-B-A, but his drawing in pl. XLVII is very inaccurate and nothing can be traced now.

The second stone (*CIIC*, no. 958) is a large upright slab with a complex cross in high relief. A cross of arcs with interlaced decoration in a circle is supported by a substantial stem which forks towards the bottom to join a club-shaped base (also described as boat-shaped).[55] In its present state, weathered and with some growth of lichen, the stone shows no inscription, but Macalister read four lines on the left of the cross stem, parallel to the stem running from bottom to top: BENDACHT|AR ART|ULURC|AIN, *bendacht ar Art U Lurcain*, 'a blessing on Art Ua Lurcáin'.[56] Ó Lurcáin (Larkin) is not a Fermanagh name but it is difficult to imagine Macalister 'making up' this inscription and we must hope it may be retrieved and confirmed in the future.

White Island (*CIIC*, II, 124, no. 960), pls 26–7

White Island in Lower Lough Erne is, like Kilcoo, historically obscure. No patron is recorded and the church site cannot be identified in any early written sources, yet it has a famous group of carved stone figures, probably of

[55] P. Lionard, 'Early Irish Grave Slabs', *Proceedings of the Royal Irish Academy* 61, C (1961), 110.

[56] Lowry-Corry, 'Killadeas', 24–6, pl. V.

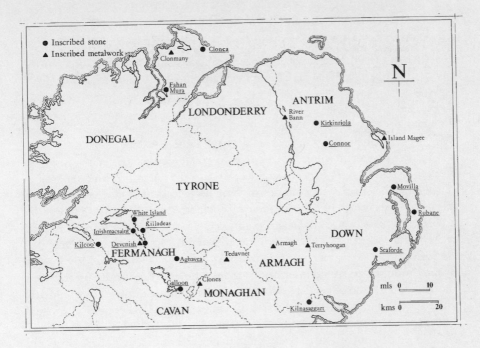

Fig. 8: Distribution of inscriptions – stones and metalwork (excluding ogham).

the ninth or tenth centuries.[57] In the 1870s Wakeman described and drew a stone with the name CORCRAIN along the top and (less well-defined) letters FOG at right angles below, but its present whereabouts is unknown.[58]

During conservation work at the site in 1958 a second inscribed stone was found, built into a fairly recently reconstructed wall. It is now mounted and displayed against the (modern) wall which encloses the church on the west side. An outline Latin cross is lightly incised on a carefully dressed trapezoidal slab, the lines crossing at the intersection to form a square. Above the cross is a single word, perhaps DELMNE, though the first and last letters are less clear than the others. It has been suggested that this could be a sept name, the Delbnae of the Westmeath/Roscommon area (modern Dealbhna, Delvin), but it may be best to regard it as an unidentified personal name.[59]

No Roman-alphabet inscriptions on stone are recorded from the other four counties of ancient Ulster (Cavan, Londonderry, Monaghan and Tyrone), though there are pieces of inscribed metalwork from the River

57   H. Hickey, *Images of Stone* (Belfast, 1976), 34–8 and 43–50.
58   W. F. Wakeman, 'White Island, Lough Erne', *Journal of the Royal Society of Antiquaries of Ireland* 15 (1879), 66 and 68.
59   J. B. Arthurs (Seán Mac Airt) in a letter in Ministry of Finance (Northern Ireland) files discussed the inscription (May 1958). It is not published except for a note and (not entirely accurate) drawing in M. Rogers, *Prospect of Erne* (Belfast, 1967), 73.

Bann, Clones and Tedavnet (*CIIC*, II, nos. 942, 966 and 967). Although I have not discussed them here, eight ogham inscriptions survive from Ulster, in the counties of Antrim, Armagh, Cavan, Fermanagh, Londonderry and Tyrone.[60]

Conclusion

Finally, from this meagre gathering of often incomplete and damaged material what general conclusions can reasonably be drawn?

First, I suggest it would not be safe to conclude that Ulster was poor in literacy or scholarship. Fig. 7 assembles some of the annal evidence for scribes and scholarship in the six counties of Northern Ireland from the seventh to the twelfth century. 'Other evidence' includes references to lectors (*fer léiginn*), books (burned at Drumbo in 1130–1) and clerics distinguished in poetry and history.[61] This map coincides with the distribution map of inscriptions (fig. 8) at four important sites – Armagh, Devenish, Movilla and Connor – but there are no inscriptions from scholarly Bangor, no inscriptions on the many cross-carved slabs at Nendrum (except the enigmatic 'runestone'), and none from Derry, Downpatrick, Clogher and elsewhere where there is evidence in written sources for literacy and scholarship.

A second conclusion is that much material has certainly been lost and sometimes destroyed – perhaps more in Ulster than in the rest of Ireland. The case of Kilcoo is particularly striking, with the reported loss of twelve or more inscribed stones and damage to two of the three recorded stones. Devenish and Inishmacsaint have only recently been added to the map through the identification of damaged stones. I find it difficult to believe that there were never any inscribed stones at Armagh or Bangor, both major centres of scholarship. This is not the place to go into the reasons for the high rate of loss and damage, but it must result at least in part from the major dislocations of population which the north has experienced and some sectarian antagonism (also seen in past attitudes to free-standing crosses).

My third point is that inscribed stones are found both at well-documented sites of clear importance, like Connor, Movilla and Devenish, and at places where the early history and sometimes even the early name are lost, like Kirkinriola, Kilcoo and White Island. It would not be safe to conclude that these, and other undocumented, sites were unimportant in the Early Christian period.

My last conclusion is that the material reviewed in this chapter, fragmentary as it is, would benefit from closer study, especially by an epigraphic specialist. The letter-forms vary considerably across the

---

[60]   *CIIC*, I (Dublin, 1945), 297-301, 303-5 (nos 309–13, 315–17).

[61]   Fig. 7 does not claim to be comprehensive; rather it presents a range of information gathered for my 1976 thesis (note 1) and my continuing use of the sources.

inscriptions and it is likely that further information remains to be extracted from specialist study.

When the survival rate of material is poor and the body of evidence is small there is obviously a limit to what conclusions can safely be drawn. But I hope that this review of the inscribed stones of Ulster has succeeded in drawing attention to a little-known group of material which, despite its problems, I would suggest still has something to teach us.

Acknowledgements
I am grateful to the Environment and Heritage Service (Department of the Environment for Northern Ireland) for permission to draw on unpublished material in its records, to my colleagues Gail Pollock and David Wilkinson for help with the illustrations, to the Ulster Museum for plate 17, to the National Museum in Dublin for access to photograph and agreement to publish plates 21 and 25, and to Fermanagh County Museum for access to photograph plate 24. The Crown Copyright photographs appear with permission of the Controller of Her Majesty's Stationery Office.

A New Edition of the Ogham Inscriptions: The Advantages and Limitations of Computers

JOST GIPPERT

When I started my investigations into ogham inscriptions in 1978, I did not expect that computers would so quickly turn out to be essential to my studies. In fact I had no idea at all of how to use them at that time, and the only instruments I then needed were a camera, pencils and paper. At that time my aims were restricted too: what I intended to take home from my first field trips, to Ireland (1978) and Scotland (1979), was mostly materials for documenting inscriptions which might be helpful for the academic teaching of the history of the Irish language. But working more thoroughly with the existing editions, especially with R. A. S. Macalister's *Corpus Inscriptionum Insularum Celticarum*,[1] I was soon convinced that a new edition of the inscriptions was an urgent task, all the more since the state of preservation of many of them was very bad.

Things had changed a bit by 1988 when I was invited to report on my work at a conference in Eichstätt. By that time I had worked out the general outline of the new edition I intended to complete, and I was glad to be able to publish it in the conference proceedings.[2] For convenience, the preliminaries

---

[1] 2 vols (Dublin, 1945 and 1949) (hereafter *CIIC*); reprint of *CIIC*, I, ed. D. McManus (Dublin, 1996). Other editions of ogham inscriptions: R. R. Brash, *The Ogam Inscribed Monuments of the Gaedhil in the British Islands* (London, 1879; posthumous ed. G. M. Atkinson); S. Ferguson, *Ogham Inscriptions in Ireland, Wales, and Scotland* (Edinburgh, 1887); R. A. S. Macalister, *Studies in Irish Epigraphy*, Vols 1-3 (London, 1897, 1902, 1907); V. E. Nash-Williams, *The Early Christian Monuments of Wales* (Cardiff, 1950). The so-called 'Pictish' inscriptions were edited by R. A. S. Macalister in his article 'The Inscriptions and Language of the Picts', in *Féilscríbhinn Eóin McNéill*, ed. J. Ryan (Dublin, 1940; repr. Dublin, 1995), 184-226. Now see also K. Forsyth, *The Ogham Inscriptions of Scotland: An Edited Corpus*, Harvard University PhD Dissertation (Ann Arbor, Michigan: UMI, 1996).

[2] 'Präliminarien zu einer Neuausgabe der Ogaminschriften', in *Britain 400-600: Language and History*, ed. A. Bammesberger and A. Wollmann, Anglistische Forschungen 205 (Heidelberg, 1990), 291-306. An announcement was published under the heading 'Towards a New Edition of the Ogam Inscriptions' in *Celtic Cultures Newsletter* 6 (August 1990), 73-4.

as established then may be summarized briefly here. They comprise: (1) all information available on the history of the inscribed monuments; (2) readings as published by former investigators; (3) older graphic representations (photographs, sketches and so on) of the monuments; (4) documentation of the present state of the monuments, supplied by colour photographs; (5) new readings of the inscriptions; (6) investigation into the relationship between linguistic and palaeographic features; and (7) verification of the readings with due consideration of linguistic, philological and historical data.[3]

By that time, computers had become a part of my work, and since then they have acquired a central rôle. As early as 1986, I had started to transfer all kinds of textual data related to the individual monuments (readings, bibliography, historical information and so on) into a computer database. The DBase-style DOS program I used for this was available until recently.[4]

Vowel letters	B-Series	Consonant letters H-Series	M-Series	"Forfeda"
A	B	*H	M	X/AE
O	L	D	G	CH/EA
U	V	T	*ŋ	P/IA
E	S	C	*Z	TH/OI
I	N	Q	R	PH/UI

Table 1: The ogham characters.

One problem that was not easy to solve in those days concerned the special fonts necessary for a one-to-one rendering of ogham characters both on the screen and with a printer. Using the EGA/VGA standard of DOS computers, this was restricted by the size of the small matrix of dots which these graphic interfaces used to represent individual characters. For ogham, this was a particular problem in that some of the characters of the ogham *beitheluisnin*, especially the ones having four or five strokes, would not fit into a matrix of 8×14 or 16 dots (cf. table 1 for the ogham characters).[5] To

---

3 Some of the problems involved were illustrated in my booklet *Ogam – Eine frühe keltische Schrifterfindung*, Lectiones eruditorum extraneorum in facultate philosophica Universitatis Carolinae Pragensis factae, 1 (Prague, 1992 [1993]). For a thorough treatment of ogham tradition cf. D. McManus's *A Guide to Ogam*, Maynooth Monographs 4 (Maynooth, 1991).

4 The program as developed by K. Boekels (Berlin/Bamberg) was first published under the name of 'Data Manager', later renamed 'Polydat'. It was available as freeware via the Internet until the end of 1999.

5 For *H* and the third and fourth characters of the *M*-Series, the traditional values are given here; a different interpretation (*Y, G^w, S*) was proposed by D. McManus in 'Ogam: Archaizing, Orthography and the Authenticity of the Manuscript Key

overcome this problem, the wider characters had to be split into two elements which made them rather awkward to use. Of course, the font also had to comprise some additional characters required for displaying Celtic language materials. The resulting VGA font can be seen in fig. 9; a screen-shot of the database is given in fig. 10.

Fig. 9: VGA font for ogham and Celtic.

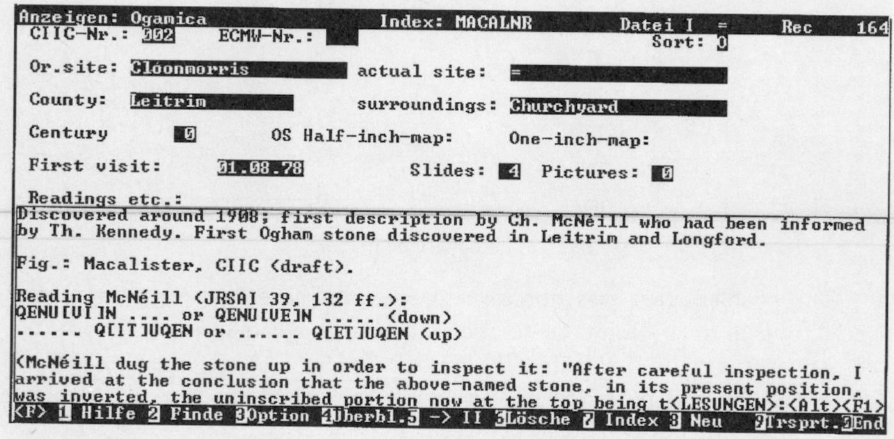

Fig. 10: The ogham database data-entry form as it appears on the screen.

An equivalent font had to be generated for printing too. Although the matrices of both 24-pin dot-matrix printers and laser-jets as available at that time were not as limited as the EGA/VGA graphics card, the ogham characters had to be arranged in a similar way, to allow for a one-to-one printout. The article mentioned in n. 2 was printed using these fonts. A scalable vectorized font to be used on today's graphic-based computers was later styled according to this principle to ensure compatibility with the data collected so far (cf. table 2). This DOS-based font was further arranged in several formats (Truetype, Postscript) to meet the requirements of different operating systems. Only recently has it become possible to convert the data

to the Alphabet', *Ériu* 37 (1986), 1–31, at 28.

into a standardized encoding scheme, since the ogham script has now been integrated into the Unicode standard.[6]

	0										1									
	0	1	2	3	4	5	6	7	8	9	0	1	2	3	4	5	6	7	8	9
000																				
020														!	"	#	$	%	&	'
040	(	)	*	+	,	-	.	/	0	1	2	3	4	5	6	7	8	9	:	;
060	<	=	>	?	@	A	B	C	D	E	F	G	H	I	J	K	L	M	N	O
080	P	Q	R	S	T	U	V	W	X	Y	Z	[	\	]	^	_	‘	a	b	c
100	d	e	f	g	h	i	j	k	l	m	n	o	p	q	r	s	t	u	v	w
120	x	y	z	{	|	}	~	⌂	Ç	ü	é	â	ä	à	å	ç	ê	ë	è	ï
140	î	ì	Ä	Å	É	æ	Æ	ô	ö	ò	û	ù	ÿ	Ö	Ü	ō	ℵ	Ŋ	η	⊢
160	á	í	ó	ú	ñ	Ñ	ā	ē	¿	⌐	¬	ī	ū	¡	«	»	Â	Á	À	Ã
180	Ă	Đ	Ê	È	Ẽ	Ë	Î	Í	Ì	Ĩ	Ï	Ô	Ó	Ò	Õ	Œ	Ø	Ǫ	Ş	Ţ
200	Þ	Û	Ú	Ù	Ũ	Ŵ	Ý	Ŷ	ã	ă	ð	ẽ	ĩ	õ	œ	ø	ǫ	ş	ţ	þ
220	ũ	ŵ	ý	ŷ	Ÿ	ß	ᚆ	ᚇ	ᚈ	ᚉ	-	ᚁ	ᚂ	ᚃ	ᚄ	┴	╨	ᚃ	╜	ᚋ
240	#	###	#	θ	ᘒ	ӿ	ӿ	≈	ᚙ	·	‾	√	⁀	‿	□					
	0	1	2	3	4	5	6	7	8	9	0	1	2	3	4	5	6	7	8	9
	0										1									

Table 2: Truetype font for printing ogham.

I entered a second level of data collection when in 1986 I started storing images in electronic form. From the beginning, I had planned that my new edition should be amply supported by photographs, since they were far from abundant in earlier editions and the state of the monuments is not improving as time goes by! Although photographs and, especially, colour slides are an excellent means of preserving visual information, electronic storage has several advantages: on the one hand, digital images can claim to have 'eternal' durability, and on the other hand, they can be handled by the computer as easily as text files, being ready for publishing, duplication, exchange, viewing and even editing.

Digitization of images requires special equipment. The fastest method is to use a digital camera right from the beginning, i.e. when recording the original monument. Although the quality of digital images produced in this way is steadily increasing, for the fullest preservation of data conventional

[6] For the standard (Unicode 3.0), see the web pages http://www.unicode.org/unicode/standard/versions/Unicode3.0.html and http://charts.unicode.org/PDF/U1680.pdf.

photographs of a high standard should not be dispensed with altogether, all the more so since they can always be used as a basis for later digitization using optical scanners.

In the course of the present project, several scanners have been used for the digitization of photographs. The choice was mostly dictated by cost (the project has never been funded), but the purposes of digitizing had to be taken into account too. A black-and-white flat-bed scanner with a resolution of 300 dots per inch may give acceptable results when a 9×11 cm (3×4") photograph is to be reproduced on a laser printer as a text illustration (the photographs accompanying the article mentioned in n. 2 were produced in this way), but a high-resolution colour scanner will be required whenever the optical data are to be stored for preservation and future analysis or when a professional printout is desired.

A special scanner is necessary for digitizing 24×36 mm (1×1½") colour slides. Since the original images are extremely small, the resolution must be much higher than that of flat-bed scanners; a minimum of 2500 dots per inch seems necessary when the data are to be preserved 'for eternity'.[7] In my experience, high-resolution scanning from colour slides yields the best results when compared with the other methods described. Incidentally, colour slide scanners can also be used for scanning ordinary negatives giving, perhaps, better results than scanning the printed photograph.

One major advantage of digitized images lies in their availability for all kinds of electronic editing. For this reason digitization is likely to develop into a principal method of epigraphic work in general. In the past epigraphists were often content to present their objects in rough sketches, drawn either from the original or from rubbings, squeezes, or even casts, thus introducing a large degree of subjectivity to what they intended to show. By comparison, photographs are usually a much better means of representing the visual impression of the original monument. The information that photography can yield depends, however, on the actual state of the monument. This is especially true in the case of ogham monuments, which are mostly not preserved in museums but have been left standing in the countryside, covered by vegetation and exposed to all kinds of weather and damage by cattle. Moreover, ogham writing itself, being arranged on the edges of the monuments, is extremely vulnerable to damage and hard to read. Under these conditions, photographs cannot always sufficiently reveal the inscription as it indeed is. Here, digitizing can help a lot: having to hand the steadily developing facilities of graphics software,[8] we can easily improve the

[7]   Since 1987 the following scanners have been used in the course of the project: (1) flat bed scanners: Xerox Datacopy 701; HP ScanJet IIp (300 dpi; b/w) / IIcx (600 dpi; colour); (2) colour slide scanner: Polaroid SprintScan 35 (2700 dpi; colour slides and negatives).

[8]   In the course of the project, I used several graphic programs such as PhotoShop

appearance of a given photograph by manually enhancing its contrast, saturation, luminance and so on, without depending on different methods of (automatic) film developing. Furthermore, we can improve the information provided by manually adding hints for the reader, for example by redrawing the strokes that constitute the ogham characters in contrast with the so-called 'stem-line' and by filtering the image thus received in order to yield the maximum contrast between the inscription and its background. Of course this too is a subjective method, but having both the original photograph and the edited one side by side, the reader can much more easily distinguish between the details on the monument and an editor's guesses, than by judging from sketches or drafts alone.

Figs. 11–20 are intended to demonstrate what can be achieved by editing digitized photographs with a view to a printed edition. The monuments in question are both to be found in Ireland. The first one, no. 54 in Macalister's corpus (*CIIC*), is now preserved in the church of Killaloe, Co. Clare.[9] Originally part of a high cross, it is a bilingual monument and contains a blessing written in late ('scholastic') ogham beside a runic inscription which denotes a Viking named ÞURKRIM who had the cross erected.[10] The second one, *CIIC* no. 104, stands in the ruined churchyard of Aghabullogue, Co. Cork, attracting attention by the large pebble attached to its top.[11] The readings that can be established in accordance with the photographs are as given below. Contrasting them with the interpretations published in Macalister's *CIIC*, we can easily see why many of the latter cannot be regarded as reliable.[12]

(Adobe), PhotoStyler (Aldus), PhotoFinish (ZSoft), or Paint Shop Professional (JASC). Although there are differences in functions and handling, all of these are usable for the tasks implied.

9   *CIIC*, I, 58–9.

10   The sketches are reproduced from R. A. S. Macalister, 'Further Notes on the Runic Inscription at Killaloe Cathedral', *Proceedings of the Royal Irish Academy* 38, C, 8-9 (1929), 237 (for the source of fig. 14, runic inscription) and *CIIC*, I, 58 (for the source of fig. 15, ogham inscription). See also now M. P. Barnes, J. R. Hagland and R. I. Page, *The Runic Inscriptions of Viking Age Dublin*, Medieval Dublin Excavations 1962–81, ser. B., 5 (Dublin, 1997), 53–6.

11   The drawings are taken from Brash, *Ogham Inscribed Monuments*, pl. IX (for fig. 16) and *CIIC*, I, 104 (for fig. 17).

12   A detailed description and argument cannot be attempted here but will be found in the Internet edition introduced below.

Figs 11–13: *CIIC*, no. 54 (Killaloe): photograph, edited photograph and filtered photograph.

Figs 14–15: *CIIC*, no. 54 (Killaloe): sketches of runic and ogham inscriptions after Macalister.

Killaloe (*CIIC*, no. 54) readings (figs 11–15):

(runic inscription)
þurkrim risti | | krus þina
'Þorgrim engraved | | this cross.'
(Macalister: [TH]URGRIM RISTI [KR]US THINA)

(ogham inscription)
B͡EANDACHT[| | TOROQ*R*[13]
'(A) blessing [upon] | Þorgrim.'
(Macalister: BENDACHT [AR] TOROQR[IM])

[13]   The second part of the ogham inscription is problematic. If the engraver took the
ornamental frame as the stem-line for this part, the two H-letters (T, Q) have
been inverted (as if V, N, cf. *VEDELMET[T] misspelt as TELEDMEV[V] in
CIIC, no. 206, for which see further n. 13 below). The drawing in *CIIC*
(reproduced in fig. 15) is misleading on this point.

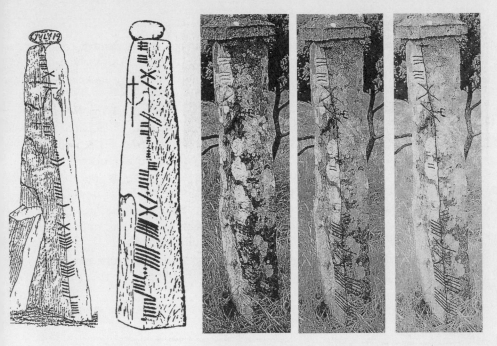

Figs. 16–20: CIIC, no. 104 (Aghabullogue): sketches by Brash and Macalister; and photograph, edited photograph and filtered photograph.

Aghabullogue (*CIIC*, no. 104) readings (figs 16–20):

—CORRE͡AMAQ V[—]D*D*[—]ME͡ATT
'[Inscription in the name] of Corr son of *Fedelmid'.[14]
(Macalister: ANM CORRE MAQVI UDD[GLO]METT)

The value of the visual information is even greater if the images thus edited can be viewed in their original colours. It seems unlikely, though, that a full-colour printed edition of the ogham inscriptions could ever be published because of the cost. There is, however, another medium of publication that can easily be used for this purpose, viz. the international data network (the 'Internet'). Although it is still far from being accessible to everyone, even today the Internet can be used for scientific publishing with much less effort and cost than traditional printing would require.

---

[14]   The name read (tentatively) as UDDGLOMETT by Macalister could be restored as *VEDDELME͡ATT[A], thus representing the genitive of the *i*-stem name *Fedelmid*. Cf. the forms VEDDELLEMETTO attested on the stone from Pilsworth, Co. Kilkenny (discovered 1969) and, with inverted letters, *VEDELMET[T] on a stone from Kilcoolaght, Co. Kerry (*CIIC*, no. 206; for these cf. McManus, *Guide*, 75).

Internet publishing has several further advantages over a printed edition, especially with regard to epigraphic material. One of these lies in the fact that the handling of both textual and graphic materials necessary in epigraphic studies is an essential feature of Internet browsers: system-independent methods of linking texts and images were indeed developed for the very purpose of Internet publishing. All kinds of epigraphic publications can especially benefit from the so-called 'hypertext' procedures. These can be used, for example, for linking interpretations of different inscriptions, linking interpretations and an extended bibliography, or linking words appearing in the inscriptions and a dictionary, an index, a commentary and so on. Linking is even possible between text and images or between different graphic files, for example between low-resolution and high-resolution pictures or between large-scale and low-scale maps for localizing monuments and so on.

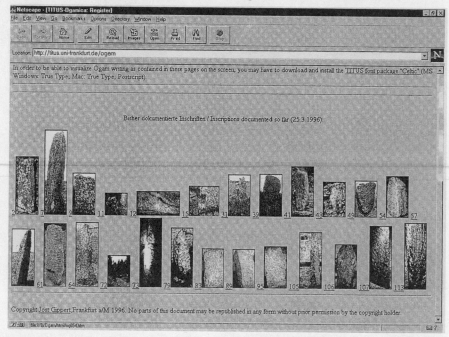

Fig. 21: Choice from a list of photographs.

Linking facilities are demonstrated in figs. 21–26. Starting from a page containing a picture catalogue (fig. 21), the descriptions of documents (for example, fig. 22: ogham monument *CIIC* no. 49) can be accessed simply by clicking on the pictures. Each description in its turn contains small-scale images (so-called 'thumb-nails') which serve as a link to their large-scale equivalents (fig. 23). Likewise, the entry concerning the current location of the ogham monument *CIIC* no. 64, 'Ballytrasna House' (fig. 24), is prepared as a link to the map of the area in question (fig. 25) and so on.

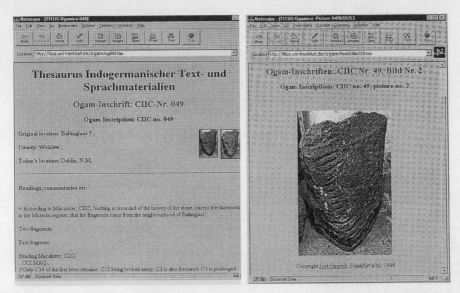

Figs 22–23: low- and high-resolution pictures.

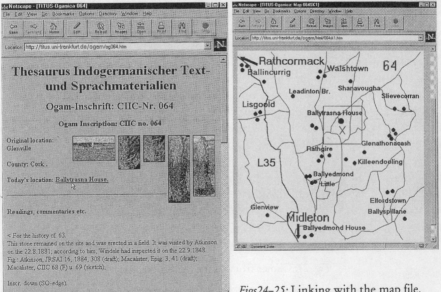

Figs 24–25: Linking with the map file.

Another advantage of an Internet edition is that it can be regarded as a 'living' edition. While a printed book is fixed, in the sense that it cannot easily be corrected after passing through the press, an electronic text can be updated perpetually with corrections, additions and the like. This has an interesting effect on readers and users, in that they will have to verify (and cite) not only the year of publication but the exact date of a published text ('page'). On the other hand, an Internet editor can immediately react to readers' criticism submitted either in a conventional way, orally or in writing, or via the same medium as that used for publication, viz. the Internet. In this way, readers and users can participate in the process of publishing to a far greater extent than when printing is required.

This is why I decided to prepare the edition of ogham inscriptions as an electronic one and to make it accessible to the public via the Internet before having completed the work in the usual way. My edition is located on a special server of the Institut für Vergleichende Sprachwissenschaft, Phonetik und Slavische Philologie, Johann Wolfgang Goethe-Universität, Frankfurt am Main (cf. fig. 26] which shows the 'homepage' of the edition; its present URL is http://titus.uni-frankfurt.de/ogam). It forms part of the so-called 'TITUS' project (the abbreviation stands for *Thesaurus Indogermanischer Text- und Sprachmaterialien*) which aims to gather textual and other linguistic resources relevant to the whole of Indo-European studies.[15] Epigraphical materials represent but a minor part of what is covered by the project. The great bulk consists of textual sources, ranging from the Old Indic Rig-Veda to Icelandic sagas. But of course, Old and Middle Irish texts fall into its scope as well, and so we can envisage that connections persisting between names mentioned in both (epic or historical) texts and ogham inscriptions will in future be revealable using hypertext links.[16]

A number of problems have still to be solved before the Internet edition of the ogham inscriptions can claim to have achieved its aims as outlined here. First, we still have to cope with the problem of font representation. Although the Truetype font designed for displaying ogham is available for downloading from the server (cf. the notice about the font package contained on the homepage, fig. 26), as was stated above this can only be regarded as a temporary expedient. Another problem resides in the fact that the legal conditions of Internet publishing have not yet been clarified in detail, at least as far as authors' rights are concerned. As long as the structure of the Internet allows not only for retrieving and copying of data (which is intended in the case of a non-commercial publication) but also for easy republishing, authors cannot rely upon their intellectual, literary and artistic property being respected by everyone. Entering a copyright notice at the end of each

---

[15] For the TITUS project, see my 'TITUS. Das Projekt eines indogermanistischen Thesaurus', *LDV-Forum* 12/2 (1995), 35–47; 'TITUS – Von der Keilschrifttafel zur Textdatenbank', *Forschung Frankfurt* 4/1995, 46–56; 'TITUS – Alte und neue Perspektiven eines indogermanistischen Thesaurus', *Studia Mesopotamica, Iranica et Anatolica* 2 (1996 [1997]), 49–76.

[16] For the time being, many of the texts in the TITUS collection cannot be made publicly accessible from the server. This is mostly due to unresolved questions of copyright.

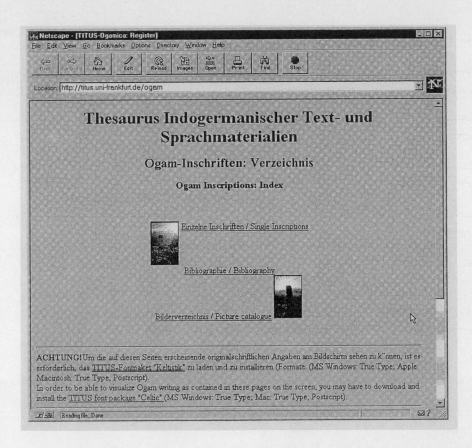

Thesaurus Indogermanischer Text- und Sprachmaterialien

Ogam-Inschriften: Verzeichnis

Ogam Inscriptions: Index

Einzelne Inschriften / Single Inscriptions

Bibliographie / Bibliography

Bilderverzeichnis / Picture catalogue

ACHTUNG! Um die auf diesen Seiten erscheinende originalschriftlichen Angaben am Bildschirm sehen zu k"nnen, ist es erforderlich, das TITUS-Fontpaket "Keltistik" zu laden und zu installieren (Formate: (MS Windows: True Type; Apple Macintosh: True Type, Postscript).
In order to be able to visualize Ogam writing as contained in these pages on the screen, you may have to download and install the TITUS font package "Celtic" (MS Windows: True Type; Mac: True Type, Postscript).

Reading file... Done

Fig.26: The Ogham 'homepage'.

document is hardly sufficient to prevent misuse. A third problem which must be noted is that the transfer of larger files becomes ever more time-consuming as more and more people get connected to and use the Internet. In the present context, this concerns mostly graphic images: a colour slide digitized at a resolution of 2700 dots per inch forms a file of 2 megabytes, even if stored in a compressed format (JPG). It seems reasonable to choose lower resolutions (which means lower quality) for Internet publications, since the quality level that should be envisaged here is the one determined by good readability on a normal computer screen, not the one needed for professional printouts.

Apart from storing graphic and textual data and publishing the results in a (printed or electronic) edition, an epigraphist's work will in future be aided by computers in several ways. The development of optical devices that are able to scan not only surfaces but three-dimensional objects, will, if applied to inscribed monuments, provide an instrument for investigating carving methods as well as chronological and palaeographical features.[17] In the case of

[17]   For perspectives on computer-aided palaeographical investigations of manuscript

ogham writing with its peculiarities, however, we must not expect too much from such a development. The script itself leaves but scanty room for palaeographical considerations, and most of the monuments are in a state of preservation that will hardly allow for reliable results when being analysed by scanning machines. The decision whether a given stroke is part of an ogham character or a mere scratch or fissure of the stone will always remain with the epigraphist.

---

writings, see my 'Paläographische Untersuchungen mit dem Computer', *Studia Mesopotamica, Iranica et Anatolica* 2 (1996 [1997]), 77–100.

Anglo-Saxon Women: The Evidence from Inscriptions

ELISABETH OKASHA

The status and condition of women in Anglo-Saxon England has received some attention from Anglo-Saxonists, in particular since the 1980s: the majority of the papers brought together by Helen Damico and Alexandra Hennessey Olsen first appeared in the preceding decade.[1] Opinion on the status of Anglo-Saxon women remains, however, divided.

In 1984 Christine Fell wrote 'it is salutary to remember that scholarship does not require us to read only, always and inevitably a history of oppression and exploitation of the female sex. The real evidence from Anglo-Saxon England presents a more attractive and indeed assertive picture'.[2] Jane Chance, however, using evidence from Old English literature, concludes that 'Anglo-Saxon society demanded passivity, rather than leadership and initiative, from most of its women'.[3] Stephanie Hollis, using the evidence of clerical literature of the eighth and ninth centuries, observes signs of 'a gradual erosion in the position of women, particularly monastic women, from at least as early as the 8th century'.[4] Barbara Yorke, writing about Wessex, concludes that, although there 'was no absolute bar on women achieving positions usually held by men', still 'women were not generally expected to take on the same roles as men and, in particular, to have a public role'.[5]

This chapter examines Anglo-Saxon inscriptions to see what can be deduced from epigraphic evidence about the position of women in Anglo-Saxon society.

The evidence Fell uses is that from archaeology, manuscripts and names, both place names and personal names. She demonstrates that in the Christian Anglo-Saxon period some occupations seem to have been gender-related while others were not. Predictably, while men fought and hunted, women spun, wove and embroidered. Less predictably, both men and women could be

[1] H. Damico and A. Hennessey Olsen (eds), *New Readings on Women in Old English Literature* (Bloomington, Indianapolis, 1990).

[2] C. Fell *et al.*, *Women in Anglo-Saxon England ...* (Oxford, 1984), 21.

[3] J. Chance, *Woman as Hero in Old English Literature* (Syracuse, 1986), 111.

[4] S. Hollis, *Anglo-Saxon Women and the Church: Sharing a Common Fate* (Woodbridge, 1992), 7.

[5] B. Yorke, *Wessex in the Early Middle Ages* (London, New York, 1995), 283.

involved in the preparation of food and both could be in charge of estates and large households. As Fell points out, single-sex monasteries and nunneries may to some extent have blurred distinctions between the occupational rôles felt to be appropriate to one sex or the other.[6]

Using evidence from personal names, whether these occur in inscriptions or elsewhere, is based on the premise that all Anglo-Saxon vernacular names are clearly masculine or feminine. It has generally been assumed that the sex of an Anglo-Saxon person corresponds to the grammatical gender of their name. Thus a dithematic name like *Aelfgifu* indicates the holder to be female because the second element, OE (Old English) *gifu*, is grammatically feminine; *Aelfraed* indicates a male name because OE *raed* is grammatically masculine. Monothematic names are similarly taken to indicate the holder's sex. This is an assumption widely made by Anglo-Saxonists, although it has recently been queried by Fran Colman.[7] Whether it was quite so clear and obvious to the Anglo-Saxons themselves deserves investigation on another occasion.

For the purposes of this chapter it is taken as a working hypothesis that grammatical gender usually indicates biological gender but that there are occasional names where the sex of the person named cannot be ascertained. It is also assumed that Anglo-Saxon inscriptions provide a unified body of evidence even though they cover various geographical areas and several centuries. This latter assumption is certainly an over-simplification but a necessary one: the number of inscriptions is so small that to subdivide the material further would render general conclusions impossible.

The evidence from Anglo-Saxon inscriptions takes the form of 136 male and female personal names. Throughout this chapter the names are given in normalized spelling. These vernacular names are those that are sufficiently legible, and occur in sufficiently complete and legible texts, that their genders are clear and the functions of their holders reasonably certain. That is, first, the names under consideration are vernacular personal names; Biblical names, the names of saints and archangels and the names of mythological and legendary figures are excluded. Secondly, the names must be sufficiently legible that their grammatical gender is certain; in practice this means that the whole of a monothematic name and at least the second element of a dithematic one must be legible. Because their genders are clear, some elements, for example, -*gyth* (Hartlepool VIII) and -*wine* (Lindisfarne VII), are included even though the first elements are lost altogether.[8] Thirdly the names have to occur in a text where the function of the person named is reasonably certain. Some quite legible names have therefore been excluded, for example

---

[6]   Fell, *Women in Anglo-Saxon England*, 50.

[7]   F. Colman, *Money Talks: Reconstructing Old English* (Berlin and New York, 1992), 54–5.

[8]   E. Okasha, *Hand-List of Anglo-Saxon Non-runic Inscriptions* (Cambridge, 1971), no. 50, p. 79 and fig.; *ibid.*, no. 80, p. 96 and fig.

that of Eadhild on a stone trial piece from Barton St David, Somerset,[9] and of Oshere on the York Coppergate helmet.[10] Eadhild might have commissioned, or made, or owned the piece of stone, as Oshere might have done with the helmet. Of course some of the names included are fully legible, their function clear and yet their grammatical gender is uncertain. Examples are the forms *abbae* (or perhaps *ahhae*) on a memorial stone from Whitby,[11] and *aelvbrh* on a bone trial piece from London where the name might represent the feminine **aelfburg* or the masculine **aelfbeorht*.[12]

The 136 vernacular personal names divide into approximately 4.5 male names to every female name.[13] Now the demographic make-up of the population of Anglo-Saxon England cannot be calculated exactly but quite certainly the population did not contain only one woman for every four and a half men. The reasons why more men than women appear in the epigraphic record, as indeed they do in the sorts of evidence examined by Fell, must be sought in the social, not the demographic, conditions of the country. A more interesting and more useful picture emerges when we examine not bare numbers but the functions of the people named in the inscriptions.

The names in the epigraphic material can be divided into six groups according to their function. These groups are listed on the Appendix along with the number of objects in each group, the number of names presented on these objects, and a list of all the female names in each group. The names are normalized and treated as if they were entirely legible, although this is not always the case. Group 1 contains the names of those who commissioned objects to be made. Group 2 contains the names of those who manufactured the objects and Group 3 the names of those who owned them. Group 4 contains the names of those deceased who are remembered in the inscriptions, and/or those for whom prayers are requested. Group 5 contains inscribed texts consisting of single names, usually on stones; the assumption is that such texts are memorial in nature even though this is not explicitly stated. Group 6 contains the names of people not directly involved with the inscriptions, for example the name of a king where a regnal date is given. Some of these six groups contain names that are mainly or exclusively male; others contain both male and female names.

The groups containing mainly or exclusively male names are Groups 1, 2 and 6. Group 1 contains 16 objects presenting us with 19 names of those who commissioned objects to be made. Typical verbs used in these texts are OE

9   E. Okasha, 'A Second Supplement to *Hand-List of Anglo-Saxon Non-runic Inscriptions*', *Anglo-Saxon England* 21 (1992), no. 186, pp. 41–2 and figs.
10   Okasha, 'Second Supplement', no. 211, pp. 58–60 and figs.
11   Okasha, *Hand-List*, no. 125, p. 122 and fig.
12   Okasha, 'Second Supplement', no. 198, pp. 50–1 and figs.
13   The actual figures are: 136 names, less 5 whose gender is uncertain; of these 131 names, 23 are female, 108 male.

het, 'ordered', *let*, 'had (made, etc.)', *sette*, 'set up' and Latin *iussit*, 'ordered'. The objects commissioned include churches: Orm son of Gamal, for example, bought the church at Kirkdale in Yorkshire when it was in a state of disrepair and had it rebuilt to Christ and St Gregory.[14] Ulf commissioned the church at Aldbrough, also in Yorkshire, for himself and for the soul of a woman Gunwaru.[15] Other objects commissioned are memorial stones, for example the runic stone Thornhill III, erected by a woman named Gilswith in memory of another woman, Beorhtswith.[16] Smaller objects were also commissioned, for instance the Alfred jewel,[17] or the Brussels cross which was ordered by two brothers, Aethelmaer and Aethelweald, for the soul of their brother Aelfric.[18]

Almost all those who are recorded as commissioning objects were men. The only certain exception is the Thornhill stone, Thornhill III mentioned above, but there is one other possible female commissioner. A stone from St Mary Castlegate, York, records the erection of the church and names three commissioners. One of the names is not now legible, one is of a man, Grim, and the third reads *aese*, a name which could be male or female.[19] Those who commissioned objects were likely to have been wealthy and of high social status in the community.[20] It certainly does not seem self-evident that all such people should be male but the epigraphic evidence suggests that very few were female.

Much the same is true of the 19 objects in Group 2. They present us with 20 names of those who actually made the objects and these names are exclusively of men. Typical verbs applied to these artisans are OE *wrohte* and Latin *fecit* both meaning 'made'. Some of the objects are of stone; for example, Hereweald constructed (*fecit*) a grave-stone from Canterbury,[21] while Lothan made (*wrohte*) the stone sundial at Great Edstone, Yorkshire.[22] Other manufactured objects are weapons and military accoutrements. Beorhthelm made the decorated iron knife from Sittingbourne[23] and Beorhtsige the leather knife sheath now in Aachen.[24] Other objects include the censer cover from Pershore made by Godric[25] and the coin-brooch from Canterbury that

[14]   Okasha, *Hand-List*, no. 64, pp. 87–8 and fig.
[15]   Okasha, *Hand-List*, no. 1, p. 47 and fig.
[16]   R. I. Page, *An Introduction to English Runes* (London, 1973), 145.
[17]   Okasha, *Hand-List*, no. 4, pp. 48–9 and figs.
[18]   Okasha, *Hand-List*, no. 17, pp. 57–8 and figs.
[19]   Okasha, *Hand-List*, no. 146, p. 131 and fig.
[20]   E. Okasha, 'The Commissioners, Makers and Owners of Anglo-Saxon Inscriptions', *Anglo-Saxon Studies in Archaeology and History* 7 (1994), 71–7.
[21]   E. Okasha, 'A Supplement to *Hand-List of Anglo-Saxon Non-runic Inscriptions*', *Anglo-Saxon England* 11 (1983), no. 161, pp. 88–9 and fig.
[22]   Okasha, *Hand-List*, no. 41, p. 73 and fig.
[23]   Okasha, *Hand-List*, no. 109, pp. 113–14 and figs.
[24]   Okasha, 'Second Supplement', no. 185, pp. 40–1 and fig.
[25]   Okasha, *Hand-List*, no. 100, p. 106 and fig.

Wuduman made.[26] It may be that in Anglo-Saxon England such objects were on occasion made by women: an obvious example might be in female monastic houses. If this were so, however, it has gone entirely unremarked in the epigraphic record.

Group 6 contains 9 objects with 13 names, all male. Some of these names are patronymics used for identification. Aethelweard, whose grave-stone is in the church of Stratfield Mortimer in Berkshire, for example, is identified as *filius kyppingus*, presumably 'son of Cypping'.[27] In a similar way Wulfmaeg, who died on 11 March 1063, is identified on a lead cross found at Canterbury by reference not to her father but to her brother, Abbot Wulfric.[28] Other names in this group are used to give dates. Eadweard, King Edward the Confessor 1042–66, is mentioned to give a regnal date on two church dedication stones, those from Deerhurst and Kirkdale.[29] On the Jarrow dedication stone, both Abbot Ceolfrith and King Ecgfrith of Northumbria are mentioned for dating purposes: the dedication was in the fifteenth year of King Ecgfrith and the fourth year of Ceolfrith's abbacy, that is, AD 685.[30] Other names in this group are on objects copied from coins, and names on Anglo-Saxon coins are almost exclusively male.[31] Coin copies include, for example, the unprovenanced 'eadward' brooch in the Ashmolean Museum, Oxford, with a text referring to Eadweard, King of the English, though to which King Edward is not altogether certain.[32]

No female names at all occur in this group, although admittedly the number of examples is not large. This may suggest to us a society where the reference points are male, a society in which both people and events are seen in relation to those of high status, all of whom are men.

However, when we turn to the other groups we do find female names occurring in the inscribed texts. Group 3 contains 21 objects each with the owner's name. Typically these contain the OE verb *ah*, 'possesses' or a Latin phrase indicating ownership such as 'the seal of so-and-so'. A few objects contain only a single name, for example the finger-rings from Sherburn and Laverstock with royal names, respectively those of Queen Aethelswith and King Aethelwulf.[33] It is possible that these names indicate personal possession but they might also record donation from the royal personage to someone else; in either case they could be described as 'owner's' names. Altogether this

[26] Okasha, *Hand-List*, no. 19, pp. 58–9 and figs.
[27] Okasha, *Hand-List*, no. 111, pp. 114–15 and fig.
[28] Okasha, *Hand-List*, no. 21, p. 60 and figs.
[29] Okasha, *Hand-List*, no. 28, pp. 63–4 and fig.; *ibid.*, no. 64, pp. 87–8 and fig.
[30] Okasha, *Hand-List*, no. 61, pp. 85–6 and fig.
[31] V. Smart, *Sylloge of Coins of the British Isles* 41. *Cumulative Index of volumes 21–40* (Oxford, 1992).
[32] Okasha, *Hand-List*, no. 154, pp. 135–6 and fig.
[33] Okasha, *Hand-List*, no. 107, pp. 112–13 and figs; *ibid.*, no. 70, pp. 91–2 and figs.

group presents us with 22 names, one of uncertain gender and the others dividing into one third female and two thirds male.

The names of both male and female owners are inscribed on finger-rings. A woman, Eawynn, owned an unprovenanced ring in the British Museum,[34] while Aedraed, a man, owned the Lancashire ring, now known to have been found in Manchester.[35] Female ownership names occur on brooches, for example Aelfgifu on the Cuxton brooch[36] and Eadwynn on the one from Sutton,[37] but there are no examples of brooches containing male ownership names. There is one example of a weaving implement inscribed with an owner's name and it is female: the weaving sword is from Wallingford and the name Eadburg is inscribed on it twice.[38]

As would be expected, the ownership names on weapons are all male; an example is the knife from Putney with the owner's name, Osmund.[39] The seal-dies contain mostly male names but there is one with a female name. It is the one from Wallingford and it contains two names, one on each side, perhaps indicating re-use. One name is male, Godwine, and the other is female, Godgyth. It might have been expected that the one woman whose seal-die survives would have been someone of high status, perhaps a queen or an abbess. Godgyth, however, is described simply as *monache deo date*, 'a nun given to God'.[40]

We might reasonably have anticipated that Anglo-Saxon women in some numbers would have owned items of jewellery and that their names would therefore have been recorded on some of these. Similarly, the fact that weapons carry only male ownership names is clearly quite predictable. More surprising perhaps is the fact that no male ownership names are recorded on brooches or weaving tools, but this may be due, at least in part, to the small number of inscribed examples that have survived.

The remaining two groups, Groups 4 and 5, can conveniently be considered together. These contain memorials, mainly in the form of stones. Some are actual grave-stones while some are in memory of deceased people. Some are objects requesting prayers for an individual, presumably someone deceased. Some are objects containing a single name where the texts appear to have a memorial function. There are 54 objects in these two groups giving us 62 names. Three of the names could be either male or female and the rest divide into one quarter female, three quarters male.

[34] Okasha, *Hand-List*, no. 155, p. 136 and figs.
[35] Okasha, *Hand-List*, no. 66, p. 89 and figs; B. J. N. Edwards, 'An Anglo-Saxon Ring Provenance Narrowed', *Antiquaries Journal* 63 (1983), 132–4.
[36] Okasha, *Hand-List*, no. 27, p. 63 and fig.
[37] Okasha, *Hand-List*, no. 114, pp. 116–17 and fig.
[38] Okasha, *Hand-List*, no. 118, p. 119 and fig.
[39] Okasha, 'A Supplement', no. 174, pp. 97–8 and figs.
[40] Okasha, *Hand-List*, no. 117, pp. 118–19 and figs.

Examples from these two groups occur on the series of memorial stones from Hartlepool, County Durham. Prayers are requested for both men and women on these stones, which is not surprising since we know that it was founded as a double monastery. Hartlepool IV, for example, reads *ora pro uermund torhtsuid*, 'pray for Wermund (and) Torhtswith', where the first name is male, the second female.[41] On other Hartlepool stones single names are inscribed, for example the male name Aethelwine, and the female name Hildithryth in runic script. On the recently found lead plate from Flixborough there are seven names, five male, one female and one of uncertain gender.[42] This lead plate was presumably memorial and may actually have marked graves.

Some of the objects discussed earlier in Group 1, under the name of the commissioner, record that the object was commissioned for the sake of someone's soul. Examples already mentioned are the church at Aldbrough, commissioned for the sake of a woman, Gunwaru, and the Brussels cross, commissioned by two men for the soul of their brother. A longer text in Old English requesting prayers for someone's soul occurs with variations on a number of stones in Groups 4 and 5. An example is the runic stone from Great Urswick which reads 'Tunwini set up a monument after Torhtred his son. Pray for his soul'.[43] Such stones may or may not have been placed above graves, but other stones were certainly actual grave-stones. This is stated in the text on the Whitchurch stone, for example, which reads *hic corpus fri(ð)burgae requiescit in (pa)ce(m) sepultum*, 'here lies Frithburg, buried in peace'.[44] Frithburg is of course a woman; a man's grave-stone is that from Winchester where the text reads *her l(i)ð g(un)n(i) eorles feolaga*, probably 'Here lies Gunni, Eorl's companion'.[45]

Both men and women then were commemorated on memorial stones and prayers were requested for their souls. However, while men and women presumably died in equal numbers and were equally mourned, they were not equally remembered in the inscribed texts that have survived. Indeed, Anglo-Saxon men were three times as likely as women to have an inscribed memorial stone raised for them. In some of the other groups of inscriptions, as we have seen, women are almost or completely absent from the record.

According to the inscriptions, for example, women rarely commissioned churches, memorial stones or other objects. This is rather surprising since we know from other evidence that women in Anglo-Saxon England did commission churches and did found religious houses. Queen Ealhswith, for example, is associated with the foundation of Nunnaminster at Winchester in

41 Okasha, *Hand-List*, no. 46, p. 77 and fig.
42 Okasha, 'Second Supplement', no. 193, pp. 46–7 and fig.
43 Page, *English Runes*, 145.
44 Okasha, *Hand-List*, no. 135, pp. 125–6 and fig.
45 Okasha *Hand-List*, no. 138, pp. 126–7 and fig.

the ninth century, Queen Aelfthryth with the founding of Amesbury and Wherwell in the tenth.[46] We must ask why the inscriptions are largely silent about such acts by women. Did men do so much more commissioning than women that inscriptions recording this are much more likely to have survived? Or is there some other reason?

When we examine the owners of inscribed objects, a different picture emerges. Clearly men would have owned weapons in much greater numbers than women and it is only to be expected that the inscribed names of owners of weapons should all be male. If we exclude weapons, women were just as likely as men to have their name inscribed on a personal possession. This is in accordance with other sorts of evidence from Anglo-Saxon England, for instance that of wills, which show that women as well as men could own and bequeath jewellery and other items. Women, according to the inscriptions, could own costly possessions just as men could; it was, however, men who made them. The artisans named in the inscriptions are without exception male, whether they were working in stone, precious metals, leather or wood.

The personal names occurring in Group 6 would seem particularly important in trying to establish the position of women. No female names at all are used as reference points in the inscriptions, neither to define moments in time nor to identify individuals. Yet we know that queens and abbesses ruled, and the importance of individuals must at least sometimes have been seen in relation to their mothers as much as to their fathers.

The picture of Anglo-Saxon England that emerges from the inscriptions is of a male world where women played a rôle, certainly, but a rôle defined and delimited by men. Is this because that was what Anglo-Saxon England was like? This may of course be so. Another possibility is that it was, at least in part, due to the fact that the written record was largely controlled by men. Certainly we know that literacy was enjoyed by both men and women in Anglo-Saxon England but the art of writing seems to have been considerably more common amongst men. Almost all the names of authors known to us from Anglo-Saxon England were male, most of the surviving letters were written by men, the few scribes known to us by name were all male, the moneyers of coins were exclusively men. If the written record, including the epigraphic record, was mostly controlled by men then it would naturally reflect their interests, their view of the world; it would be, in a word, male-dominated. Women, then, would be 'allowed', at least on occasion, to own possessions and have stones raised in their memory; as seen through male

[46] The evidence associating Queen Ealhswith with the foundation of Nunnaminster is discussed in Fell, *Women in Anglo-Saxon England*, 127. On Amesbury and Wherwell, see Yorke, *Wessex*, 218, 220, and N. E. S. A. Hamilton (ed.), *Willelmi Malmesbiriensis monachi de gestis pontificum Anglorum libri quinque*, Rolls Series 52 (London, 1870), II, 87, p. 188. I am most grateful to Barbara Yorke for providing me with the reference to William of Malmesbury.

eyes, these were recognized functions of women. But perhaps such functions did not include the commissioning of churches and other objects; nor, perhaps, did men see women as people by reference to whom time was defined or individuals were identified.

Christine Fell's view quoted at the beginning of this chapter suggests that the picture of women in Anglo-Saxon England is 'more attractive and ... assertive' than that of oppression and exploitation.[47] The evidence from the inscriptions does not, however, support Fell's view of the assertive rôle of Anglo-Saxon women. On the other hand, the evidence does not point either to Anglo-Saxon women as the victims of exploitation and oppression. More insidiously, and perhaps equally depressingly, the world which is suggested is one where male interests were paramount and where women and their rôles were drawn and delimited through male eyes and from a male perspective.

APPENDIX

The numbers I, II and so on are those assigned to the inscriptions by Page[48] and Okasha.[49]

Group 1: Names of commissioners
16 objects
19 names: 17 male, 1 female, 1 gender uncertain
Female name: Gilswith (runic, Thornhill III)

Group 2: Names of makers
19 objects
20 names: 20 male

Group 3: Names of owners
21 objects
22 names: 14 male, 7 female, 1 gender uncertain
Female names: Eadwynn (Sutton)
    Aelfgifu (Cuxton)
    Aethelswith (Sherburn)
    Burgthryth (Swindon)
    Eadburg (Wallingford II)
    Eawynn ('eawen' ring)
    Godgyth (Wallingford I)

---

[47] Fell, *Women in Anglo-Saxon England*, 21.
[48] Page, *English Runes*.
[49] Okasha, *Hand-List*; Okasha, 'A Supplement'; Okasha, 'Second Supplement'.

Group 4: Names of the dead remembered and/or those for whom prayers are requested
28 objects
29 names: 22 male, 7 female
Female names: Aethelswith (Hartlepool V)
    Beorhtswith (runic, Thornhill III)
    Frithburg (Whitchurch)
    Gunwaru (Aldbrough)
    Torhtswith (Hartlepool IV)
    Wulfmaeg (Canterbury III)
    -swith (runic, Collingham)

Group 5: Single names on memorials
26 objects
33 names: 22 male, 8 female, 3 gender uncertain
Female names: Aethelgyth (Flixborough)
    Beorhtgyth (Hartlepool VI)
    Cynburg (Whitby XIV)
    Helmgyth (Jarrow VI)
    Hildigyth (runic, Hartlepool II)
    Hildithryth (runic, Hartlepool I)
    Osgyth (Lindisfarne II)
    -ugyth (Hartlepool VIII)

Group 6: Names of those not directly involved with the inscription
9 objects
13 names: 13 male.

Form and Focus in the Deerhurst Dedication Inscription

JOHN HIGGITT

The dedication inscription that was found in 1675 in an orchard in the Gloucestershire village of Deerhurst is one of the best known Anglo-Saxon inscriptions (pl. 28).[1] Its fine capitals stand out as unusually classical in form in the context of late Anglo-Saxon inscriptions on stone. It has also attracted interest because all of the individuals referred to in its text are known from other historical sources. I discuss this inscription more fully in another publication but would like in this chapter to draw attention to aspects of its layout that seem not to have been noticed before, in the hope that this may lead to the identification of parallels.[2]

The village of Deerhurst contains two Anglo-Saxon churches, of which the larger, older and more complex is St Mary's, which became the church of a Benedictine priory and is now the parish church.[3] The other is a small private church, which was founded by Earl Odda, a kinsman of Edward the Confessor, and was dedicated to the Holy Trinity in 1056. This building, now known as 'Odda's Chapel', was converted into a house following the Reformation and was only recognized as an Anglo-Saxon church in 1885. The dedication inscription, which had earlier been associated with St Mary's, could now be identified as having belonged to 'Odda's Chapel' because it bears the same, at that time still novel, dedication to the Holy Trinity as another, fragmentary, inscription that was found re-used in the fabric of the converted church. This second inscription can be reconstructed as having

---

[1]   E. Okasha, *Hand-List of Anglo-Saxon Non-Runic Inscriptions* (Cambridge, 1971), 63–4 (no. 28); J. Backhouse, D. H. Turner and L. Webster (ed.), *The Golden Age of Anglo-Saxon Art 966–1066*, exhibition catalogue (London, 1984), 131–2 (no. 138).

[2]   The Deerhurst dedication inscription was the subject of the paper that I gave at the Oxford conference. I discuss the inscription more fully and in a broader context in: J. Higgitt, *Odda, Orm and Others: Patrons and Inscriptions in Later Anglo-Saxon England*, Deerhurst Lecture 1999 (The Friends of Deerhurst Church, forthcoming).

[3]   H. M. Taylor and J. Taylor, *Anglo-Saxon Architecture*, 3 vols (Cambridge, 1965 and 1978), I, 193–209.; P. Rahtz and L. Watts with H. Taylor and L. Butler, *St Mary's Church Deerhurst, Gloucestershire: Fieldwork, Excavations and Structural Analysis 1971–1984* (Woodbridge, 1997).

recorded the dedication of an altar.[4] The link with 'Odda's Chapel' is confirmed by an earlier reference to the principal dedication inscription, the one discovered in 1675, in a rather garbled passage in a late medieval chronicle of Tewkesbury Abbey, according to which it was then positioned in the wall over a door of a small chapel opposite the gate of Deerhurst Priory, a clear reference to 'Odda's Chapel'. We are not, however, told which door is meant nor whether the inscribed stone was on the inside or outside of the building.[5]

The well preserved dedication inscription is on a stone panel of approximately 99 cm. by 69 cm. and is now in the Ashmolean Museum in Oxford. The text is in Latin and consists of seven principal sections. It opens with an incised cross, an abbreviated invocation of God. This is followed by the name of the patron of the building, *Odda dux* (Earl Odda), and a statement that he ordered this *regia aula*, literally a royal hall or palace but here a church or chapel,[6] to be built (*iussit hanc regiam aulam construi*). The text continues with Odda's ordering the church to be dedicated in honour of the Holy Trinity (*dedicari in honore Sanctae Trinitatis*). The next phrase (*pro anima germani sui Ælfrici qui de hoc loco as(s)umpta*) is a statement of Odda's purpose in having the church built, namely to benefit the soul of his brother Ælfric, which had been taken up from this place. Then comes the presiding bishop: *Ealdredus vero episcopus qui eandem dedicavit* ('and Bishop Ealdred who dedicated it'). This is followed by a dating formula: the day of the month (the day before the Ides of April, that is the 12 April); and the regnal year, which was the fourteenth of Edward the Confessor (*quarto decimo autem anno regni Eadwardi regis Anglorum*). As Edward was crowned on 3 April 1043, 12 April 1056 would have fallen in the fourteenth year of Edward's reign.

The inscription displays the information that the church has been canonically consecrated. It also records the name in which it was dedicated (the Holy Trinity), the name of the officiating bishop and the date (to allow for annual commemoration). These are matters of particular concern to the clergy. The text, however, emphasizes the role and intentions of the secular

[4] G. Butterworth, 'Newly Discovered Saxon Chapel, Deerhurst, Gloucestershire', *Journal of the British Archaeological Association* 41 (1885), 413–18; J. H. Middleton, 'On a Saxon Chapel at Deerhurst, Gloucestershire', *Archaeologia* 50 (1887), 66–71; Taylor and Taylor, *Anglo-Saxon Architecture*, I, 209–11, III, 738–9; Okasha, *Hand-List*, 65 (no. 29).

[5] W. Dugdale, *Monasticon Anglicanum...*, 8 vols (London, 1846), II, 59–60; L. Toulmin Smith (ed.), *The Itinerary of John Leland in or about the Years 1535–1543...*, 5 vols (London, 1907–10), IV, 150–1.

[6] For arguments that *regia aula* should be understood as referring simply to a church building rather than, as has often been thought, to some kind of secular hall or centre with royal connections, see D. Parsons, 'Odda's Chapel, Deerhurst: Place of Worship or Royal Hall?', *Medieval Arachaeology* 54 (2000), 225–8. See also Higgitt, *Odda, Orm and Others*.

founder, Earl Odda.[7] We are told that Odda ordered the construction and dedication of the church and that his purpose in founding the church was to aid the soul of his brother Ælfric, who had died at Deerhurst (one of Odda's estates).

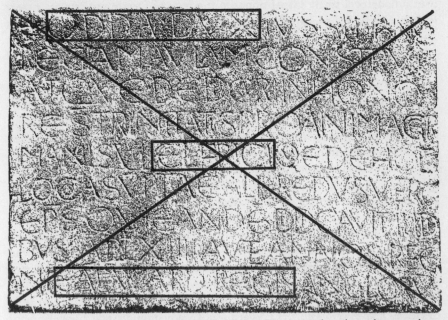

Fig. 27: Symmetries in the Deerhurst dedication inscription based on photograph (copyright Ashmolean Museum, Oxford).

There is nothing very surprising about these emphases. What is interesting is that the designer of the inscription has laid out the text in a way that seems deliberately to highlight the patron, family interests and secular authority (fig. 27). The first two words of the inscription, which are more generously spaced than the rest, are the patron's name and office (ODDA DVX). The final words are the name and office of King Edward. Thus the inscription closes with the name of Odda's royal kinsman. The text therefore both opens and closes with names of members of the same kin and with references to secular power. The name of Odda's brother, for the benefit of whose soul the church was founded, is placed in the middle of the middle line. The middle letter of his name (R), as it appears in the genitive (ÆLFRICI), lies at the centre of the stone, that is the crossing point of diagonals drawn from the corners of the stone. Care also seems to have been taken in arranging the details of the dedication symmetrically around the focal name of Ælfric.

7 For Odda, his family and his estates see: A. Williams, *Land, Power and Politics: The Family and Career of Odda of Deerhurst*, Deerhurst Lecture 1996 (The Friends of Deerhurst Church, 1997).

Forms of the verb of dedication (*dedicare*) appear two lines above and two lines below his name. Similarly the names of the dedicatee, the Holy Trinity, and of the officiating bishop, Ealdred, are in the lines immediately above and below. This *could* all have happened by chance but it is much more likely that it is a matter of careful calculation, especially in the context of such a neatly lettered, carefully laid out and well cut inscription.

There are of course other Anglo-Saxon inscriptions that show that thought was given to the positioning of the whole inscription or to words within the inscription, in order achieve particular effects or emphases.[8] I do not, however, know of any other example of such strict yet subtle symmetry being used to focus the text visually on a single name or word. If we assume that the central positioning of Ælfric's name was intended, we have to admit that it does not leap to the eye; it has instead to be discovered and is in a sense encoded into the inscription. It is unclear whether the reader was meant to 'discover' and appreciate the pattern or whether it was simply thought of as effective and satisfying composition. In spite of the secular and family concerns of this embedded subtext in the Deerhurst inscription the careful manipulation of the Latin text and its layout strongly suggest that the composer/designer of the inscription had been trained in clerical latinity.[9] The letter-cutter, who was probably a different individual, was skilled but did not need such a training. The composer/designer was perhaps a member of the circle of Ealdred, the well-travelled and sophisticated bishop of Worcester who presided at the dedication. Ealdred had recently returned from a year in Germany and it is possible that one should look amongst the inscriptions of the Ottonian Empire for the background to the visual rhetoric employed in this inscription.[10]

[8] See, for example, discussions in: J. Higgitt, 'Words and Crosses: The Inscribed Stone Cross in Early Medieval Britain and Ireland', in *Early Medieval Sculpture in Britain and Ireland*, ed. J. Higgitt, British Archaeological Reports, British Series, 152 (Oxford, 1986), 125–52; R. Gameson, *The Role of Art in the Late Anglo-Saxon Church* (Oxford, 1995), 70–104, especially 94–104.

[9] The text was carefully composed in competent Latin, although there are a couple of errors either in the drafting of the text or in the copying of it onto the stone. The verb *est* seems to have been omitted from the sixth line, perhaps because the copyist's eye jumped from an abbreviated *est* to the first letter of Ealdred's name. The other clear error is an ungrammatical S on the end of *annos* in the penultimate line. An S has also been omitted from *as(s)u(m)pta*, again apparently inadvertently.

[10] For the range of Ealdred's activities and interests see: M. Lapidge, 'Ealdred of York and MS. Cotton Vitellius E.XII', *Yorkshire Archaeological Journal* 55 (1983), 11–25 (reprinted in M. Lapidge, *Anglo-Latin Literature 900–1066* (London and Rio Grande, 1993), 453–67, 492; M. Hare, *The Two Anglo-Saxon Minsters of Gloucester*, Deerhurst Lecture 1992 (The Friends of Deerhurst Church, 1993); M. Hare, 'Kings, Crowns and Festivals: The Origins of Gloucester as a Royal Ceremonial

The essential characteristic of this device is that it is visual and is therefore quite distinct from the types of embedded messages that Charles Thomas has argued for in several early medieval inscriptions in British Latin in Wales, Cornwall and south-west Scotland. His interpretations are based on the assumption that the composers were familiar with 'biblical style' and that there are hidden meanings behind the literal meaning of the text.[11] These are to be discovered in various aspects of the text and particularly in arithmetical and numerological patterns encoded into the letters, syllables and words of the surface text. He also argues that the composers of these inscriptions sometimes intended 'mental images' (diagrams or pictures) to be read by following similar clues. It is striking, however, that most of the inscriptions that he discusses are very informal in execution and show little obvious concern for visual effect. The kind of subtext that is proposed here is much simpler than those proposed by Charles Thomas. It can also be tested visually and is therefore easier to verify.

These observations lead to a further conclusion. The efforts that the designer of this inscription made to link the foundation with Odda and his brother Ælfric verbally and visually allow us to dismiss the idea that the inscription might be later than the events that it describes. Odda died on 31 August 1056, only a few months after the dedication on 12 April. Odda's estates at Deerhurst and elsewhere then passed to the king, who gave the part of the estate on which Odda's Chapel lies to Westminster Abbey.[12] Neither Edward nor the monks of Westminster would have gone to such lengths to commemorate Odda and Ælfric in this way. The Deerhurst dedication inscription can therefore be dated with considerable confidence to 1056.

Addendum and Acknowledgements
Since writing the above, I have found parallels in Rome for Deerhurst's centrally placed name (e.g. the mosaic inscription in Santa Sabina) and, for Deerhurst's symmetries, on the epitaph of Pope Hadrian I at St Peter's. See J. Higgitt, 'Design and Meaning in Early Medieval Inscriptions in Britain and Ireland', in *The Age of Conversion in Northern Europe*, ed. M. Carver (forthcoming).

I am very grateful to Michael Hare for his advice on Ealdred and various aspects of Deerhurst and to David Parsons for showing me a draft of his forthcoming paper on the meaning of the *aula regia* of the Deerhurst inscription.

Centre', *Transactions of the Bristol and Gloucestershire Archaeological Society* 115 (1997), 41–78.

[11] For explanations, examples, illustrations and further references see: C. Thomas, *Christian Celts: Messages and Images* (Stroud, 1998). For the concept of 'biblical style' see also: D. Howlett, *The Celtic Latin Tradition of Biblical Style* (Dublin and Portland, Or., 1995), 1–54, and A. B. E. Hood, 'Review Article: Lighten Our Darkness – Biblical Style in Early Medieval Britain and Ireland', *Early Medieval Europe* 8.2 (1999), 283–96.

[12] Williams, *Land, Power and Politics: The Family and Career of Odda of Deerhurst*.

Inscriptions and Archives

R. I. PAGE

This chapter has a general title but a limited topic. Though it claims to discuss 'inscriptions', it treats chiefly those in the runic character, only marginally those in Roman script, and exclusively examples from the British Isles. But what I say may be relevant to other regions and studies.

It is many years since I first heard Erik Moltke distinguish two types of runologist, the *feltrunolog* and the *skrivebordsrunolog*, field runologist and desk runologist. His experience made him favour the first, the runic scholar who spends most of his time in immediate contact with the inscribed object and observes conditions of working and survival, materials, tools and methods used, and so on. He distrusted the desk runologist, who, he contended, took an inscription out of context, often treating it simply as a philological specimen and viewing it in a transliterated version. It is easy to sympathize with Moltke's view, yet it is a simplistic one. At times even field runologists must behave like desk runologists, inevitably when studying material that survives today only in written/archival form.

In the British Isles it was not until quite late in the nineteenth century that formal collections of Anglo-Saxon and Norse inscriptions appeared. Before that individual scholars reported on individual texts, sometimes wisely but seldom too well. For instance, Reginald Bainbrigg first drew the mixed runic and Roman text of the Bridekirk font c.1600,[1] and since his day numbers of gentlemen scholars have engaged its problems. William Nicolson of Carlisle (1655–1727) searched his diocese for runic inscriptions and made valuable records.[2] In the absence of the great and planned corpora of Scandinavia, like Ole Worm's *Danicorum Monumentorum Libri Sex* (Copenhagen, 1643) or the surveys of Johan Peringskiöld (1654–1720) in Sweden and the Norwegian *Stavangriensia* of Thomas Wegner (1639), we have to rely for our earliest reports on such individual or chance encounters, and we often find them by serendipity rather than search.

[1]   London, British Library, Ms. Cotton Julius F VI, fol. 305, published in W. Camden, *Britannia*, rev. edn (London, 1607), 632.
[2]   Preserved in several places: for example the drawings accompanying a letter from Nicolson to Thoresby, 9 September 1691, in the Yorkshire Archaeological Society's library.

With runic inscriptions the modern English scholar is confused by the variety of meanings attached, in earlier centuries, to the words 'rune' and 'runic(k)', for they often carry no precise epigraphical significance.[3] A supposed report of a runic inscription may be no such matter. For instance, in John Aubrey's manuscript *Monumenta Britannica* (Oxford, Bodleian, Ms. Top. Gen. c 24–5) is the entry:

> *Memorandum* Mr Webster (Divine & Schoolmaster | London) tells me, that there is a | Runique Inscription in a Church-yard at Folsham in Norfolk | within twelve miles of Norwich. qu*ære* Sr Tho: Browne for it. | Item. qu*ære* his sonne.[4]

Certainly there is a stone monument, in fact a fifteenth(?)-century table tomb with curious lettering on it, north-west of the tower of Foulsham church, but these are not runes. They are crowned Lombardic capitals in no obviously meaningful sequence. Is this the inscription Aubrey meant? How can we know? And what could he have meant by 'Runique'?

There are many such cases where runes are mentioned with little likelihood of our confirming the identification. Sometimes, however, we can accept that 'rune/runic' is imprecisely applied. In the archive left by Bruce Dickins (d. 1978) are responses to an advertisement for information issued by G. B. Brown and Dickins preliminary to their planned runic corpus, *c*.1920. One records:

> ... in Innerleithen [Borders/Peeblesshire] ... a house called 'Runic Cross.' The reason that was given for the name was that when the builder ... was digging the foundations, he found either a runic cross or a portion of one.

The house remains, still called *Runic Cross*, but this find-account is wrong. In fact, the builder discovered the stone in the foundations of the old church at Innerleithen when it was demolished in 1871. It now stands outside the new church. It is neither runic nor a cross; it is a shaft fragment, probably Celtic, without inscription.[5]

Or again there is the famous case of Humfrey Wanley's annotation in a copy of William Nicolson's *English Historical Library* (London, 1714) in the Bodleian Library. It notes that Sir Andrew Fountaine brought from Ireland 'a Wooden Hand or Scepter of an Irish or Danish King with many Runic Letters on it.'[6] Continuity of ownership shows that this was almost certainly the

---

3   R. I. Page, 'Runes and Non-runes', in *Medieval Literature and Civilisation: Studies in Memory of G.N. Garmonsway*, ed. D. A. Pearsall and R. A. Waldron (London, 1969), 28–54, at 49–51; C. E. Fell, 'Runes and Semantics', in *Old English Runes and their Continental Background*, ed. A. Bammesberger, Anglistische Forschungen 217 (Heidelberg, 1991), 195–229, at 199–205.

4   J. Fowles and R. Legge (ed. and annot.), *John Aubrey's Monumenta Britannica* (Sherborne, 1980–2), 849.

5   Royal Commission on the Ancient and Historical Monuments of Scotland, *Peeblesshire* (1967), I, 177–8, no. 378.

shrine of St Lachtin's arm from Donaghmore, Co. Cork, which has a copper-alloy cladding with texts inscribed upon it, though none in runes. The shrine was bought at the Fountaine sale in 1884, presented to the Royal Irish Academy and transferred to the National Museum of Ireland, Dublin, where it remains for us to check.

Somewhat different is the case of the Thornaby-on-Tees rune-stone. This is reported in George Stephens's catalogue, *The Runes, Whence Came They* (London and Copenhagen, 1894), chap. vi, no. 5, with the improbable reading IT BISTR IS AN BI-UIK, *This is the best at Bi-wik*. The stone is no longer extant, for the east end of the church where it was embedded was demolished and remodelled early in the twentieth century as a letter from the vicar in the Dickins archive records. Perhaps luckily, a photograph survives among the George Stephens papers in the University Library, Lund, Sweden. It is hard to interpret, because the picture was taken at an angle to the stone face. Its 'inscription' comprises a series of vertical and sloping straight lines cut or scratched across the stone face, some of them intersecting, some dotted. They do not form runes or even resemble them much. Stephens's reading could hardly have derived from this without extensive editing. Certainly the accompanying letter from T. M. Fallow, October 1893, is not encouraging. Describing the east wall it says:

> You will see a small dial and <u>on a stone below that with the dial</u> there are some marks which I have thought may have a significance of some kind. Neither stone is *in situ* and I think the stone with the markings is upside down. It looks to me as if the marks may have been a lightly scratched inscription in runes – now much worn ... rather a scribble in runes by some one.

W. G. Collingwood published a drawing quite different in effect; it shows a group of indistinct individual graphs, which could include runic 'b' and 's'.[7] Apparently either a much edited version of the stone photographed or a different bit of stone altogether. What did Stephens base his reading on?

Not all investigations are so fruitless. In *The Runes, Whence Came They*, chap. xx, entry no. 119 reads: 'Dublin Museum, Ireland. The *later* runes. On a wooden Cavel. Apparently only a scribble. Cannot be further dated.' Stephens's name for the museum is hardly precise, and no museum in Dublin admitted to holding this object. Serendipity succeeded where questioning failed. Looking through the Lund Stephens papers I came upon a full-scale drawing, beautifully executed, addressed from the Science and Art Museum, Dublin; with the annotation in Stephens's characteristically aggressive hand: 'A wooden Kevel. Apparently only a scribble. Cannot be further dated.' The

[6] Page, 'Runes and Non-runes', 52.
[7] W. G. Collingwood, 'Anglian and Anglo-Danish Sculpture in the North Riding of Yorkshire', *Yorkshire Archæological Journal* 19 (1907), 402 and drawing on opposite page.

drawing is of a stick with elegantly shaped and turned ends, perhaps eighteenth-century. Its inscription, running along two of the sides, is not genuinely runic though it includes runic forms taken from various alphabets. The stick was sometime in the Museum of the Royal Dublin Society but its ultimate origin is unknown. The Science and Art Museum, Leinster House, holdings were dispersed decades ago. Where this piece is now I have not been able to find, but it need worry the runologist no more.

Just as Stephens is our most prolific collector of runic data hitherto (though not its most reliable interpreter), so his correspondence and papers in two great collections, Lund University Library and the Royal Library, Stockholm (formerly dep.189, now Acc.1980/142), are most impressive repositories of runic information and misinformation. An example is that of the Coquet Island, Northumberland, lead ring. This came to light in the 1860s, and was recorded in *The Old-Northern Runic Monuments of Scandinavia and England, now first Collected and Deciphered*, by which time it was in the Duke of Northumberland's collection of antiquities.[8] (He exhibited it at the November 1863 meeting of the Society of Antiquaries of Newcastle-upon-Tyne.) When I was assembling the material of the Anglo-Saxon runic corpus many years ago I wrote to the Duke asking permission to see the ring. I received a gracious 'yes', soon followed by an embarrassed 'no'. The change of mind followed his consultation with his keeper of collections, when it was found that the ring no longer existed, having disintegrated into a white powder later identified as basic lead carbonate, a natural corrosion product. It was believed this resulted from storing the ring in an oaken box: indeed, the powder is, I understand, in the British Museum Research Laboratory so labelled.

There is more to the story than this. The ring is not in the 1880 published catalogue of the Duke's antiquities, nor was it available to Vietor when he visited Alnwick in 1894;[9] which may imply that it had disintegrated even within twenty years of its discovery. Again Stephens's archive (Royal Library) is revealing. A letter dated March 1863 from the antiquary Edward Charlton claims:

> I have at present lying before me, a ring of lead with an inscription in Anglo-Saxon Runes, and which was found on the finger of a skeleton in the old monastic burial ground on Coquet Island off the coast of Northd ... I dare not do much at it as the ring belongs to the Duke of Northd.

There is a related group of letters dating from September and November 1863 telling how Albert Way, antiquary and cataloguer of the collection, had sent the ring to Charlton for examination unknown to the Duke (and

8   G. Stephens, *Handbook of the Old-Northern Runic Monuments of Scandinavia and England* (London, Copenhagen and Lund, 1866–1901), I–II, 481–2.

9   W. Vietor, *Die Northumbrischen Runensteine. Beiträge zur Textkritik. Grammatik und Glossar* (Marburg in Hessen, 1895), 18, n. 1.

apparently also to his official keeper of antiquities). This rather tense correspondence both discusses the importance of the ring and expresses fear lest the Duke find out what they were up to. Eventually the well-regarded runologist and antiquary Daniel Henry Haigh dared to inform the Duke, prevailing upon him to release the ring to Stephens in Copenhagen, whence his published account.

But this is not the whole tale the letters tell. Before it went abroad it was first cleaned 'by gentle treatment with Nitric Acid', or, as another version says, 'by the skilful use of nitric acid'. What the ultimate effect of such treatment might be I do not know; but the ring does not survive. What remains (in the letters) are drawings of it before and after cleaning, and on these any study must be based. There is also a manuscript catalogue of 1867 which records the find in markedly different and more cautious terms than Charlton's.

> A rudely fashioned massive ring of lead found in Coquet Island, Northumberland, in or near an ancient burial-place that adjoins the buildings now occupied by the keeper of the lighthouse. These stand probably on the site of a small cell of Benedictine monks that was associated with Tynemouth Priory ... It was stated by the light-keeper that the Ring with other relics of some antiquity had been found by him in digging in a spot cultivated as a Garden, and in which human bones were frequently disinterred.

So much for 'on the finger of a skeleton in the old monastic burial ground'! Any work on this lost object must note the archival (as well as the published) accounts, with their drawings of the ring before its acid ordeal and after. It would help if archaeologists would look at the possibilities of the Coquet Island site (if it can be identified), but there seems little enthusiasm for it.

So far the information I have adduced from archives has been minimally helpful. However, sometimes even a small addition of fact can be useful. Recently, for instance, B. J. N. Edwards traced the find-place of a partly runic ring which for many years had been given only a general provenance, Lancashire. He showed there was evidence to put it specifically in Manchester, his source being an eighteenth-century annotation to a Stukeley notebook (Society of Antiquaries of London, Ms. 265, 80).[10] The importance of this discovery is that the ring can now be plotted on a distribution map of the later, post-650, inscriptions – 'Lancashire' was too imprecise for that.

Parallel but more important epigraphically is an entry in the Minute Book of the Spalding Gentlemen's Society, 9 November 1732. This records a member's exhibition of a 'Small Gold Medal found at Folkestone in Kent'. There is a careful drawing of its legend alone, in retrograde runes with a few, residual, Roman characters; and another of the obverse and reverse of the

[10] B. J. N. Edwards, 'An Anglo-Saxon Ring Provenance Narrowed', *Antiquaries Journal* 63 (1983), 132–4.

piece.[11] The legend appears to contain a personal name form, **aniwulufu**/'æniwulufu'. The medal (or rather coin) is now lost, but casts of it from the eighteenth and nineteenth centuries survive to confirm the drawings' accuracy. More recently another specimen (apparently a die-duplicate) has emerged from the Hunterian cabinet in Glasgow University: one of William Hunter's pieces but with no provenance recorded. The importance of the Spalding minute is its naming of the find-spot, Folkestone, for there is dispute over whether such early (*c*.600) gold coins are Anglo-Saxon or Frisian and every bit of evidence which helps with the problem is welcome.[12]

Here an archive preserves a text that no longer exists, or at any rate is not known to exist. Another case involves material from Dearham, Cumbria, when the well-known antiquary W. S. Calverley was incumbent. The Royal Library Stephens archive has a number of letters from him, some complaining of his lack of professional advancement, the more important from our point of view recounting the work of church restoration he was organizing. This resulted in the rediscovery in 1882, 'over the North doorway', of the well-known ADAM slab with its Scandinavian runic graffito.[13] In December of that year he reported he had found more runes, scribbles on building stones; and produced two drawings of them. One shows three Norse graphs, **ank**, the other five runes perhaps divided into two groups by a cross, apparently **nan✱+f**. These have not, as far as I know, been seen since, and a search for them is called for. They could be anywhere, built into the present fabric. A more modern example of a lost monument would be the Conishead Priory rune-stone, which Michael Barnes and I have sought in vain and which we know from a 1930 photograph and a drawing of about the same date.[14]

Or an archive could keep an earlier and clearer form of an inscription that is now severely decayed or damaged, as we hope some drawings of the Bewcastle Cross may do. There is a converse to this. An early drawing may confirm the validity of a present-day reading. A clear case is the Falstone, Northumberland, stone. This has weather-worn remains of a pair of related texts, one runic, one Roman, now partly illegible or uncertain in detail. Stephens's picture shows the object in sharper condition, with texts that can

[11]   P. Grierson and M. Blackburn, *Medieval European Coinage: With a Catalogue of the Coins in the Fitzwilliam Museum, Cambridge* (Cambridge, 1986), I, 641–2.

[12]   The point is discussed in several of the articles in *Frisian Runes and Neighbouring Traditions. Proceedings of the First International Symposium on Frisian Runes ... January 1994*, ed. T. Looijenga and A. Quak, Amsterdamer Beiträge zur älteren Germanistik 45 (Amsterdam and Atlanta, 1996).

[13]   Stephens, *Old-Northern Runic Monuments*, III, 420–4.

[14]   P. V. Kelly, 'Excavations at Conishead Priory', *Transactions of the Cumberland and Westmorland Antiquarian and Archæological Society* 30 (1930), 149–68, pl. iii, facing p. 157. Drawing in B. Dickins's contribution to A. Fell, *A Furness Manor: Pennington and its Church* (Ulverston, 1929), 219–21.

be read with confidence. We would think the stone had deteriorated since his time were it not that the earliest known picture, a splendid engraving from 1822, depicts it in much the same state as it now is.[15] Stephens's versions are wish-fulfilment.

A parallel case is that of the Sandwich/Richborough stone, whose text has traditionally been read **rahabul**/'ræhæbul', leaving scholars much exercised as to how to make an Old English personal name from this unpromising sequence. The graphs are in fact very difficult to make out, yet Stephens's engraving shows them clear and precise. The monument is of loose-grained stone which has certainly suffered from its former mounting in the Royal Museum, Canterbury. Clearly the inscription could have lost its precise detail in quite recent years. However, David Parsons examined the stone's known history, pointing out that the earliest drawing, from 1844, shows the runes rather as they are now.[16] He accuses Daniel Henry Haigh of originating the mistaken but hopeful reading **rahabul** (based on his identification of an Old English personal name), citing his book of 1861.[17] This seems true enough as far as it goes, but the Stephens archive (Royal Library) can add to it. It holds a letter from the Kentish antiquary J. Brent, dated May 1862. This tells that 'about five years since' Brent corresponded with Haigh about the Richborough stones, 'and with some misgiving, and hesitative, he read the inscription on the smaller stone'. At that time Haigh identified the sequence of graphs **rahwrul**/'ræhwrul', 'being very doubtful however as to the characters, those marked with asterisks', that is, runes 1, 4: 'r', 'w'. In other words, Haigh came to his reading **rahabul** only after some consideration and rejecting an earlier attempt. This is in accordance with his practice elsewhere, which often shows imagination step by step triumphing over observation.

Archives may also reveal the technical abilities of earlier scholars, and their reliability. They can help us assess the precision of their accounts. We can, for instance, compare Stephens's printing of the discovery of the Aith Voe, Cunningsburgh, Shetland, runic text (Barnes's Cunningsburgh 1)[18] with

15 Cf. Stephens, *Old-Northern Runic Monuments*, I–II, 456 (which, curiously enough, R. W. V. Elliott chose to illustrate the Falstone stone, beneath a more recent though not very clear photograph, in *Runes: An Introduction*, 2nd edn (Manchester and New York, 1989), fig. 32) with J. Wood, 'Some Account of a Saxon Inscription, on a Stone found near Falstone, in the County of Northumberland', *Archæologia Æliana* I (1822), 103–4 and engraving.

16 D. Parsons, 'Sandwich: The Oldest Scandinavian Rune-stone in England?', in *Developments around the Baltic and the North Sea in the Viking Age*, ed. B. Ambrosiani and H. Clark, Birka Studies 3 (Stockholm, 1994), 310–20.

17 D. H. Haigh, *The Conquest of Britain by the Saxons* (London, 1861), 52 and the (retrograde!) drawing of the runes, pl. iii, 31.

18 G. Stephens, 'Note of a Fragment of a Rune-inscribed Stone from Aith's Voe, Cunningsburgh, Shetland, now in the Museum', *Proceedings of the Society of Antiquaries of Scotland* 10 (1875), 425–30, at 426. M. P. Barnes's numbering system

his source, J. Anderson's copy (November 1873) of the finder's original letter (Royal Library). Stephens is accurate in essentials, faulty only in occasional lapses of punctuation. Can we therefore trust other statements of his for which no source survives?

This brief survey shows some of the variety of archival material related to English runic inscriptions, and also some of the problems of finding and assessing it. There are obvious places to search: the major manuscript collections, early modern private archives, particularly those of antiquaries. Some are not so obvious. Who knows if and where there is a Haigh archive parallel to that of Stephens? There is no mention in his *Dictionary of National Biography* entry, and enquiries at Erdington and Oscott College have been fruitless. There are many local antiquaries, like Ralph Thoresby and William Nicolson, whose papers would be interesting to search, but time-consuming. John Aubrey is an obvious case, but where among his confused creations does relevant material repose? Moreover, even this brief selection of examples affords an important lesson: that you never know what you might find in an unlikely place. Who would have guessed that a primary piece of runic information from Kent resided in an eighteenth-century minute book of a Lincolnshire learned society? Or, as for that, that an early account of the finding of the Bramham Moor, Yorkshire, runic ring could be found in the papers, in Cambridge University Library, of Thomas Baker (1656–1740), *socius eiectus* of St John's College, Cambridge?[19] A difficulty is knowing which threads are worth following. It is unlikely, for instance, that it is worth pursuing J. Anderson's note (Royal Library): 'There are two gold rings in the collection at the Advocates Library here [Edinburgh] which seem to have Runes upon them judging from a hasty glance.' Or G. M. Atkinson's, '[I] send you a little stick. I got [it] last year at a very wild place in the South of Ireland. The peasantry that come to pray at the Holy Lake (Wells and Ruins/at Gougaune Barra [Co. Kerry]) use such to number their prayers ... This is the only relick of the Rune Staff I have seen in Ireland.' (Royal Library).

On the other hand, what about the printed page that records first, briefly, the Ruthwell Cross, next 'Two LATIN MONUMENTS in the Library at the College of Glasgow', and then adds, 'This Page is from a loose Paper apart whereon are many Runnic Letters'?[20] The original is in the National Library

---

is in 'Towards an Edition of the Scandinavian Runic Inscriptions of the British Isles – Some Thoughts', *NOWELE (North-Western Language Evolution)* 21/22 (1993), 21–36, at 32–4.

[19] R. I. Page, 'The Finding of the "Bramham Moor" Runic Ring', *Notes and Queries* 9 (1962), 450–2.

[20] W. MacFarlane, *Geographical Collections Relating to Scotland*, ed. Sir Arthur Mitchell and J. T. Clark, Publications of the Scottish History Society 51–3 (Edinburgh, 1906–8), III, 225.

of Scotland, Advocates' Library, Ms. Sibbald 33. 5. 15.[21] Enquiry produced no trace of the 'loose Paper apart'; a pity because in this context the reference looks promising. Perhaps serendipity will discover it. Perhaps too we may light upon more about the lost Leeds rune-stone. All we have are drawings derived ultimately from R. D. Chantrell, the architect who controlled the demolition and rebuilding of Leeds parish church in 1837–41.[22] We know he lectured on his finds there to learned and professional societies, but I have not traced any text of his discourse.

A final observation. It is natural to students of our century to assume that manuscript texts have precedence over printed – they are earlier and therefore more authoritative. It is a mistaken assumption in runic studies. This was brought home to me when I was given a xerox of a drawing, from a major library, of the Manx Andreas II, Braddan IV, Kirk Michael III and V rune-stones (Manx Museum nos. 131, 135, 130, 132). With delight I showed it to Sir David Wilson, who observed that it resembled the depiction of these stones in Gibson's edition of Camden's *Britannia*.[23] Unlikely as it may seem, he was right. Theoretically the drawing could be the original from which Gibson made his print; it is more likely a copy from the print. 'A Warning to the Curious', as that distinguished desk-runological scholar M. R. James put it.

[21] National Library of Scotland, *Summary Catalogue of the Advocates' Manuscripts* (Edinburgh, 1971), no. 1856.
[22] Haigh, *Conquest of Britain*, pl. ii, 16 and Stephens *Old-Northern Runic Monuments*, I–II, 487–8.
[23] W. Camden, *Britannia*, 2nd edn by E. Gibson (London, 1722), cols 1457–60.

Aspects of the Scandinavian Runes of the British Isles

MICHAEL P. BARNES

In 1993 I published a brief paper on the Scandinavian runic inscriptions of the British Isles.[1] I stressed there the various deficiencies that marred existing treatments of this material, and discussed the shape and content of what all but the most critical of my runologist colleagues might be persuaded to regard as a satisfactory edition. As an appendix, I included a list of the Scandinavian runic inscriptions of the British Isles then known to me. (See fig. 28, overleaf, for a map of find-spots that includes more recent additions to the list.)

Given the existence of this general survey, the most profitable approach in the present context would seem to be, first, to provide an update on the corpus, and, second, to air a few tentative conclusions concerning the nature of Scandinavian runic activity in the British Isles (largely absent from the earlier account).

Nothing, least of all runology, stands still. In the years since I wrote the 1993 paper several inscriptions have been discovered, and some rediscovered. Rediscovery, unfortunately, has thrown into disarray the system I proposed for designating individual inscriptions: a letter or letters to denote the country of origin of the find[2] and a number based on the date of discovery (1 = earliest, and so on). This seemed to me beautifully simple and appeared to allow new finds to be added with no disturbance to established designations. However, I can now report the existence of an Irish inscription recognized before any of those excavated in Dublin in the 1970s and 1980s (IR 4–14, 16), and of one from Shetland noted long before the discovery of what I designated SH 1.

The Irish inscription is on the Roosky bracelet from Donegal. It consists of an r and possibly one further rune, and was first mentioned in 1973.[3] The Shetland case is the Eshaness gravestone, described and illustrated by George

---

[1] M. P. Barnes, 'Towards an Edition of the Scandinavian Runic Inscriptions of the British Isles: Some Thoughts', *Northern Studies* 29 (1992, published 1993), 32–42. (An earlier version of this paper was published in *NOWELE* 21/22 (1993), 21–36.)

[2] SH = Shetland, OR = Orkney, SC = Scotland, E = England, IR = Ireland.

[3] R. Hall, 'A Hoard of Viking Silver Bracelets from Cushalogurt, Co. Mayo', *Journal of the Royal Society of Antiquaries of Ireland* 103, C (1973), 78–85, at 83.

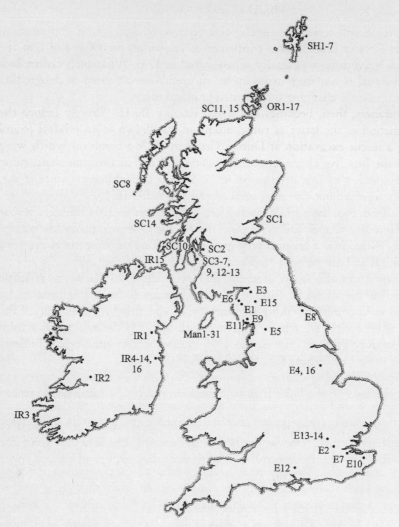

Fig. 28: Map of find-spots of Scandinavian runic inscriptions of the British Isles (drawn by Caitlin Evans). See fig. 29, p. 113, for a detailed map of the Shetland inscriptions.

Low following his trip to Shetland in 1774,[4] but subsequently thought to be lost, and dismissed as non-runic by many. Recent examination has confirmed Low's original observation that the stone is inscribed with both runes and Roman letters,[5] but both have proved extremely hard to read.

With the connivance of two of my fellow runologists I have chosen to employ subterfuge to meet the challenge posed by these two inscriptions to

4   G. Low, *A Tour through the Islands of Orkney and Schetland* (Kirkwall, 1879), 135–6.

5   Cf. M. P. Barnes, 'The Runic Stone at Cross Kirk, Eshaness, Shetland', *Nytt om runer* 8 (1993), 12–14.

what overall still seems a neat and clear system of designation. I thus claim that the Roosky bracelet was confirmed as runic only in 1994, and that the Eshaness gravestone was finally rehabilitated in 1993. What such claims lack in intellectual rigour they make up for in usefulness: a system of designation that is constantly changing is of limited practical value.

Eshaness, then, becomes SH 6 and Roosky IR 15.[6] Shortly before the confirmation of the latter as runic, attention was drawn to an artefact found during a rescue excavation at Dublin Castle in 1985: a comb on which were incised the first five characters of the *fuþark* and one further uncertain rune. The designation of this inscription as IR 14 was unproblematic since it was not only reported but also excavated several years after IR 13.

Shetland, too, has a fresh inscription: SH 7, found in 1994 during a rescue excavation at a chapel and graveyard site on the Gungstie peninsula on the island of Noss. It is a fragmentary graffito consisting of some six runes on a loose stone, and can be both read and interpreted in different ways.

Orkney can also boast a recent find, with the 1995 discovery at Little Isegarth on the island of Sanday of what appears to be a fragment of an inscription of common Viking-Age memorial type, detailing the name of the carver. This is OR 17, which, together with SH 7, is the subject of a joint notice by Ray Page and me in the 1995 number of the runological bulletin *Nytt om runer* (concerning OR 16, see below).[7]

The same number contains a notice by John McKinnell of the excavation in Lincoln in 1994 of a bone fragment containing part of a runic inscription – E 16.[8]

Another recent discovery is of three additional runes on the wall of Carlisle Cathedral, 41 cm. to the left of the existing E3. Whether these are part of E3 or a separate inscription is at present unclear, but pending a more detailed examination it has been decided not to give them their own designation.

Most recently a further inscription from the Dublin excavations has come to light. It consists of six or so very indistinct characters placed on a bone artefact – possibly a pin or an owner's tag. The likelihood is that the characters are runes, but there is a chance they are merely 'rune-like'; the bone is so worn it is difficult to tell. The inscription is provisionally designated IR 16.

---

[6]   A supplementary list detailing these and other inscriptions discovered or brought to light since the 1993 account was compiled is presented on p. 111.

[7]   M. Barnes and R. I. Page, 'Two Runic Inscriptions from the Northern Isles', *Nytt om runer* 10 (1995, published 1996), 12–13.

[8]   J. McKinnell, 'A Runic Fragment from Lincoln', *Nytt om runer* 10 (1995, published 1996), 10–11.

Reports from Orkney (September 1996) indicate the discovery of a new runic stone on Mainland. To date, however, no runologist has examined the object, so nothing definite can be said about the nature of the carving.

Some nine additions to the corpus in four years is a respectable total. Further inscriptions are clearly to be expected in the future. Indeed, some may already be with us. When Page and I were examining the myriad scratchings on the wall of St Molaise's cave on Holy Island, Arran, we thought we could discern other runic carvings there than have appeared in the published accounts (SC 3–7, 9, 12–13) – though what we could make out was so faint that decipherment looked a daunting, possibly hopeless, task.

As well as an adding of inscriptions to the 1993 list, there may have to be a taking away – potentially more serious for the system of designation. A recent investigation I have made suggests that E 5, the Settle stone, may have been carved by James Farrer in the 1860s or 1870s.[9] Farrer was the excavator of Maeshowe, the rune-inscribed Orkney cairn.[10] He lived close to Settle, and E 5, which bears a striking but seemingly not perfect resemblance to a section of the shattered Maeshowe no. 17, is most plausibly explained as an imitation of one of the missing pieces of that inscription. Whatever the true genesis of E 5, there is little doubt that, like the relevant part of Maeshowe no. 17, its runes read oframr, not afr(al)fr as indicated in my 1993 list. Some of the Orkney twig-rune inscriptions also give cause for concern.[11] Devoid of find reports as several such inscriptions are, it would not be surprising to discover there were modern carvings among them. To be sure, the use of twig-runes as a cryptic device was very much part of Scandinavian runic tradition, but the extraordinarily high percentage of inscriptions from Orkney in which they feature may reflect post-1861 awareness of the prominent occurrence of twig-runes in Maeshowe rather than any Viking-Age or medieval practice.

The Settle stone and most of the Orkney twig-rune carvings are at least available for examination. Two Orkney inscriptions, however, OR 1, Stackrue, and OR 5, Ring of Brogar II, together with E 11, Conishead (Cumbria), cannot at present be located. Fortunately, photographs of all three

9   M. P. Barnes, 'The Strange Case of the Settle Stone', in *A Frisian and Germanic Miscellany Published in Honour of Nils Århammar on his Sixty-Fifth Birthday, 7 August 1996*, ed. A. Petersen and H. F. Nielsen (Odense, 1996), 297–313.

10   Cf. M. P. Barnes, *The Runic Inscriptions of Maeshowe, Orkney*, Runrön 8 (Uppsala, 1994).

11   Cf. M. P. Barnes, 'Twigging the Twig-runes: Orkney and the Wider Scandinavian World', in *Frejas Psalter til brug for Jonna Louis-Jensen*, ed. Bergljót S. Kristjánsdóttir and P. Springborg (Copenhagen, 1997), 14–18. Twig-runes are a runic cypher based on a division of the *fuþark* into three groups, for example: **fuþark:hnias:tbmlz**. Twigs or branches are placed on either side of a vertical, the total number on one side denoting the group, on the other position within the group.

exist, and, as long as the originals remain in hiding, these constitute our primary evidence. Two fragmentary inscriptions also feared lost, OR 8 and 9, turn out to have been left behind in the transfer of exhibits from the now abandoned site museum on Birsay, Orkney, to Kirkwall. They currently lie forgotten and unattended, though mercifully locked up, in the shack that once housed the collection. In the wall of the ruined church on Birsay, close to the ground, can be seen a further stone with what appear to be the remains of runes running along its narrow edge (seemingly first observed by Anders Bæksted in 1955). No characters can be clearly identified, but in general appearance the stone is remarkably like the two in the shack, and I have little hesitation in designating it OR 16. It is to be hoped it can be removed and taken into safe keeping, where it should also be possible for it to be more thoroughly examined. Regrettably, I am unaware of any plans to effectuate its removal. The same goes for SC 15, Thurso II, discovered in 1989 and currently still high up in the wall of Old St Peter's Church, where the inscription is rapidly flaking off under the onslaught of the Pentland weather.

On a more cheerful note, it is good to be able to report scholarly progress since 1993. My edition of the runic inscriptions of Maeshowe (see note 10) appeared in 1994, and a volume dealing with the Irish runic inscriptions in 1997.[12] A sizeable part of the Scandinavian runic material from the British Isles is thus at last becoming available in modern, scholarly form.

Having updated the preliminary outline of the corpus I gave in 1993, I now turn to the question of the general inferences to be drawn from it.

First and most obviously: the inscriptions indicate the presence of people from Scandinavia, or their descendants. Scarcely an exciting conclusion in itself, it does prompt the further questions: what sort of people and what sort of presence? Cursory examination of the data shows that Scandinavian runic activity in the British Isles took a number of different forms. More thorough investigation of these forms may reveal something of the context of particular inscriptions or groups of inscriptions.

In some cases we are clearly dealing with stable rune-using communities, in others with people passing by who left evidence of their ability to use the script. Occasionally we may have indications of both types of activity in the same place, or we may not be able easily to distinguish the one type from the other. Now and again things become considerably murkier, and it can be diffi-cult to suggest a plausible context at all for texts that have come down to us.

The best example of a stable British-Isles community using Scandinavian runes is probably that which existed in Viking-Age Man. This relatively small island preserves a remarkably homogeneous collection of upwards of thirty runic inscriptions, mostly commemorative crosses said to be from the tenth

[12]   M. P. Barnes, J. R. Hagland and R. I. Page, *The Runic Inscriptions of Viking Age Dublin* (Dublin, 1997). The work also contains an appendix on the runic inscriptions in Ireland outside Dublin.

century.[13] Considerable time and effort went into the making of these monuments, they were not easily transported, and they clearly addressed a local audience. From them, moreover, emerge indications that the Scandinavian spoken on Man may have been starting to come under the influence of Gaelic, which in turn suggests that Scandinavian already had some antiquity on the island at the time the inscriptions were made.

There are several other areas in the British Isles where the epigraphic remains show Scandinavian runes being used for the purpose of public commemoration, thus suggesting or confirming the existence of a settled, Scandinavian speech community. This is true of Shetland, where only one of the seven known inscriptions seems inconsistent with the supposition of a memorial stone or gravestone. It must also apply to north-eastern Caithness: one of the two Thurso inscriptions is a memorial cross and the other may well be of memorial type. Apart from the collection on Holy Island, Arran – of which more below – only three runic inscriptions are known from the Hebrides and the Firth of Clyde: SC 8, Kilbar, SC 10, Inchmarnock, SC 14, Iona. All appear to commemorate the dead. Iona is a gravestone, Kilbar a memorial cross. Inchmarnock is a cross too, and was therefore presumably made in memory of a deceased relative, but not enough of the inscription now remains to confirm this.

Given what we know of the patterns of Viking settlement in the British Isles, it is of course scarcely surprising to find evidence of stable rune-using communities in north-eastern Caithness and various parts of the west of Scotland. More unexpected is IR 2, the Killaloe cross, from an inland site in the west of Ireland, and IR 3, the Beginish stone, from an island off the Kerry coast. Killaloe, however, is only some twelve miles distant from the Scandinavian settlement of Limerick, and the original location and purpose of the Beginish stone are unknown: when found, it was being re-used as a lintel. Perhaps somewhat unexpected, too, is the occurrence of one certain and one highly probable memorial inscription in south-east England, E 2, St Paul's, and E 12, Winchester. Neither London nor Winchester are areas associated with long-term Scandinavian settlement, and it has therefore been surmised that both these inscriptions are to be connected with the campaign of Canute the Great early in the eleventh century. This is a plausible enough idea, but its acceptance must lead to doubts about the evidential value of memorial stones for the existence of settled rune-using Scandinavian communities. Of course, there may well have been an expectation of linguistic permanence on the part of those who commissioned the St Paul's and Winchester stones, but it is also possible that they were simply observing a custom familiar to them from their Scandinavian homelands: the raising or laying of a memorial stone was

---

[13]   A succinct account of the Manx runic material is: R. I. Page, 'The Manx Rune Stones', in *The Viking Age in the Isle of Man*, ed. C. Fell *et al.* (London, 1983), 133–46.

perhaps something a person of status was expected to organize, irrespective of the potential readership.

If we had to rely solely on runic evidence for our knowledge of Scandinavian involvement in Orkney, we would gain a wholly false impression. It is only with the 1995 discovery of the Isegarth fragment, OR 17, that we get any sort of evidence for the raising of memorial stones in the islands. Beyond that, and excepting the vast collection in Maeshowe (see below), the runic material from Orkney is an incongruous and puzzling collection of odds and ends: twig-rune finds, many of uncertain provenance and all of uncertain interpretation; two stones with unlikely sequences of plain runes, and another with an apparent graffito; three further stones with inscriptions so damaged hardly a single rune can be recognized with certainty; portable objects with non-linguistic messages or graffiti. Quite apart from the fact, alluded to earlier, that some of these carvings may be modern, they do not give the impression of a society that used runes as a regular means of communication – either for commemorating the dead or for practical, everyday purposes. Indeed, such is the nature of much of the Orcadian runic material, it is hard to see why it should have been carved at all.

Maeshowe presents an entirely different picture. In this prehistoric chambered cairn may be found in excess of thirty inscriptions that make perfectly good sense, even twig-runes bearing straightforward linguistic messages – and an otherwise unknown series of cryptic runes that can be interpreted with a fair degree of certainty. The orthography is remarkably consistent and there are also indications of orthographic innovation. Runes are embellished for particular purposes, and in two cases written right to left. In short, Maeshowe represents a rare display of runic competence and versatility. The contrast with the rest of Orkney is stark – one of the reasons why I believe the Maeshowe inscriptions are the product largely or wholly of imported skill. What we otherwise suspect or know of their background suggests much of the skill was Norwegian: the cairn seems to have been broken into in the winter of 1150–1, while a group of adventurers mainly recruited from Norway was preparing to depart with the Orkney earl, Rǫgnvaldr Kali, on a crusade to the Holy Land. Indeed, one inscription states: 'Jerusalem-men broke [open] this mound', and another: 'Jerusalem-travellers broke [open] Orkhaugr [i.e., Maeshowe]'. As regards content, the inscriptions appear to be light-hearted graffiti, which may offer us further insight into their genesis. Maeshowe is an unusually large cairn, and affords excellent shelter from the Orkney weather for smaller or larger groups of people. To the extent that some of the carvings stem from the period after the initial break-in, they may be the work of visitors who, inspired by what was already there, felt the urge to while away an idle hour by incising their names into the walls, along with other bits of trivial information such as that they 'carved runes'.

Holy Island, off Arran, offers a similar environment. The sound between the two islands provides a tolerably safe haven in a storm, and what better to do while waiting there for fair weather than go ashore and carve one's name into the rock face of one of the few natural shelters on the island. The Holy Island inscriptions are in no way as versatile as those in Maeshowe, but like them, they are clearly the work of visitors passing through, not of an established community.

How far the recently excavated Dublin inscriptions reflect a settled rune-using community is unclear. The evidence for Scandinavian settlement in the city is of course unambiguous. Sporadic indications of literacy are also to be found: not only are there runic inscriptions, but one or two in the Roman alphabet with Anglo-Saxon or Latin texts, and one in ogham possibly recording a Scandinavian name. Nevertheless, we cannot be sure that the rune-inscribed objects that have come to light were written by people permanently resident in the city. Given that a feature of many of these inscriptions is their incomprehensibility, it would certainly be hard to argue that runes were an established medium of written communication in late Viking-Age and early medieval Dublin.

Scandinavian runic activity in England as it manifests itself in the preserved artefacts is oddly fragmented. As well as the St Paul's and Winchester stones, referred to earlier, E 7, Rochester, and E 10, Canterbury, provide possible indications of memorial stone raising in the south-east. Also from this area, but of very different type, are the two rune-inscribed bones, E 13 and 14, found in St Albans. One has some curious letter combinations, perhaps a kind of code, the other sports a w among its Scandinavian characters, a feature that may indicate influence from Anglo-Saxon runic writing. What connection these inscriptions have to St Albans is unclear, but it is worth remembering that the city was very close to the southern boundary of the Danelaw.

The other cluster of English inscriptions in Scandinavian runes comes from the north-west. E 1, the Bridekirk font, with its Middle English text, E 3, Carlisle Cathedral, and E 9, the Pennington tympanum, with their aberrant linguistic forms, and the incomprehensible E 6, Dearham, and E 11, Conishead, both on stone, suggest the existence of a rune-using community, but what sort of community it was and how long it had been using runes are matters about which one can at the moment only speculate. Four of these five inscriptions appear to be from the twelfth century (Conishead is possibly from the thirteenth), and have been taken to show how far assimilation of the Scandinavians into English culture had gone. The ungrammatical Norse of Carlisle and Pennington may indicate a language under siege from a more prestigious rival, while Bridekirk with its Norse runes and Middle English text could be evidence of the complete adoption of English by at least some twelfth-century descendants of the settlers.

Another inscription from the north-west is E 15, the Penrith *fuþark*, but this is on a loose object, a ninth- or tenth-century penannular brooch, and its runes were probably inscribed far from the spot where it was found. The two Lincoln inscriptions, E 4 and E 16, both likewise on loose objects, are also of uncertain provenance, though Lincoln is a place where the use of Scandinavian runes would not be unexpected. From the north-east, E 8, Skelton, is something of an oddity. In its complete state the sundial which bore the inscription must have been a heavy object, and it is therefore reasonable to suppose that it was made not far from where it now stands. What kind of milieu it reflects is at present impossible to say. It is perhaps worth noting, however, that Yorkshire and the north-east have the heaviest concentration of Anglo-Saxon rune-stones, and in its mixture of Roman and runic the Skelton sundial parallels a number of these.

Much detailed work remains to be done on the runes of the British Isles, which may to some degree improve our understanding of the contexts in which they were made. Nevertheless, the broad outlines of the account I have given here are, I believe, likely to stand.

APPENDIX

Supplementary list of Scandinavian runic inscriptions in the British Isles
(see p. 105)

SH 6   Eshaness II (gravestone): þïnnastaïn (followed by an extensive sequence of runes, most of which have so far proved impossible to read because of wear or damage).

SH 7   Gungstie (stone). The most likely reading is: –[.]*u*kãktu

OR 16   Birsay V (stone fragment): the lower quarter of about 14 runes, some of which appear to be u or r.

OR 17   Little Isegarth (stone fragment): –n:in:ãsk[*a*..]:r–

E 3   (additional runes): ai[*f*]

E 16   Lincoln II (rib bone): [*b*–]*l*:hitir:stin:

IR 14   Dublin Castle (bone comb): fuþãr[.]

IR 15   Roosky (silver bracelet): r[.]

IR 16   Mostly illegible, but perhaps containing an s, b and þ.

The new Orkney find reported in September 1996 has yet to be examined.

Reading the Runes:
Epigraphy and History in the Northern Isles

KATHERINE HOLMAN

The archipelagos of Shetland and Orkney lie on the major sailing routes south from Norway to the British mainland, the Western Isles, and Ireland, a situation of great importance in the Viking Age. The islands were first settled by a Norse population in the course of the ninth century, and belonged to the Norwegian crown until they were pledged to Scotland in 1468–9. Although there is little written evidence for this settlement, it has left its mark on the archaeology, place-names and language of the two island groups. Almost all of the place-names in the Northern Isles are of Norse origin, and the Norse dialect, Norn, was spoken in the islands, at least by some individuals, into the eighteenth century. In contrast, the islands' pre-existing Pictish population had disappeared from the historical and archaeological record by about the eleventh century.

The historical and cultural background to the fifty-seven separate inscriptions in Scandinavian runes found in the Northern Isles is thus clearly and overwhelmingly Scandinavian. At first sight, these inscriptions appear to be rather unevenly distributed between the two island groups: seven have been found on Shetland, compared with fifty on Orkney. However, thirty-three of Orkney's fifty inscriptions are carved in one place, on the walls of the prehistoric chamber tomb, Maeshowe, in central Mainland. This collection of light-hearted graffiti appears to have been carved over a fairly short period in the middle of the twelfth century. Michael Barnes has suggested that the inspiration behind the Maeshowe inscriptions may well have been Norwegian, as there is little evidence for the thriving runic culture that lies behind these inscriptions in twelfth-century Orkney.[1] If we exclude Maeshowe, Orkney is left with eighteen inscriptions, eight of which consist of merely a few cryptic runes. As a cryptic rune is usually simply a vertical line with between one and six diagonal cuts on either side, it is possible that they may have been cut by someone ignorant of Scandinavian runes and the principle behind the cryptographs.[2] Certainly, these eight cryptic inscriptions

---

[1]   M. P. Barnes, *The Runic Inscriptions of Maeshowe, Orkney*, Runrön 8 (Uppsala, 1994), 60. See above, p. 109.

[2]   See above, p. 106.

do not appear to make sense in any Scandinavian language. I have therefore chosen to omit them from this discussion. I have also excluded an inscribed spindle-whorl, purchased in Stromness in the nineteenth century, but otherwise of uncertain provenance. This leaves ten runic inscriptions from Orkney, a figure that is more in line with the Shetland total.

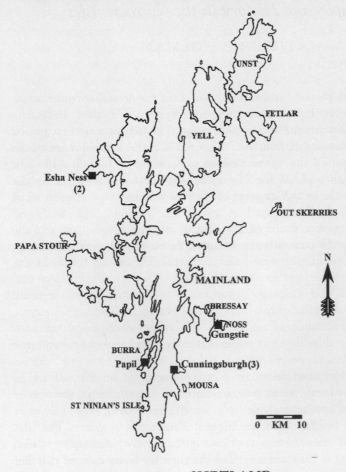

Fig. 29: Map of Scandinavian runic inscriptions found on Shetland.

SHETLAND

Three fragmentary runic inscriptions on stone have been found in the cemetery at Mail in Cunningsburgh. Amateur archaeological investigations in the mid-nineteenth century uncovered the remains of occupational debris on and around the site.[3] As well as the runic inscriptions, three ogham inscriptions and, more recently, a Pictish stone decorated with a wolf-headed

---

[3] For details of this site see G. Goudie, 'On Rune-inscribed Relics of the Norsemen in Shetland', *Proceedings of the Society of Antiquaries of Scotland* 13 (1878–9), 136–64; A. Ritchie, *Viking Scotland* (London, 1993), 62.

figure have been found at Mail. These finds suggest a high-status site with some ecclesiastical function, and the place-name Cunningsburgh, 'king's stronghold', also suggests secular importance. The soapstone quarries at nearby Catspund Burn were an important centre for the production of soapstone artefacts in the Norse period. This soft rock was one of the most important natural resources in Scandinavian Shetland, and the place-name and finds may reflect the economic significance of this resource.

Unfortunately, both Cunningsburgh I and II are extremely fragmentary, consisting of the lower part of five and four runes respectively. Although Cunningsburgh I has been identified as the remains of a male personal name,[4] it is not possible to read either inscription with any certainty. However, Cunningsburgh III can be identified as the end of a memorial inscription, —eftir fǫður sinn Þorbjǫrn, '—in memory of his/her father Þorbjǫrn'. Although the personal name Þorbjǫrn is given after the information that he was X's father, this inscription otherwise follows the common memorial formula found on Viking-Age rune-stones throughout Scandinavia. The beginning of the inscription would presumably have contained the usual information about the person responsible for the monument, in the form, X reisti stein þensi, 'X raised this stone'.

One runic inscription has been found at the Early Christian site of Papil on the island of West Burra. As the place-name Papil, 'priests' lot or dwelling', suggests, this site was an important Early Christian religious centre, and some thirteen pieces of worked stone in the Christian/Celtic tradition have also been found there.[5] This sculpture continued to be produced into the tenth century, that is, after Scandinavian raids and settlement had begun. The runic inscription is fairly certainly a fragment of a Viking-Age memorial stone, with the verb reisti, 'raised', followed by the beginning of what was probably the word st(ein) 'stone'.

Two runic inscriptions on stone have been found in the churchyard of Esha Ness (also Eshaness) in north-west Mainland. Late medieval activity on the site is suggested by the discovery of a small bronze figurine of a horse, a Scandinavian scale-weight, dated to the early fourteenth century.[6] The first inscription from Esha Ness is so fragmentary that nothing can really be said about it, consisting as it does of the upper part of seven runes: -[..] :

[4]   A. Liestøl, 'Runes', in The Northern and Western Isles in the Viking World, ed. A. Fenton and H. Pálsson (Edinburgh, 1984), 224–38, at 227; M. P. Barnes, 'Towards an Edition of the Scandinavian Runic Inscriptions of the British Isles – Some Thoughts', NOWELE (North-Western Language Evolution) 21/22 (1993), 21–36, at 32.

[5]   C. Thomas, 'Sculptured Stones and Crosses from St Ninian's Isle and Papil', in St. Ninian's Isle and its Treasure I, ed. A. Small et al. (Oxford, 1973), 8–44, at 10 and 39–43.

[6]   Royal Commission on the Ancient Monuments of Scotland, Orkney and Shetland (Edinburgh, 1946), III, 89.

[.]kku[.]–. However, it can be noted that doubled consonants are most often found in post-Viking-Age inscriptions. The other runic inscription from Esha Ness, the so-called Cross Kirk stone, is also barely legible. The inscription apparently begins with the words þenna stein 'this stone', but it is no longer possible to identify any of the remaining runes with certainty.[7] An inscription in Roman letters accompanies the runic inscription, and the forms of these, and of the recumbent grave slab, suggest a date in the later medieval period.[8]

Most recently, a rune-inscribed slate fragment was found during excavations at Gungstie on the island of Noss.[9] The discovery of a corner-post from an Early Christian shrine suggests an ecclesiastical function for the site, possibly as early as the eighth century. In addition, there were indications that the site had been intensively used and re-used for burial, and the foundations of what may have been a twelfth-century round chapel were also discovered. Other finds from the site include a small sandstone slab, decorated with an interlaced cross, and a steatite spindle-whorl of characteristic Scandinavian form. The inscription is the only known example of runic graffiti on Shetland, and consists of five lightly scratched runes. No translation can be suggested, although it is possible that the text contains the Norse word ok, 'and'.

ORKNEY

Five of the ten Orkney inscriptions were found on the Brough of Birsay, a tidal island which lies off the north-west coast of Mainland. Although the island has often been associated with an Early Christian monastic site, recent excavations have not been able to confirm this, and archaeological excavations have instead revealed an important eighth-century bronze-working industry on the Brough. Three ogham inscriptions, two of which are casual ninth-century graffiti, a Pictish symbol stone and two carved grave-stones have also been found on the site.[10] In addition, a complex of high-status buildings, dated to the tenth and eleventh centuries, has been excavated, as have some more conventional Norse longhouses, occupied from the ninth into the thirteenth or fourteenth century. The ruined twelfth-century stone church on the Brough overlies an earlier structure, but whether this was the site of Earl Þorfinnr's Christchurch, the foundation of which is described in

---

[7] M. P. Barnes, 'The Runic Stone at Cross Kirk, Eshaness, Shetland', *Nytt om runer* 8 (1993), 12–14. Cf. above, pp. 103–4, 111.

[8] C. S. Calder, 'A Recumbent Grave-slab from Breckon, Esha Ness, Shetland', *Proceedings of the Society of Antiquaries of Scotland* 92 (1958–9), 114–15.

[9] I would like to thank Tommy Watt and Carol Anderson of the Shetland Museum for the information about this site and for a photograph of the inscription. A short description of the inscription by M. P. Barnes and R. I. Page can be found in *Nytt om runer* 10 (1995), 12–13.

[10] A. Ritchie, 'Orkney in the Pictish Kingdom', in *The Prehistory of Orkney*, ed. C. Renfrew (Edinburgh, 1985), 183–204, at 192.

Orkneyinga Saga (ch. 31), is a question that is still debated.[11]

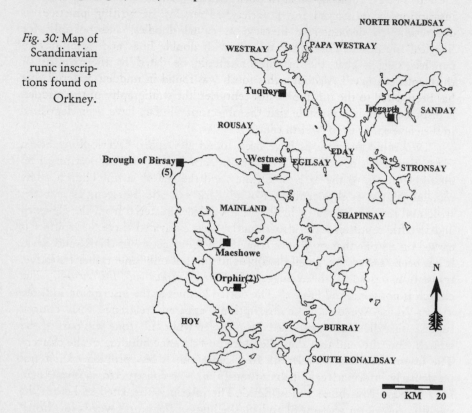

Fig. 30: Map of Scandinavian runic inscriptions found on Orkney.

Four of the Brough inscriptions were found in the structure of this twelfth-century church. There are three consecutive inscriptions on the stone slab known as Birsay I, only the last of which can be confidently transcribed as a runic text. This begins with the personal name, Philippus, and is followed by what might be an abbreviated or confused form of the words *reist rúnar* 'carved runes' (**ranru**).[12] Birsay II, III, and V are carved on split flagstones, and only the lower parts of twelve, ten and fourteen runes respectively remain. These inscriptions are too damaged to be reconstructed, but the slabs appear to have been split, and also therefore inscribed with runes, before being placed in the structure of the twelfth-century church. The fifth and final inscription from the Brough of Birsay is carved on a seal's tooth, and consists of the first

11 *Orkneyinga saga*, ed. Finnbogi Guðmundsson (Reykjavik, 1965); *Orkneyinga Saga: The History of the Earls of Orkney*, trans. H. Pálsson and P. Edwards (Harmondsworth, 1981), 75.
12 M. Olsen, 'Runic Inscriptions in Great Britain, Ireland and the Isle of Man', in *Viking Antiquities in Great Britain and Ireland*, ed. H. Shetelig, VI (Oslo, 1954), 163.

six letters of the runic alphabet (**fuþork**) and an additional vertical cut. *Fuþork* inscriptions were carved for a variety of reasons: as writing practice, as decoration, to demonstrate literacy, as casual doodles, and possibly for 'magical' purposes. The runes are cut with double lines and Scandinavian parallels suggest that the inscription should be dated to the twelfth or thirteenth century.[13] Although this tooth was found in midden material that has been dated to the ninth or tenth centuries, the stratigraphy of the midden is disturbed and it is possible that the object may in fact have been deposited in the eleventh or even twelfth century.[14]

Two runic inscriptions have been found at Orphir. Overlooking Scapa Flow, this site is described in *Orkneyinga Saga* (ch. 66) as the location of an estate belonging to the earls of Orkney and the site of 'a fine church'. The remains of the twelfth-century Round Kirk can still be seen, as can the structural remains of a large hall. Mill and midden material from the eleventh and twelfth centuries have also recently been excavated there.[15] Orphir I is carved on a stone that may have come from the structure of the Round Kirk. It has been read as: **ikergirgi(a)k(a)þ(us)ufs[u]**, but only one, rather tentative, translation has so far been suggested: *Ekki er kirkia góð, liúf sv(a)—*, 'The church is not good, mild as—'.[16] The dotted k-runes in the inscription indicate a post-Viking-Age date. The inscription's apparent reference to a church suggests that the runes could have been carved while the stone was part of the church structure, and that they therefore post-date the building of the church. The fragmented text on Orphir II, a cattle rib, is less problematic, if not particularly informative: **–[.]a:bain:uas:i[þ]u[..]–**, reconstructed as (*Þett)a bein uas í þv(esti)*, 'This bone was in flesh'. The inscription is dated to before the twelfth century on account of archaic spellings of the Norse words for 'bone' and 'was'.[17]

Excavations at the settlement and cemetery site of Westness on the island of Rousay have uncovered a bone pin inscribed with three a-runes.[18] The repetition of runes without any recognized linguistic meaning is well-evidenced in the runic material, particularly in the pre-Viking and medieval

13 A. Liestøl in C. L. Curle, *Pictish and Norse Finds from the Brough of Birsay 1934–74*, Society of Antiquaries of Scotland Monograph Series 1 (Edinburgh, 1982), 59–60.

14 K. Holman, *Scandinavian Runic Inscriptions in the British Isles: Their Historical Context*, Senter for middelalderstudier skrifter 4 (Trondheim, 1996), 238–9.

15 C. E. Batey with C. Freeman, 'Lavacroon, Orphir, Orkney', *Proceedings of the Society of Antiquaries of Scotland* 116 (1986), 285–300.

16 J. R. Hagland, 'Two Runic Inscriptions from Orphir', in *The Viking Age in Caithness, Orkney and the North Atlantic*, ed. C. E. Batey et al. (Edinburgh, 1993), 370–4, at 372.

17 J. McKinnell, 'A New Find from Orkney', *Nytt om runer* 4 (1989), 15.

18 S. H. H. Kaland, 'Westnessutgravingene på Rousay, Orknøyene', *Viking* 37 (1973), 77–102, at 99.

periods. The purpose of such inscriptions is unclear: they may have served some kind of magical purpose, perhaps with each letter representing the initial of a longer word, or they may have been purely decorative. No details are known about the archaeological dating of the pin, although occupational and burial material on the site spans the Viking Age.

A rune-inscribed stone was found during rescue excavations at Tuquoy on the island of Westray.[19] These excavations revealed a monumental twelfth-century stone hall adjacent to the twelfth-century Crosskirk, evidence which suggests that this was a high-status site. The stone was found, upside-down, in the structure of this stone hall, and it is inscribed with the graffito: Þorsteinn Einarssonr reist rúnar þessar, 'Þorsteinn Einarssonr carved these runes'. This sort of text is perhaps the most common form of runic graffiti: there are seven such inscriptions in Maeshowe, one from Birsay and numerous examples from Scandinavia. The rune-forms and orthography of the inscription suggest a date early in the twelfth century.

A further inscription on a dressed stone slab has recently been found in a wall at Isegarth on the island of Sanday. This site has otherwise yielded only a few odd domestic finds from the Norse period.[20] The text is fragmentary: –n:in:ãsk[a..]:r–, but the word en, 'and/but' at the beginning of the fragment suggests that this is the end of a longer inscription, perhaps the beginning of a rune-carver's signature following a commemorative text.[21]

DISCUSSION

As this survey has revealed, several runic inscriptions were found on sites that were Early Christian centres and where ogham inscriptions have also been found. Particularly striking is the number of ogham and runic inscriptions found on the Brough of Birsay and at Cunningsburgh, both of which were clearly important sites in the pre-Scandinavian and Viking periods. Given the difficulties in precisely dating both sorts of inscriptions, it is unfortunately not possible to say whether or not the relationship between the runic and ogham inscriptions is more than geographical. Certainly, carved stones in the Christian Pictish tradition continued to be produced in Shetland after Norse raids and settlement had begun (see above), although there is no evidence that this was the case in Orkney. The word dividers used in the Bressay, Lunnasting and Cunningsburgh 3 oghams from Shetland have also generally been regarded as imitations of the dividers used in Scandinavian runic inscriptions. It is possible that the discovery of ogham inscriptions at certain locations encouraged Norse interest in their own script. However, there is

[19] O. Owen and J. McKinnell, 'A Runic Inscription from Tuquoy, Westray, Orkney', Medieval Archaeology 33 (1989), 53–9, at 55.

[20] The Orcadian, Thursday 12 October 1995.

[21] M. Barnes and R. I. Page, 'Two Runic Inscriptions from the Northern Isles', Nytt om runer 10 (1995), 12–13, at 12.

nothing in any of the runic inscriptions from Shetland or Orkney which suggests interaction with a Pictish population. Given the apparently Scandinavian features of these oghams from Shetland, and the rather experimental nature of the Cunningsburgh oghams, it has instead been suggested that Scandinavian epigraphy stimulated interest in the ogham script.[22] This evidence also seems to suggest that there was initially greater Pictish survival on Shetland than on Orkney.

Indeed, although Orkney and Shetland are frequently presented as a single unit in historical and archaeological accounts, there are important differences in their geography, topography, and history. The geology and landscape of Shetland is in stark contrast to that of fertile, low-lying Orkney. The landscape is hilly, and while there are some outcrops of sandstone and limestone on mainland Shetland, the underlying rocks are, for the most part, hard metamorphosed gneisses and schists, supporting poor quality, acidic peat soils. This must have made Shetland a less attractive destination for prospective settlers than Orkney. There are certainly significant differences in the social and territorial organization of Orkney and Shetland which support such a conclusion. Several parishes or parts of parishes in Shetland have names in -ting 'local assembly', suggesting local self-governing communities. These divisions also formed the basis of the twelve to fifteen priest districts (prestegjeld) into which Shetland was divided for ecclesiastical purposes. In contrast, Orkney's local divisions appear to have been imposed on communities from above, presumably by the powerful earls of Orkney.

These differences also appear to be reflected in the locations where the runic inscriptions are found. The Shetland inscriptions are largely found on ecclesiastical sites, although it is not clear if Mail also had a secular rôle, but the Orkney group come from high-status secular sites that often had churches built on them by wealthy patrons. Another difference between the inscriptions from the two archipelagos is that while three of the meagre runic corpus from Shetland are clearly memorial stones and as such appear to have served some formal or practical function, most of the Orkney inscriptions appear to be casual graffiti. This is clearly a small sample, but there is no good reason to believe the Orkney group is any more unrepresentative than the Shetland one. Indeed, there is a plentiful supply of easily split sandstone on Orkney, making the re-use and destruction of stone monuments less likely there.[23] In addition, there has been considerable archaeological work on

22   K. Forsyth, *The Ogham Inscriptions of Scotland: An Edited Corpus*, Harvard University Ph.D. dissertation (Ann Arbor, Michigan: UMI, 1996), 225, and pers. comm.

23   Local conditions may nevertheless háve varied. For example, the abundant supply of stone on the beach by the Brough of Birsay was difficult to transport up the cliff to the island; see J. R. Hunter, *Rescue Excavations on the Brough of Birsay 1974–82*, Society of Antiquaries of Scotland Monograph Series 4 (Edinburgh,

Orkney, and we would expect this to have revealed more runic finds than on the comparatively unexplored Shetland.

The runic inscriptions from Orkney and Shetland are a fairly disparate collection in terms of their texts, the objects on which they are carved, and, to judge from the scant evidence, their date. This suggests that there were varying sources of inspiration behind the runic inscriptions of the Northern Isles. As mentioned above, the inspiration behind the Maeshowe inscriptions may have been Norwegian. The Cross Kirk inscription from Shetland, datable to the later medieval period, also appears to represent a later import of the runic script. Orphir I may be the work of an outsider as well: the dotted k-rune suggests a carver who was aware of post-Viking-Age runic innovations, and the inscription also suggests a carver who was used to inscribing more creative texts than the usual 'X carved these runes' sort of inscription. In this connection, I would like to draw attention to the fact that Orphir I also has a distinctive form of the r-rune, which in the British Isles is also found in Maeshowe and on Holy Island off the Isle of Arran. Holy Island VIII was carved by a man called Vigleikr *stallari* ('steward'), who has been identified with a member of the Norwegian fleet that embarked upon the fateful Scottish campaign of 1263. Following the Norwegian defeat at Largs, this Norwegian fleet wintered at the Bay of Howton, at Orphir.[24] Is it possible that Orphir I should also be connected with a member of this fleet?

Finally, I would like to conclude by contrasting the inscriptions from Shetland and Orkney with those from the Isle of Man. Man was also settled by a Scandinavian population in the ninth century, but greater Celtic survival or revival there is suggested by linguistic and place-name evidence. However, thirty-three Scandinavian runic inscriptions on stone have been found on the Isle of Man, almost all of which are memorial texts carved on cross-slabs. The inscriptions are based on the Viking-Age runic formula, 'X raised this stone in memory of Y', followed by the relationship between X and Y. However, there is one important variation: the word 'cross' is used instead of 'stone'. 'Cross' is also found on runic inscriptions from Kilbar (Barra) and Inchmarnock off Bute, but on only one Viking-Age inscription in Scandinavia.[25] The distinctiveness and comparative uniformity of the Manx group suggests that the island was looking inwards rather than outwards for its inspiration, developing its own runic conventions. Runes were clearly known in Shetland and Orkney but, unlike on Man, there seems to have been no impulse to develop a distinctive runic culture. Paradoxically, this might reflect the relative proximity of the Northern Isles to the Norwegian homeland, and more frequent contact with outsiders.

1986), 61.

[24] *Hákonar saga Hákonarsonar*, ed. M. Mundt (Oslo, 1977), ch. 128.

[25] M. Olsen *et al.*, *Norges innskrifter med de yngre runer* (Oslo, 1941–), IV, 222–4 (N417).

Scandinavian Medieval Runic Inscriptions – an Interface Between Literacy and Orality?

T. SPURKLAND

When the Scandinavians came into contact with the Latin alphabet they had been carving runes for about 800 years. It was therefore no scriptless community that was introduced to the Roman script some time in the tenth or eleventh century. Nor were runes immediately displaced by Latin literary culture. In Norway they were used for another 300 years. How did the cultural meeting between the 800-year-old local writing-tradition – the runes – and the new literary book-writing – Roman script – turn out? To what extent were the writing and reading of runes and Roman script parallel activities? Did 'read' and 'write' have the same meaning for both scripts?

The Two-Script Culture of Medieval Norway

Let me start by taking you back to the church green outside the Lom stave church one Sunday in the late 1200s or early 1300s. The local people are going to church; among them is Håvard, as well as Gudny and her family. Gudny is not quite herself today; in fact she is rather upset. It's about the rune-stick Håvard gave her before entering the church – she got so confused by the subject that she started to whittle on it at once to erase the carving. On the other hand, it was also so exciting that she did not want to let either the stick or the inscription go immediately. She therefore put it into her pocket. But now, during the mass, she became ashamed of not having turned down Håvard's advances at once. After all, she was intended for Kolbein; that was decided a long time ago. Now it was as if the stick was burning in her pocket. She carefully slipped it out and dropped it down between the cracks in the floor. Fortunately, no one had noticed anything. And that was the end of Håvard ...

Some 700 years later, in 1973, the time had come to replace the worn-out floor of Lom stave church. Under the old floor the archaeologists, among many objects, came across the rune-stick that made Gudny so upset, and now we can read why. The stick has runic carvings on all four sides (pl. 29), and the language is Old Norse:[1]

---

[1]   The rune-stick is numbered A74 in the Runic Archives in Oslo.

121

1. ᛭᛭] ᚨᚢ ᚨᚱᚦᚨᚱ : sender : gu [᛭] : g[.] ᚦᚨᚱᛋ : kueᚦiu oksinaⁱuigan

—] aů arþær : sender : gu [—] : g[.] þærs : kueþiu oksinauigan

2. oknuerminfuleruili : at : biþiaþin : efþuuilt : æihimeþ

oknuerminfuleruili : at : biþiaþin : efþuuilt : æihimeþ

3. [———]bæini : uer[.] : [—] a : þitraþ : oklatsehiamer

[—]bæini : uer[.] : [—] a : þitraþ : oklatsehiamer

4. þinuilia

þinuilia

In normalized Old Norse:

Hávarðr sendir G(uðnýju) Guðs kveðju ok sína vingan. Ok nú er min fullr vili at biðja þín, ef þú vilt eigi með (Kol)beini vera. Huga þitt ráð, ok lát segja mér þinn vilja.

In a modern translation:

Håvard is sending Gudny God's regards and his friendship. Now it is my intention to make you an offer of marriage, provided that you do not prefer Kolbein. Think the matter over and let me know your will.

No wonder Gudny was knocked off her perch!

How the story ended, we do not know. Nor do we know if it really took place in this way. What we do know is that the message was written, carved in wood from Håvard to Gudny, that it was a marriage proposal, that Kolbein is also involved, and that it all happened some time in the thirteenth or fourteenth century. From the shape of the stick we can infer that it was the lower part of a cane. It tapers towards the end, which is obtuse, a little splintered with soil and pebbles pressed into the wood. Håvard simply cut off a part of his cane and used it as writing-material when the need to inform Gudny of his innermost feelings became urgent. It is evident that Håvard had mastered Latin lettering on parchment as well; the style of his runic letter is an indication of that. The opening phrase (*Hávarðr sendir Guðnýju*) *Guðs kveðju ok sína vingan* corresponds to the *salutatio* known from vernacular charter-manuscripts *Q(ueðju) G(uðs) ok s(ína)*, 'God's and his greetings'. At that moment, however, he did not have pen, ink and parchment to hand; but he had his knife, and the cane. Moreover, it was clear that the type of letter he was going to write was inappropriate for parchment, and Gudny would have to destroy it once she had read the message.

There are reasons to assume that at first the Roman alphabet was restricted to a very narrow social stratum connected to the church and secular power. As Roman script came gradually to be used for the vernacular, and those proficient in the Latin language carved runes, the demarcation between runes and Roman letters was reduced in the sense that the same person might master both scripts. It is, however, only under special circumstances that the two writing systems overlap, that they are used in the same contexts. Runes were made to be cut in wood; they are composed of vertical and sloping lines which go across the grain. Roman letters, however, were less appropriate for carving in wood, because of the rounded curves and horizontal lines. Roman script demanded parchment, pen and ink. There is still a distinction, therefore, but it is not to the same degree dependent on social conditions. The conditioning factor could be the availability of material: wooden sticks and a knife were more accessible than parchment, pen and ink, especially in conditions that called for urgent written communication. The explanation for the complementary distribution of the two scripts might also lie in the nature of the communication: some things were more fit to be expressed in wood than on parchment. Yet there are instances of overlapping, where the two writing systems operate side by side. We have inscriptions – memorials – with texts both in runes and Roman letters. In some cases it is exactly the same text that is expressed in the two systems. From time to time runes are used for marginal notes in manuscripts; runic signs may also operate as abbreviations or additional letters in otherwise literary manuscripts. Around the year 1300 runes were used as book-script in Skåne in the south of Sweden.

In Norway there are some 1400 epigraphic runic inscriptions altogether, dating from 1150 to the end of the fourteenth century. This is more than the sum total of inscriptions from the other Scandinavian countries in the same period. The majority of the Norwegian material consists of rune-sticks dug out from the medieval soil of the cities of Oslo, Bergen, Trondheim and Tønsberg. They range from religious and secular texts in Latin language to old Norse poetry and business correspondence. There are name-tags, alphabet-inscriptions, writing exercises, incomprehensible hocus-pocus, everyday messages, confidential intimacies and pure obscenities. Every conceivable use for writing is represented in this material. The scope of the finds shows clearly that a good proportion of medieval runic carvers were also literate in Roman script.

Mutually Independent Textual Communities

Let us return to Håvard in Lom. One relevant question is: if Håvard on one occasion used runes and on another Roman script, was there a one-to-one correspondence between the Roman letters and the corresponding runes? Were words spelled the same way in the two writing systems? In other words, to what extent might we argue that rune-carving became a transliterating of Roman letters? And if there are any discrepancies between runic and Roman orthography, how are they to be interpreted?

From Bryggen in Bergen we have a rune-stick (pl. 30) with the following fragmentary inscription:[2]

1. ᛑᛋᛁᛏᛁ:ᛏᛁᛁᚱᚱᛁᛏᛁ:ᚾᛁᛏ ᚤ:ᚠᚦ:[..]ᚻ.--
d͡ucite ⫶ diskrete : uita͡m ⫶ ku͡e ⫶ [..]n[.--

2. ᚾᛏᛁ ᚱᛁ:ᛋᛁᚾᛁᛁ:ᚤᛁᛏᛁ:ᛋᛁᛒ:ᚻᛏᛋᛁᛁ:[--
uæstra ⫶ salus ⫶ mete:siþ:næcia:[--

1) *ducite discrete vitam, que—*
2) *vestra salus mete sit nescia—*

'Conduct (pl.) in a sensible way a life which ...! May your health be unrestricted!'

When the Latin language is written in Roman letters /e(:)/ is marked by <e>, while the runic script varies between ᛁ <e> and ᚠ <æ>, <uærsum> *versum*, <ua͡estra> *vestra*, <mete> *mete*. The Roman letter <c> is carved ᚻ <c> before front vowels and ᚴ <k> in other contexts: <d͡ucite> *ducite*, <diskrete> *discrete*. In Roman script unaccented /t/ is spelled <t> while in runic script we often find þ: <siþ> *sit*, <æþ> *et*. These features are found in other Latin runic inscriptions as well, and similar alternations appear when the written and carved language is Old Norse. These, almost systematic, grapho-phonological distinctions between runic and Roman script may indicate that the rune-carver was more accustomed to adapt his spelling to his pronunciation. The writer of Roman script, on the other hand, carried the weight of classical literary tradition on his shoulders.

Even when the two scripts appear side by side expressing the same text, there is still no one-to-one relationship between runic character and corresponding Roman letter. On a grave-slab from southern Sweden we find this epitaph:[3]

ᚱᛁᚼᛁᚾᛘᚢᚦ:ᛚᛏᛏ:ᚵᛁᚱᛁ:ᚼᚢᛁᚱᚠ:ᛁᚠᛁᚱ:ᚵᚢᚾᛏᛏᚱ:ᛏᛋᛒᛁᛏᚱᚠ ᚱ·ᛋᚠ:
rehinmoþ : læt : gera : hualf : ifir : gunnar : æsbeornar : so͡n:

Reginmot lét gera hvalf yfir Gunnar, Æsbjarnar son
'Reginmot had this grave made for Gunnar, the son of Åsbjørn.'

On the opposite side of the monument the text is written in Roman letters:

REGINMOT : LET : GERA : HVALF : IFIR : GVNNAR : ESBEORNAR
: SON .

[2] *Norges innskrifter med de yngre runer*, ed. M. Olsen *et al.* (Oslo, 1941–), no. 604.
[3] *Västergötlands runinskrifter*, ed. H. Jungner and E. Svärdström, Sveriges runinskrifter 5 (Stockholm, 1940–70), no. 95.

The orthographic disparities are familiar. The runic inscription has two signs for /e/, ┤ and ┼, and the unaccented /t/ is rendered ▶; not so in the Roman script variant. In addition we find ⁎ <h> for <g> in the runic version. In both Old Norse and Latin runic inscriptions there is a tendency to carve <h> for Latin <g>, in order to indicate that the phoneme /g/ was a fricative in certain environments. There is also a craftman's signature on the stone, written in Latin with Roman letters:

HARALDUS : ME : FECIT : MAHISTER

Note that Master Harald writes the Latin word *magister* with an <h> and not with a <g>; he is spelling the word in the runic way. It is noteworthy that the runic spelling has influenced the Latin writing and not the other way around. So even when used beside one another, runic and Roman script stick to their idiosyncratic spelling conventions, which may indicate that the path from speech to writing was shorter when you carved runes than when you were dealing with Roman letters. And we might also conclude that runes and Roman script constituted mutually independent textual communities. I follow Stock's definition of 'textual community':[4] 'a society that makes use of texts, both to structure the internal behaviour of the members of the society and to provide solidarity against the outside world'.

Rune-Carving and Handwriting – Expressions of Different Mentalities

Medieval terminology for the production and decoding of written communication strengthens the assumption that runes and Roman letters reflect the divergent mentalities of different textual communities.[5] In the corpus of Norwegian medieval runic inscriptions there are 123 instances of a verb meaning, broadly, 'write' where the direct object is 'runes' or the inscription itself. Three verbs are predominant: the strong verb *rísta* with 80 occurrences, the weak verb *rista* and the strong verb *ríta* with 15 occurrences each. In manuscripts the common word for writing a letter is the weak verb *rita*. Consequently the runic carver most often *reist* his runes, but sometimes he *risti* or *reit*. The Roman-literate scribe, however, *ritaði* his letters. The action of the runic carver should therefore be translated 'carved', 'incised' or the like, to reflect the idea of the physical work, while *ritaði* in the manuscripts should be translated 'wrote', indicating that the concrete instrumental meaning of the word is no longer present.

4   B. Stock, *The Implications of Literacy: Written Language and Models of Interpretation in the Eleventh and Twelfth Centuries* (Princeton, 1983), 90.

5   On the terminology of reading and writing dealt with in this section, see further T. Spurkland, '"Måtte Herren hjelpe den mann som ristet disse runer og likeså hans om leser dem!" Ett mentalitetshistorisk blikk på "skrive" og "lese" i norsk middelalder', *Norsk lingvistisk tidsskrift* 12.i (1994), 3–15. See also E. Ebel, *Die Terminologie der Runentechnik* (Göttingen, 1963).

Turning to decoding, the reading of runes is almost always expressed by the verb *ráða*. The basic meaning is 'decide', 'govern', 'take care of' or 'advise'. In connection with writing the common meaning is 'interpret', 'decipher'. However, in many instances both the direct object and the wider context make the concrete meaning of *ráða* uncertain. It is apparent that in some contexts the meaning is 'read', but elsewhere it is a more concrete 'interpret' or 'decipher'. This is found particularly when the carver wants to put the addressee to the test by name-riddles, cryptic runes or the like. Then the message is *ráð rett rúnar*, 'interpret the runes correctly'. However, *ráða* (*rúnar*) may in some cases have a meaning 'master', 'be proficient in handling' runic script. The famous stanza of Egill Skallagrimsson:[6]

> *Skalat maðr rúnar rista*
> *nema ráða vel kunni*

is in several instances translated 'You should not carve runes unless you read them well'. In consideration of the context this must be wrong. Egill was visiting a farmer whose daughter was ill in bed. The father had runes carved on a stick and put it into the bed in the belief that magic words carved in runes would cure the girl. But the magic apparently did not work, since the girl was not cured. When Egill examined the rune-stick, he found that the inscription was not carved correctly. So he erased the carving and carved new runes himself. And then he pronounced the stanza. This situation does not reflect a matter of correct interpretation, it is rather a question of carving correctly. It should therefore be interpreted as 'You should not carve runes unless you master them well'. Consequently, depending on context, the meaning of *ráða rúnar* is either 'interpret', 'decipher', 'read' or 'master', 'know how to write' runes. It is this extended meaning of the word that we find in the following injunction on a rune-stick from Bryggen in Bergen:[7]

sæst : niþær : ok : rat : runar͡ : ris : uP : ok : fis : uit:
Setz niðr ok ráð rúnar, rís upp ok fís við,
'Sit down, carve runes, stand up and fart'.
The sender must have believed that dealing with runes could have a relieving effect on gastrospasms!

In the manuscripts the common word for decoding script is *lesa*. The contexts indicate that in practice the meaning is 'read aloud to convey a message to many persons present'. Silent reading is most often expressed by *lesa* plus particle: *yfirlesa, fyrirlesa*. In connection with authorized transcripts of charters, so-called *vidimi*, the formula of corroboration is *ver saom ok*

---

[6] See further F. Genzmer, 'Die Geheimrunen der Egilssaga', *Archiv för nordisk filologi* 67 (1957), 39–47.

[7] Numbered B584 in the Runic Archives in Oslo.

ifirlasom bref, 'we saw and read through the letter'. When *lesa* occurs without a particle in the charters, it seems clear that it is matter of reading aloud. Most charters were intended for the public; they announce facts relevant to everyone or a group of people. That is evident from the formula of address, the *inscriptio: ǫllum mǫnnum þeim sem sem þetta bref sjá eða heyra,* 'to all who shall see and hear this charter'.

It is commonly assumed that literacy came into being as a result of the need to extend and materially preserve the collective memory. But, texts that were directed to posterity, such as laws, religious texts, legends, historical narratives and charters, were written in order to be read out loud on special occasions. The reader took over the function of the teller in oral culture. It takes time before script is perceived as a visual means of communication. As Clanchy puts it:[8]

> Although writing had the potential [...] to change the perception of language by making it visual as well as auditory, [...] preliterate habits of mind persisted long after documents became common. Books and letters continued to be read aloud and listened to, instead of being silently scrutinized by the eye, and authors went on thinking of composition in terms of dictation rather than of manipulating a pen.

Those 'preliterate habits of mind' manifest themselves in large measure when we compare runic inscriptions and contemporary Roman literacy in the Middle Ages. Literate reading was first of all an auditory performance intended for a group of people or God. It is not until the invention of printing that reading changes character to an individual, visual activity. Not so for runic script. It had a quite different purpose. What was carved in runes, was not primarily intended for reading aloud, but for silent scrutinizing by the eye. This implies that runic script from the outset had the very function that Roman script did not obtain until the end of the Middle Ages. And this functional difference is manifested by the verbs *lesa* and *ráða.*

Conclusion

In the light of the dichotomy between orality and literacy it is conspicuous that runes and Roman alphabet writing in medieval Scandinavia constitute a two-script culture where the two writing systems represent different mentalities. Handling runes, one was still conscious of the handicraft, you were 'carving' or 'incising'. Writing Roman letters, however, was a learned, 'literate' activity; the instrumental conception was weaker, you were 'writing'. As for the decoding, the situation was the opposite. To read Roman script was an auditory or oral activity; what was written was intended for many persons and should be mediated by loud reading. The addressee of most of the runic inscriptions was not the collective but the individual. The text

8   M. T. Clanchy, *From Memory to Written Record: England 1066–1307,* 2nd edn (Oxford and Cambridge, Mass., 1993), 278.

should not be broadcast but mediated from eye to eye. Runic script was a 'literate', visual means of communication while the decoding of the Latin alphabet still stood with one foot in orality. By the end of the Middle Ages the literate mentality seems to have made a breakthrough in both scripts, expressed by the modern Scandinavian verbs *skrive* and *lese*, with the generalized meaning of 'write' and 'read'. We have evidence for that in a runic inscription from the island of Öland, from the 1500s:[9]

ᚥᚢᚨᛦ:ᛋᚢᛘ:ᛏᚨᛏᛏᚨ:ᛚᚨᛋ
huør : søm : thættæ : læs

ᛏᚨᚾᚨ:ᚠᛁᚱᚠᛁᚨ:ᚼᚨᛏᚨᛦ:ᚱᚢᚾᚨᛋᛏᚨᚾ:ᛏᚨᛚ:ᛒᚬᛦ:ᛋᚬᚳᚾᚨ:
tanæ : kirkia : hætar : runastæn : tal : bør :socna :

ᚼᚨᛦᚨᚾ:ᚠᚢᚾᚾᚨ:ᚱᚢ ᚨ:ᚱᚢᚾᚨᛦ:ᛁᛚ:ᚢ ᚱᛁᚠᚢᚨ:ᚼᚨᛚ
haræn : kunnæ : runær : læsæ : oc : scrifuæ : hæc

ᛁᚨ:ᚨᛚᚨ:ᛚᛅᛚᛘ ᚱᚾ
io : ola : calmarn

'To those who read this; this church is called Runsten. The parish priest should know how to read and write runes. This (wrote) Johan Olofsson from Kalmar.'

9   *Ölands runinskrifter*, ed. E. Brate and S. Söderberg, Sveriges runinskrifter 1 (Stockholm, 1900–6), no. 34.

Computerizing Rune-Forms

ESPEN S. ORE & ANNE HAAVALDSEN

Abstract
Runic scripts have so far not had any standard transliteration scheme. Various schemes have been used at various places and at various times. Transliterations of runic inscriptions often include a choice of reading. This makes it difficult, for example, to establish international – or even national – databases of runic inscriptions.

Our project has experimented with tools – partly computer-based – that can be used to establish a graphic typology of rune-forms. Such a typology can be used to define a transliteration table based on the graphic forms of runes.

As part of the project a database of all medieval runic inscriptions from Bergen, Norway has been produced and photographs of the inscriptions have been digitized. This database has been made available on the Internet via the WWW (World Wide Web). The text data in the database are linked to photographs of the inscriptions.

Background
Runic script comprises a family of related writing systems. Runes were used from at least the second century CE to the sixteenth century. Branching out from a common system of 24 runes there developed the Anglo-Saxon/Frisian system on the one hand and the Scandinavian on the other. The Scandinavian 16-rune system was further developed so that eventually there was a more or less one-to-one correspondence between runic and Roman characters.

Due to the changes in the runic writing systems and in the languages involved, runic inscriptions have traditionally been transliterated – or rather transcribed – in different ways according to knowledge or assumptions about the relations between the characters and the phonetic system they represent. To facilitate comparison of computerized runic texts we aim to develop a transliteration system – or a basis for a transliteration scheme – that is wholly dependent on the symbols' graphic form and makes no assumptions about their phonetic value.

To do this we have started by inputting the runic inscriptions from excavations in Bergen (about 600 inscriptions) and will later add Swedish and Danish inscriptions. We have entered the texts in the traditional transcription(s), along with photographs and drawings and some archaeo-logical reference material. From the image data we will look into the possibilities of defining a set of distinctive factors for grouping the graphic forms, and this will be the basis for a transliteration scheme.

A Database of Runic Inscriptions from Bergen

In 1993, a database in HyperCard on a Macintosh computer was made, based on the archive files at the medieval collection at the Historical Museum in Bergen and on published material. This database was converted to FileMakerPro in 1994. In addition, the photographs from the museum archive were scanned.

The archive consists of photocopied index cards, most of them written by the late Aslak Liestøl. The archive will therefore be referred to as the Liestøl Archive. The originals are in the Runic Archive in Oslo. Since the copies were made, the information has in some cases been updated. This applies both to the reading of the inscriptions and the datings. We have chosen to exclude these corrections, mainly because: (1) the aim of computerization was to get a survey of the material (text and photographs) good enough to choose suitable inscriptions for a graphical analysis of the rune-forms; (2) the revised information in the Runic Archive will be transferred to the University of Oslo's database on language and culture (The Documentary Project).

Although we only intended to computerize the Liestøl Archive, useful visits have been paid to the Runic Archive when the information offered by the Liestøl Archive turned out to be unclear or insufficient.

The database of the medieval excavations at the Historical Museum (made in Mapper – a system originally used on Unisys mainframe computers) contains corrections on the find data for all the runic inscriptions, based on information from the Runic Archive. A copy of the runic database with corrections made up to spring 1993 was transferred from Mapper to Omnis7. The copy has now been converted to FileMakerPro. The Mapper database contains principally data on finds rather than information on the texts or the condition of the artefacts. Therefore, it seemed natural to us to base our information on relevant data from the Liestøl Archive.

The Liestøl Archive contains information on the Bergen inscriptions B1–B655. The Runic Archive holds information on the B-numbers up to and including B670. B656–B670 were therefore registered on information taken from the Runic Archive or from their journal *Nytt om Runer*.[1]

The Liestøl Archive also contains photographs up to and including B578. In addition there are photographs of several other inscriptions. Most of these were made to give an overview of the inscription. Even if they do not always

---

[1]   *Nytt om runer: Meldingsblad om runeforskning* [News about Runes: Bulletin of Runic Research], The Runic Archives at IAKN, University of Oslo, ed. J. Knirk.

allow a detailed study of the runes, they are clear enough for us to decide if an inscription is fit for the project or not. One of the premises for a classification system based on graphical form is that there must be no doubt about the forms that make up the basis of the system. Unclear or worn inscriptions are therefore of no use. The photographs in the Liestøl Archive are mostly copies of originals in the Runic Archive. There are also detailed photographs of most inscriptions.

The Liestøl Archive made up the main body of the database. Subsequently, information on inscriptions published in *NIYR*[2] and information from other sources was registered. In addition, remarks and alternative readings were also registered, mainly taken from Terje Spurkland's unpublished doctoral thesis.[3]

The FileMakerPro database from the Liestøl Archive is now available on WorldWideWeb at: http://gonzo.hd.uib.no/NCCH-docs/Runes.html.

A Database of Runic Forms

For the planned typology based on graphic forms a database of individual runes has been considered necessary. This database should hold all the information that is needed for grouping based on statistical methods. Since we have not as yet decided what the distinctive factors will be, the database now holds a large number of values for each rune (see fig. 31, overleaf).

Some of the values here are measurements in pixels taken from a digitized photograph. Since the photographs have not been taken according to any standard scale, these measurements are not directly comparable. Instead fractions and other relations between measurements can be used. Fig. 32 shows one possible relative measurement from a hypothetical rune.

Earlier graphematic analyses of runic inscriptions have used similar but simpler methods, such as for instance Loman, whose work on the Swedish Rök inscription has influenced all later work.[4]

External Users of the Databases

The database of individual runes does not contain enough runes yet for statistical analysis, but the database of inscriptions from Bergen together with photos of about 50 inscriptions has been available on the Internet since the spring of 1995. It is slightly surprising to us that this has become a popular web site. In 1995 the database search form was accessed 5000 times; in 1996 more than 7000 times.

[2] *Norges innskrifter med de yngre runer*, ed. M. Olsen *et al.*, vols I–VI (Oslo, 1941–90).

[3] T. Spurkland, 'En fonografematisk analyse av runematerialet fra Bryggen i Bergen', unpublished doctoral thesis, Oslo (1991).

[4] B. Loman, 'Rökrunorna som grafematiskt system', *Arkiv för nordisk filologi* 80 (1965), 1–60.

Fig. 31: Database
record for an
individual rune

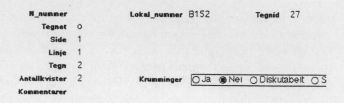

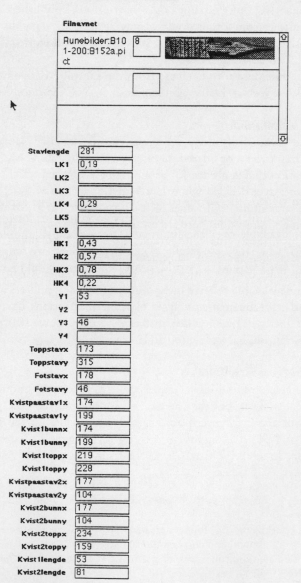

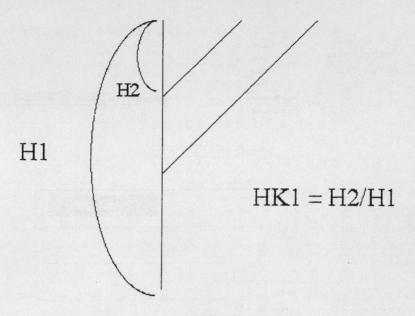

Fig. 32: Relative measurement from a rune

Apart from the curiosity factor which probably explains much of the interest we think that there are two very good reasons for making this kind of database available over the Internet: (1) the originals should not be handled too much since they are fragile; (2) given that there are only an estimated 100 runologists all around the world, print publication would be expensive.

The Fascination with Runes in Nineteenth- and Early Twentieth-Century Poland

KRZYSZTOF MACIEJ KOWALSKI

The aim of this chapter is to discuss the runic inscriptions of Poland and other Slavonic countries; it will be especially concerned with nineteenth-century Polish forgeries, as well as with the whole question of so-called 'Slavonic runes'.

David Diringer, in his well-known book, *The Alphabet: A Key to the History of Mankind*,[1] devotes only a single paragraph of the chapter on runes and ogham to Slavonic runes. He notes that the matter has been the subject of much discussion, but is not convinced that specifically Slavonic runes existed, or that runes were ever used to represent Slavonic language. The question remains controversial. This chapter will focus instead on the fascination with runes in Poland over the past two hundred years. At the end of the nineteenth century, in particular, discussion of so-called 'Slavonic runology' was very lively, and the interest generated led to the fabrication of antiquities. We still do not know what exactly lay behind the forgeries, or why historians were so naïve and uncritical in their treatment of them; why they were inclined to accept, not only the fakes, but also fantastic stories about the supposed origins of authentic medieval objects.[2]

Nineteenth-century Polish researchers examined the corpus of rune-inscribed artefacts and came up with various classifications. Objects were often uncritically accepted as genuine, but there were some attempts to differentiate authentic medieval objects from fakes. Judgements were hardly ever made on the basis of technical analysis, however, but usually depended rather on interpretation of the inscriptions.[3]

---

[1]   D. Diringer, *The Alphabet: A Key to the History of Mankind*, 3rd edn, 2 vols (London, 1968), I, 405.

[2]   J. Kostrzewski, *Dzieje polskich badań prehistorycznych* [The History of Polish Prehistoric Research] (Poznań, 1949); A. Abramowicz, *Historia archeologii polskiej. XIX i XX wiek* [The History of Polish Archaeology: Nineteenth and Twentieth Centuries] (Warsaw and Łódź, 1991).

[3]   W. Surowiecki, *O charakterach pisma runicznego* [The Character of the Runic Alphabet] (Warsaw, 1822); T. Wolański, *Schrift-Denkmäler der Slaven vor Christi Geburt* (Gnesen, 1850–2); J. Łepkowski, *Obecny stan nauki o runach słowiańskich i*

The high-point of research arrived with Leciejewski's classification of Slavonic runic monuments in 1906.[4] Five categories were identified:

1. monuments wrongly identified as rune-inscribed
2. forgeries
3. runic inscriptions wrongly identified as Slavonic
4. runic inscriptions of uncertain origin
5. authentic Slavonic runic inscriptions.

This classification systematizes the observations and conclusions of Leciejewski and his predecessors. It also indicates that the methodology of research was not far behind the present. The following review considers Leciejewski's work and the state of Polish runology at the beginning of the twentieth century.

The first category of objects comprised those that had been erroneously considered runic by nineteenth-century researchers. These included two Styrian helmets with inscriptions that proved to be Etruscan,[5] and a stone lion in Bamberg cathedral, the 'runes' of which were identified as the effects of erosion (fig. 33).[6] There were also mysterious signs around the shoulders of urns from Gdansk (fig. 34)[7] and Bieganin;[8] these came to be judged not inscriptions but ornamentation. Finally, the inscription on a golden cup from Szent-Miklos in Transylvania was identified, a hundred years after its discovery, as Greek.[9]

---

napisach [The Current State of Knowledge about Slavonic Runes and Inscriptions] (Poznań, 1860); W. Cybulski, 'Obecny stan nauki o runach słowiańskich' [The Current State of Knowledge about Slavonic Runes], Roczniki Towarzystwa Przyjaciół Nauk w Poznaniu 1 (1860), 32–64; A. H. Kirkor, 'O runach słowiańskich' [The Slavonic Runes], Przegląd Literacki (Kraków, 1872), 400–3; K. Estreicher, 'Runy słowiańskie' [The Slavonic Runes], Józefa Ungra kalendarz ilustrowany na rok zwyczajny 1873 (Warsaw, 1872), 92–7; R. Zawiliński, Kwestya run słowiańskich ze stanowiska lingwistycznego [The Question of Slavonic Runes from a Linguistic Standpoint] (Kraków, 1883); R. Zawiliński, 'O tak zwanych runach słowiańskich' [The so-called Slavonic Runes], Archiwum do dziejów Literatury i Oświaty w Polsce 5 (1886), 191–209; V. Jagič, 'Zur slavischen Runenfrage', Archiv für slavische Philologie 5 (1886).

[4] J. Leciejewski, Runy i runiczne pomniki słowiańskie [The Runes and Slavonic Runic Monuments] (Lwów, 1906).

[5] Ibid., 39–40.

[6] Cybulski, 'Obecny stan nauki', 420–30.

[7] Th. S. Bayer, Opuscula, 509; W. K. Grimm, Deutsche Runen, 291.

[8] R. Zenkteler, Ein Beitrag zu den Ausgrabungen in der Provinz Posen (Ostrów, 1884), 14 and fig. 1.

[9] J. Hampel, Der Goldfund von Nagy Szent-Miklos (Budapest, 1886), 47.

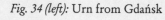

Fig. 33 (above): Lion from Bamberg Cathedral.

Fig. 34 (left): Urn from Gdańsk

The second category, forgeries, included above all the 'Prylvick [Prillwitz] Idols' (fig. 35)[10] and the stones from Neustrelitz (fig. 36),[11] both finds supposedly linked to the Slavonic tribe, the Obotriten. They were discussed in both Slavonic and German archaeological literature; over thirty authors argued over their authenticity, until it came to be accepted that the objects had been made by Gedeon Sponholz and Neumann,[12] who took their runes from the work of Clüver and Arnkiel (Table 3).[13] Perhaps the most interesting feature of these forgeries was the imaginative creation of a pantheon of Slavonic gods including, beside Radegast, such names as Wotan, Thor, Sybil and Mitra.[14]

The third category, monuments that had wrongly been considered Slavonic, comprised a variety of objects. They included a banner which had

[10]   A. G. Masch, *Die gottesdienstlichen Alterthümer der Obotriten aus dem Tempel zu Rhetra am Tollenzer See* (Berlin, 1771).

[11]   F. Hagenow, *Beschreibung der auf der Grossherzoglichen Bibliothek zu Neustrelitz befindlichen Runensteine* (Loitz and Greifswald, 1826).

[12]   K. Lewezow, *Über die Echtheit der sogenannten Obotritischen Runendenkmäler zu Neustrelitz* (Berlin, 1835).

[13]   T. Arnkiel, *Cimbrische Heyden-Religion* (Hamburg, 1691); Clüver, *Beschreibung des Herzogtums Mecklenburg* (Hamburg, 1757).

[14]   Leciejewski, *Runy*, 48–9.

136

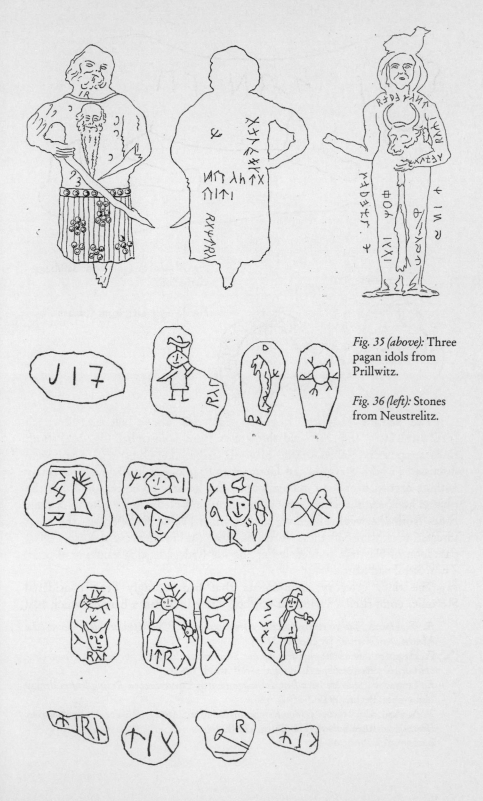

Fig. 35 (above): Three pagan idols from Prillwitz.

Fig. 36 (left): Stones from Neustrelitz.

Table 3: Runic Alphabets according to Arnkiel and Klüwer and from inscriptions of Mikorzyn and Prillwitz.

Arnkiel	Klüwer		Mikorzyn	Prillwice
ᚼ	A	ᚼᚤ	ᚦᚼ	ᚾᚠᚤᚴᚿᚼᚦᚼᛏᚿᛇᚼᚤᚾᚦᚱ
ᛒ ᛏ	B	ᛒᛉ		ᚴᛐᚴᛐᛐᚤᛐᚤ φ
ᚤᛁ	C	ᚤᛁ		ᚤ
}ᚦᚾ	Dᛈ	ᚦᚾ	ᚦᚹᚹᛤ	ᚼᛈᛈᚦᚼ
ᛏᚼ	E	ᚼᚼ	ᛖ	ᚼᛪᚾᚠᛏᛤᚼᚤᚠᚤ×ᛁᛐ
ᚤᚹ	F	ᛏᚤ		ᚠ
ᚤᛈ	G	ᚤᛈ	×	ᚤ×ᛁᚤᚤ
ᚼᛏ	H	ᚼᚼ		ᚼᚼᛏᚤ
ᛁ	I	ᛁ	ᛁ	ᛁ
ᚤ	K	ᚤ		ᛉᛁᛐᚤᚤ
ᚵ	L	ᚤ	ᚔᚤ	ᚾᚾᚤᚾᚤ
ᚤφ	M	ᛏφ		ᚤᛏφᚤ
ᚼᚻ	N	ᚤᚻ		ᛏᚻᚤᚼᚼ
ᛂᚼ	O	ᚼᛂ	ᛣ	ᛣᛂᛏᛂᛁᛂᚼᚼᛏᛏᛁ
ᛒᚿ	P	ᛒᚿ		ᚿᚿ
ᛣᛉ	R	ᛉ	ᛣ	ᛉᛏ
ᚤᚿ	S	ᚤᚿ	ᚿᚤ	ᚿᚤᚤ
ᛏᛏ	T	ᛏᚵ	ᛐᛏᛏ	ᛏᚤᛏ
}ᚿᚿ	UV	ᚿᚿ	ᚼᛏᚼᚿ	ᚿᚿᚿᚢ
φ	X	φ		φᚤ
ᚤ	Y	ᚤ		ᚔ
ᚼ	Z	ᚻ		ᚤᚼᛏᚼ

been taken from the Prussians by the Knights of the Teutonic Order,[15] a number of seals,[16] and some coins, including Lithuanian coins with a runic inscription mentioning Prince Mendog[17] which were found in the Czech Republic, apparently taken there by Scandinavians.[18] There was also the famous spear-head from Suszyczno (Kowel) (pl. 31),[19] one of the most precious runic monuments found on Slavonic territory, still recognized by

[15] T. Narbutt, *Dzieje starożytne narodu litewskiego* [The Oldest History of the Lithuanian Nation] (Wilno, 1835) I, pl. 6, fig. 10.

[16] Amongst others, *ibid.*, pl. 4, fig. 31.

[17] *Ibid.*, pl. 3, fig. 10.

[18] G. Stephens, *Old-Northern Runic Monuments of Scandinavia and England* (London and Copenhagen, 1866–1901) II, 520.

[19] A. Szumowski, 'Grot z runicznym napisem z Suszyczna' [The Rune-inscribed Spear-head from Suszyczno], *Wiadomości archeologiczne* 3 (Warsaw, 1876), 49–62, pl. 1.

runological publications today.[20] This category brought together inscriptions thought to be genuine Scandinavian pieces under their find-places, and was often used to support the argument that runes were known and used on Slavonic territory.

The fourth category, runic monuments of uncertain origin, comprised pieces whose affiliations could not be securely identified. They included some spear-heads (pl. 32) and the famous knife found in Grunówko, near Leszno,[21] an iron axe from Biezdrów, near Szamotuły,[22] and an urn from Kobielice.[23] These inscriptions were either unintelligible or had been variously interpreted; the urn from Kobielice, for instance, gave rise to such disparate readings as the absurd *Belbog kleal Kaja* and the inappropriate *eva gamm ksansoa*, 'here is the cave/grave of the prince'.[24] It was recognized that there was insufficient evidence to consider these monuments genuine Scandinavian runic inscriptions.

The ambition of scholars in the nineteenth and early twentieth centuries was to identify authentic Slavonic runic inscriptions. Numerous reports and interpretations of inscribed artefacts were published, but most of them were very inaccurate. Various unclassified antiquities were also attributed, rather hastily, to the runic corpus. Leciejewski, on the other hand, attempted to limit the number of objects; he did not claim to have assembled a complete corpus of Slavonic runic inscriptions, but he hoped that the ones he had left were reliable. He divided the real Slavonic monuments into Polish, Czech, Slovak, Russian and Ruthenian finds. We are most interested in the Polish inscriptions, comprising the famous bracteate from Wapno, the medal kept in Cracow, the figure from Lednica and the famous stones from Mikorzyn.

The bracteate fround in the village of Wapno in 1852 was identified as the only Slavonic runic bracteate (pl. 33).[25] Leciejewski argued that 'the golden bracteate is no doubt of Scandinavian origin', yet nonetheless interpreted the text as Sabaw (Zabaw), an archaic Polish masculine personal name. It is

[20] Stephens, *Old-Northern Runic Monuments* III, 266; L. F. A. Wimmer, *Die Runenschrift* (Berlin, 1887), 62; M. A. Tichanova, 'Starszeruničeskije nadpisi' [The Oldest Runic Inscriptions], in E. A. Melnikova, *Skandinavskije runičeskije nadpisi* [The Scandinavian Runic Inscriptions] (Moscow, 1977), 134–41 and pl. 71.

[21] B. Erzepki, 'Znaleziska we wsi Grunówko pod Lesznem' [The Finds from the Village of Grunówko in the Neighbourhood of Leszno], *Zapiski archeologiczne poznańskie* 1, pl. 17, figs 1–3.

[22] Anon. in *Zapiski archeologiczne poznańskie* 1, p. 35 and pl. 12, figs 13a, b.

[23] *Sitzungberichte der königlichen böhmischen Gesellschaft der Wissenschaftlichen zu Prag* 8 (1834); *Mémoires de la societé royale des antiquaires du nord* (Copenhagen, 1852), 353–7.

[24] Leciejewski, *Runy*, 63–6.

[25] G. A. Kruger, *Über die im Regierungsbezirk Bromberg aufgefundenen Alterthümer* (Mainz, 1872), 17; Wolański, *Schrift-Denkmäler der Slaven*; Leciejewski, *Runy*, 68–73 and fig. 29.

paralleled by the heraldic name-proclamation Zabawa, an analogy which suggested a date of 850–875. As a result, the bracteate was described as the oldest monument in the Polish language and as one of the oldest historic documents relating to knights' proclamations and the keeping of a public register of arms. Even when trying very hard to understand Leciejewski's intentions it is extremely difficult to accept his interpretation of the bracteate as evidence of medieval Polish culture.

Great significance was also attached to the medal in the collection of Professor Friedlein of Cracow (pl. 34).[26] Scandinavian runologists were not able to read its inscriptions, but Leciejewski produced imaginative readings that led him to the conclusion that the medal depicted the Virgin Mary and Prince Mieszko I, the first Polish ruler. Moreover, he believed that it was issued to commemorate the Christianization of Poland in 966, and that the Polish texts were rendered by the runic script supposedly used in the Prince's Chambers in Gniezno.

The wooden figure resembling a goat found on Ostrów Lednicki island was held to bear an inscription which could be interpreted 'Heal, figure!'. It was identified as the only Polish runic amulet (pl. 35).[27]

Undoubtedly the most famous Slavonic runic monuments were the two stones from Mikorzyn (pl. 36).[28] They were said to have been discovered in 1855 (fig. 37) and 1856 (fig. 38), and proved to be authentic quern-stones that had been covered with runic inscriptions and primitive drawings by an unknown forger (probably Piotr Droszewski). This major forgery, one of the greatest historical deceptions perpetrated in Poland, provoked long-lasting scholarly debate. By 1872 the inscriptions were widely regarded as fakes, due mainly to the efforts of a well-known bibliographer, Karol Estreicher, and a linguist, J. Baudoin de Courtenay, who was unable to find language, grammar or sense in the interpretations hitherto suggested.[29] Later authors, however,

26 Leciejewski, *Runy*, 74–92.
27 Zenkteler, *Ein Beitrag*, 21; Leciejewski, *Runy*, 92–7.
28 P. Droszewski, 'Mikorzyńskie kamienie runiczne' [The Runic Stones from Mikorzyn], *Czas* 242 (1858); J. Przyborowski, 'Prowe Wielkopolski' [Prowe from Wielkopolska], *Gazeta Warszawska* 182 (1856); Cybulski, 'Obecny stan nauki', 432–64; A. Małecki, 'Co rozumieć o runach słowiańskich' [On Slavonic Runes and the Authenticity of the Mikorzyn Inscriptions], *Roczniki Towarzystwa Przyjaciół Nauk w Poznaniu* 7 (1872), 226–46; K. Szulc, 'Autentyczność kamieni mikorzyńskich zbadana na miejscu' [The Authenticity of the Stones from Mikorzyn Examined on the Spot], *Roczniki Towarzystwa Przyjaciół Nauk w Poznaniu* 9 (1876), 71–222; A. Kohn, 'Die mikorzyner Runensteine', *Zeitschrift für Ethnologie* 8 (1876); Fligier, 'Runensteine in der Provinz Posen', *Mitteilungen der antropologischen Gesellschaft in Wien* 8 (1878).
29 K. Estreicher, 'Runów słowiańskich w Mikorzynie fałszerstwo' [The Forgery of the Slavonic Runes from Mikorzyn], *Kalendarz warszawski* (1869), 73; J. Badouin de Courtenay, Letter to Prof. J. Łepkowski (19.3.1872), in Szulc, 'Autentyczność'.

Figs. 37–8: The first (left) and second (right) stones from Mikorzyn.

Fig. 39: Tombstone from Skalsk.

did not always accept these arguments: various works of F. Piekosiński and J. Leciejewski argued at length that the inscriptions were reliable and valuable evidence for the existence of runes in the medieval Slavonic world.[30] The 'believers' held that the texts on the stone depicting a human figure were connected with the Slavonic god Prowe, while the language of the inscriptions on both stones was considered by both Polish and Ukrainian researchers to be Old Polish.

Among the monuments from other Slavonic-speaking territories, Czech and Slovak inscriptions had a high profile. One of a pair of stones making up a grave-marker found in Skalsk in 1852 bore an inscription which was interpreted as a runic text enumerating gods, mainly Slavonic, such as

---

[30] F. Piekosiński, *Kamienie mikorzyńskie* [The Stones from Mikorzyn] (Kraków, 1897); Leciejewski, *Runy*, 97–155.

Radegast, Nisz, Jamar and Ziw (fig. 39).[31] Mysterious signs found in 1896 on a boundary-stone from Bodin, Slovakia, were also considered runic. Leciejewski believed this stone to be important evidence for the use of runes with numeric values. He established the values on the basis of the order of the Scandinavian *futhark*, and claimed that the runes on one surface of the stone added up to a total of 200977.[32] He also identified an inaccurately specified measurement of 77 A 76, and on another surface read the inscription WT as 2000. He accepted, however, that these (rather fantastic) calculations were insufficient to prove that the Scandinavian and Slavonic *futharks* were identically ordered, but expressed a willingness to believe that in borrowing the runic script, the Slavs had maintained the order of the *futhark*. Leciejewski stressed that the runes of the Bodin stone were specifically Slavonic; nonetheless, although recognizing that the numbers on known medieval runic calendars were represented in a different way, he argued that this inscription – which he dated to the ninth century – might be a significant aid to identifying numbers in Scandinavian runic inscriptions.

In Russia, runes were identified on (whole and fragmentary) cremation urns. The most significant came from the village of Alekanowo,[33] while from Czechy came a piece with a symbol identified as an l-rune.[34] The appearance of runes on both Russian and Ruthenian urns suggested that the script may have been widespread in this context among the Slavs.

As a result of the research into inscriptions in Poland, scholars divided into two camps over the question of the existence of Slavonic runes. Opponents of the view identified genuine runes as imports from Scandinavia, and sought to reveal other inscriptions as forgeries. Supporters of Slavonic runology, on the other hand, presented evidence for the use of runes to render texts in Polish and other Slavonic languages. They also set up such institutions as the Runological Committee at the Skills Academy in Cracow,[35] and tried to underpin their belief by scientific study of the script. Thus it came about that J. Leciejewski, having examined a number of individual texts, wrote a chapter on Slavonic runes.

[31] W. Krolmus, *Posledni božiště Cernoboha s runami na Skalsku* [The Last Pagan Black-god with Runes in Skalsk] (Prague, 1857); Leciejewski, *Runy*, 158–70, fig. 38.

[32] P. Križko, 'Zprawa o bodinskom medzniku v Trenčianskoj stolici' [Report on the Boundary-stone from Bodin in the Trencin Land], *Sbornik musealnej slovenskoj spoločnosti* 1 (1896), 196–200; Leciejewski, *Runy*, 173–82.

[33] W. A. Gorodcev, 'Zametka o glinianom sosude s zagadočnymi znakami' [Note about a Clay Vessel with Enigmatic Signs], *Archeologičeskije izvestija i zametki* 5 (1897), 12, 385–90; Leciejewski, *Runy*, 183–88.

[34] J. Szaraniewicz, 'Cmentarzyska przedhistoryczne we wsiach Czechy i Wysocko w powiecie brodzkim' [The Prehistoric Burial Ground in the Villages of Czechy and Wysocko in the District of Brody], *Teka Konserwatorska* 2 (Lwów, 1898).

[35] Established in 1869; see Abramowicz, *Historia archeologii polskiej*, 49.

At the beginning of the third section of his work, Leciejewski stated his belief in the existence of Slavonic runes.[36] He argued that the number of medieval runic inscriptions found in Poland, and the variety of materials in which they were cut (stone, metal, clay and wood), suggested a native tradition. He also believed he could identify a detailed system in the use of runes by Slavs. By a combination of slight changes to the corresponding Scandinavian characters, and a number of specifically Slavonic additions to the *futhark*, all the sounds of the Slavonic languages could be precisely represented. Indeed, he felt that tenth-century runic did a better job of rendering Slavonic language than modern script.

Leciejewski also considered the dissemination of runes among the Slavonic people. The surviving inscriptions suggested that the script was used by Poles, Czechs, Slavs and Ruthenians, as well as Baltic Slavs. From the works of ancient chroniclers he deduced that Southern Slavs must also have known runes. The Slavs of Laba seemed to him likely to be responsible for taking the script from the Baltic to the Czech people. Finally, like his predecessors, Leciejewski thought that the Eastern Slavs of Ruthenia got their knowledge of runes either directly from the north, or via Poles or Lithuanians.

The system of Slavonic runes may be of interest to modern runologists. Leciejewski drew up a table which equates all the symbols found in the Slavonic runic inscriptions with the Polish alphabet (Table 4). In order to accommodate Slavonic sounds that are not found in Germanic languages, he suggested that the following procedures had been followed:

1. where more than one Scandinavian rune-form existed, one shape – usually the most frequently attested – was chosen to give the sound common to both Germanic and Slavonic languages; variant shapes were then given new values in the Slavonic system.

2. the original rune-form was altered by the addition of a line, or was turned upside-down.

He also argued, as we have seen, that numbers were expressed in runes. From the Bodin boundary-stone, he concluded that the Slavs used a decimal system, because only the first ten runes are used as numbers.

A separate chapter was devoted to the bind-runes, ligatures, which appeared relatively often in the small corpus. Table 5 gives twenty-four examples of bind-runes in the Slavonic inscriptions. Abbreviations of Polish words were identified (Table 6 gives six examples), as were reversed, or retrograde, runes: the Wapno bracteate and Alekanowo urn have wholly retrograde texts, while the inscription on the medal from Cracow is mixed, with two runes facing right to left, the others left to right. Finally, there were

[36] Leciejewski, *Runy*, 193–207.

Number	Polish Alphabet	Scandinavian Runes	Bracteate of Wapno	Border Stone of Bodin	Amulet of Ostrów	Medal of Cracow	Stones of Mikorzyn	Tombstone of Skalsk	Russian urns
1	a	ᚠᛘᛏᛣᛃ	ᚠ	+		ᛦ	ᛣ	ᛃ	+
2	ã (an)					ᛉ	ᛉ		
3	b	ᛒ B	ᛒ					ᛒ ⊟	
4	c	ᛏᚲ			ᛏ	U	Lᚲ		
5	ć	ᛌᚦD'				D	ᚦ		
6	cz (č)	ᛠᛞᚦD			ᛐ··	ᛌ			
7	d	ᛏ						ᗡ	
8	dz (d)								
9	dż (d)					ᛑ			
10	dž (d)						ᚷ		
11	e	ᛝᛡᛏᛏ			ᛏ	+	ᛝ	+	
12	ě (czeskie¹)							ᛠ +	
13	g	ᚷᚢ		ᚷ +			ᚷ		
14	h	ᚻᚺ᛭		ᚻ					ᚻ
15	i, j	ᛁ			ᛁ	ᛢᚻ···	ᛁ	ᛁ	ᛁ
16	k	ᛌᚴ				ᛣ		ᚴᚢᛚ	
17	l	ᚱ			ᚱ		ᚱ		ᚱ
18	ł = l					ᚱᚦ		ᚱ	
19	m	ᛘᚦᛡᛏ				ᚦ	ᛉ	ᛡᛠ	ᛡ
20	n	+ ᚱ		ᛡ			+	ᛡ +	
21	o	ᚷᛡᛡ				ᚷ ᛡ	ᛡᛉ	ᛉ	
22	p	ᛒ ᚴ							
23	r	ᚱ R		ᛙ		R	ᚱᚱᚱ	ᚱ	
24	rz					R ᚺ			
25	s	ᚻᛉᛌ				ᛁᛌ	ᛁᛌ	ᛌ	
26	sz (š)²)							ᛌ	
27	t	ᛏᛋ				ᛏ	ᛏᛋ	ᛋ	
28	u	ᚢᚢᚼ		ᚢᚼ			ᚼ	ᚢᚢᚼ	ᚹᚢ
29	w	ᛈᚢ:ᛈ	ᛈ			ᚹᚼᚺ	ᚹ	ᚱᛋ	
30	y	ᛉᚼ				ᛉ ::	ᚼ	ᛁᛢᚱ	
31	z	ᛌ ;·	ᛙ			ᛌ			
32	ž	ᚱᛁ ᛁ:					ᚱ	ᛁᛁ	
33	ъ (ь)							ᛁ = ᛁ	

Table 4: Runic alphabet from Slavonic monuments, according to Leciejewski.

Number	Ligatures	Border Stone of Bodin	Medal of Cracow	Stones of Mikorzyn	Tombstone of Skalsk	Russian urns
1	an	⚡				
2	at (ta)					⍏
3	aw					⍏
4	ba				♉	
5	bratr				⊕	
6	de				♉	
7	et			⍏		
8	ja (aj)					⍴
9	kamn				ⅩⅩ	
10	ko				Ⅹ	
11	le			⍢		
12	ln (nl)					⍕
13	lu					⍍
14	ma					⍍
15	mu				⍭	
16	nu					⍦
17	oć			⅋		
18	ra				⍴	
19	st					⍯
20	te			Ⲧ		
21	we		⋀			
22	ze		↳			
23	żd					⍻
24	żi (ży)			M [M]		

Table 5: Ligatures from the Slavonic runic monuments, according to Leciejewski.

1	dź(e)w'(i)ca	⌐∪Υ				
2	m(a)ći	⏀D⅄				
3	s(lavu)				⌠	
4	sv(é)mu				⌠∩⅄	
5	synowi			S=⍴	⌠⊥ʜ	
6	um(eršemu)					∩⅄

Table 6: Abbreviations from the Slavonic runic monuments, according to Leciejewski.

145

symbolic signs: two pagan (swastika, symbol of Thor) and one Christian (triangle with sun).

Leciejewski discussed the origin of Slavonic runes: were they native or had they been adopted from elsewhere? He argued that comparison between Slavonic and Scandinavian runes suggested that the Slavs did not invent the script, but probably adopted it from Scandinavia. Both the forms of the runes and the nature of the Slavonic monuments showed similarities to Scandinavian runes and monuments. Common sounds were represented by the same runic characters, and specifically Slavonic sounds were rendered by modifications of runes used in Scandinavia. Since the earliest Slavonic runic inscription was attributed to the end of the eighth century, while the earliest Scandinavian runes were thought to be fifth-century, it followed that the Slavs could not have invented the script.

Nonetheless, he accepted that the limited number of surviving inscriptions did not allow the date of the script's adoption by the Slavs to be precisely fixed. He also allowed that some Slavonic peoples may not have learned runes at all, in particular perhaps those who could have learned Latin script from the Romans at an early date.

Leciejewski supposed that knowledge of the runes may have reached the Poles in the eighth century, allowing some time to elapse before their earliest runic inscription, the ninth-century Wapno bracteate. He regarded the fact that all the known monuments came from the Wielkopolska region (Polonia Maior) as a strange coincidence. And he argued that runes developed along similar lines in Poland and Scandinavia, basing his analysis primarily on the forms of the a-rune.

It was regarded as self-evident that runes could not have reached Poland from the north without first being adopted by the Baltic Slavs, who may, therefore, have learned the script in the eighth, or even the seventh, century. Because of their close contacts with the Danes, the Laba Slavs may have been the first of all. Elsewhere, it was argued that the Czechs, Moravians and Slovaks received runes from the Western Slavs, while the Southern Slavs may instead have adopted the script from the Germanic population that inhabited their territory before them – the runes on the Kowel spear-head, for instance, may derive from a South Germanic tradition.

The final question Leciejewski considered was the date at which the Slavs stopped using runes. This seemed relatively easy to determine since he connected the decline of the script with the introduction of Christianity (though the explicitly Christian Cracow medal and Skalsk tombstone demonstrated that the correlation was not absolute). He argued that the Southern Slavs stopped using the runic script in the ninth century, Czechs in the eleventh century, Poles at the end of the eleventh century, Western Slavs also in the eleventh century, and – finally – the Baltic Slavs, probably at the beginning of the twelfth century.

J. Leciejewski's research and projects were not continued. His work was criticized by linguists such as Henryk Ułaszyn, who published his own study of Slavonic runes in 1909,[37] an article which proved to be the last extensive treatment of the subject. Controversy between followers and opponents of Slavonic runology faded away, and nothing was published on the question after the First World War. In recent years there has been some revival of interest in runes, though principally in publications concerned with magic and fortune-telling. In scholarly archaeological and epigraphical literature there have been very few references to runic script, and where they are found, they usually concern the history of Scandinavian monuments.[38] But even Scandinavian runology is little studied by contemporary historians and linguists in Poland.

The debate over Slavonic runes is an interesting episode in the course of Polish historical scholarship in the nineteenth and early twentieth centuries. This fascination with the script, the startling readings of authentic monuments and nineteenth-century forgeries alike, and the various fantastic hypotheses, may surprise us now. In the epoch of Romanticism, however, and in the circumstances of a loss of independence, Polish historians and archaeologists were eager to demonstrate close early links between Poland and Western civilization. It is against this background that we should set the theory of a widespread Slavonic adoption of runes, leading in turn to the earliest Polish inscriptions.

[37] H. Ułaszyn, 'Runy słowiańskie' [The Slavonic Runes], *Materiały i Prace Komisji Językowej Akademii Umiejętności* 4 (1909), 41–71.
[38] M. Adamus, *Tajemnice sag i urn* [The Mysteries of the Sagas and the Runes] (Warsaw, 1971); A. Gieysztor, *Zarys dziejów pisma łacińskiego* [The History of Latin Script in Outline] (Warsaw, 1973).

147

Insular Influences in Inscriptions on the Continent

WALTER KOCH

One of the most fruitful cultural phenomena of pre-Carolingian and early Carolingian times on the Continent was the Irish and Anglo-Saxon mission. The influence of Irish and above all Anglo-Saxon missionaries – in many cases long-lasting – on the script and book-production in the monastic settlements that they founded on the Continent is well known and has been much studied.[1] Such centres as Luxeuil in Burgundy and Bobbio near Piacenza in the kingdom of the Lombards in northern Italy, both foundations of the migrating Irish monk Columbanus who died in 615, became highly influential in ecclesiastical politics and culture. While in Echternach, which was founded in 698, Northumbrian calligraphy flourished throughout the eighth century, a missionary region reaching from Franconia and Hesse to Westphalia was nearly unanimous in its use of southern English script. Similarly in Bavarian and Alemannic scriptoria Insular scribes or scribes trained in the Insular tradition are to be found up to the late eighth or early ninth centuries, when – frequently following a long transitional phase – Carolingian minuscule finally took over. Whether these missionaries and scribes or products of their scriptoria exercised influence on inscribed monuments and on Continental traditions of epigraphic script of the seventh and eighth centuries is a question still to be settled.[2] The background to be considered in such a study is the immense variety in the lettering of inscriptions in the British Isles on the one hand and the many connections between epigraphic writing and the forms of

---

[1] B. Bischoff, *Latin Palaeography: Antiquity and the Middle Ages*, trans. D. Ó Cróinín and D. Ganz (Cambridge, 1991), 88–9, 92–5 (= *Paläographie des römischen Altertums und des lateinischen Mittelalters*, Grundlagen der Germanistik 24, 2nd edn (Berlin 1986), 120 and 126–9).

[2] This question was posed in R. M. Kloos, 'Die frühmittelalterliche lateinische Epigraphik', in *La cultura in Italia fra tardo antico e alto medioevo, Atti del Convegno tenuto a Roma, Consiglio Nazionale delle Ricerche, dal 12 al 16 Novembre 1979* (Rome, 1981), 893–901, at 900, n. 26. See also R. M. Kloos, *Einführung in die Epigraphik des Mittelalters und der frühen Neuzeit*, 2nd edn (Darmstadt 1992), 117. For some thoughts on the subjects see W. Koch, *Auszeichnungsschrift und Epigraphik. Zu zwei Westschweizer Inschriften der Zeit um 700*, Sitzungsberichte der Bayerischen Akademie der Wissenschaften. Phil.-hist. Klasse. Jg. 1994, Heft 6 (Munich, 1994), 28–34.

script on vellum in this region on the other. Apart from some isolated remarks in the literature, there has never been full discussion of this question. To anticipate, the results of our search for Insular influences in Continental inscriptions will be quite modest. This is hardly surprising, considering that the Irish and Anglo-Saxons crossed the Channel as missionaries and scribes of books intended to spread the faith, or as gifted organizers, but not as stone-cutters nor, as far as we may infer from the private charters which have survived, as writers of charters.

In the epigraphic field the newcomers met with an established tradition based on monumental capital script. In the seventh and early eighth centuries this tradition had reached a very low level in both quality and quantity, but nevertheless it had survived and was well rooted in the Late Antique and Early Christian epigraphic world, even if the Migration Period had brought some marked changes that can be seen in a considerable number of the surviving monuments. What may be attempted, however, is to investigate indications, which – unlike the broad tradition of Continental epigraphy – may possibly show some Insular influences. I am using this very cautious formulation deliberately.

Let us first look at Luxeuil and its environment. The scriptorium of this monastery which was founded in 590 in the Vosges will without any doubt have followed Irish styles in the beginning. It is evident, however, that with the development and consolidation of its own calligraphic style of writing based on Continental traditions this Insular heritage was very soon abandoned.[3] The oldest examples of script that can be connected with Luxeuil date from no earlier than the late seventh century. In these there are only a few features that E. A. Lowe saw as having been inherited from Irish calligraphy and Insular book production.[4] The most important of these are the wedge-shaped serifs in uncial, half-uncial as well as in display texts of the Luxeuil group. We should also consider Ms. Morgan 334 of the Pierpont Morgan Library in New York, the oldest codex from Luxeuil (c.669), written in uncial with a display page (fol. 1v),[5] of which the alphabet is an early form of the fine decorative alphabet that was used later. The spiral curve of G, the greater use of uncial forms, a tendency towards variety in forms, the

[3]   B. Bischoff, 'Irische Schreiber im Karolingerreich', in Bischoff, *Mittelalterliche Studien. Ausgewählte Aufsätze zur Schriftkunde und Literaturgeschichte* (Stuttgart, 1981), III, 41. See also Bischoff, *Palaeography*, 194–5 (= Bischoff, *Paläographie*, 254).

[4]   E. A. Lowe, 'The "Script of Luxeuil": A Title Vindicated', in Lowe, *Palaeographical Papers 1907–1965*, ed. L. Bieler (Oxford, 1972), II, 389–98, at 396. See also Françoise Henry, 'Les débuts de la miniature irlandaise', in F. Henry and G. Marsh-Micheli, *Studies in Early Christian and Medieval Irish Art, II, Manuscript Illumination* (London, 1984), 33–4.

[5]   Lowe, *Palaeographical Papers*, II, pl. 74A.

rectangular break at the bottom of uncial T (also to be found in Insular writing) – these are all features that may reflect the Insular heritage. As early as 1926 two inscriptions from Yverdon and Baulmes in western Switzerland, dating from around 700, and discovered near the Neuenburger See[6] were associated with the Insular tradition by Konrad F. Bauer,[7] and following him by Wilhelm Berges.[8] What is particularly significant is that both tomb inscriptions were clearly influenced by the characteristic display script of Luxeuil and are therefore rare examples of a clear and unambiguous relationship between display script on vellum and an inscription in stone within the context of early medieval Continental epigraphy.[9] Let us be clear: these are not inscriptions that immediately recall the Insular tradition. If there are any such Insular symptoms they will have to be looked for in small details occasionally to be found in the script of Luxeuil. In addition to a tendency towards a variety of forms there can be seen here or there some kind of wedge-shaped termination, but they do not appear systematically or in great numbers. But in the context of our search for Insular influence on the Continent these things count for more than a little.

Unlike Luxeuil, Bobbio and other scriptoria of northern Italy, such as Verona, are represented by manuscripts of the seventh and also of the eighth centuries which are written in Irish script or show clear Insular influence, for example in their system of abbreviations.[10] We have a rather good epigraphic coverage of northern Italian inscriptions, especially those of the kingdom of the Lombards thanks to the collections of plates by Silvagni[11] and Rugo,[12] and

6   C. Jörg, *Corpus Inscriptionum Medii Aevi Helvetiae II. Die Inschriften der Kantone Freiburg, Genf, Jura, Neuenburg und Waadt*, Scrinium Friburgense, Sonderband 2 (Freiburg 1984), nos. 46 and 47 (pls 59 and 60).

7   K. F. Bauer, 'Mainzer Epigraphik. Beiträge zur Geschichte der mittelalterlichen Monumentalschrift', *Zeitschrift des deutschen Vereins für Buchwesen und Schrifttum* 9, no. 2/3 (1926), 19.

8   W. Berges, *Die älteren Hildesheimer Inschriften bis zum Tode Bischof Hezilos*, ed. H. J. Rieckenberg, Abh. der Akademie der Wissenschaften in Göttingen. Philol.-hist. Klasse 3. Folge Nr. 131 (Göttingen, 1983), 32–3.

9   Manuscripts with comparable lettering include: London, British Museum, Ms. Add. 11878 (E. H. Zimmermann, *Vorkarolingische Miniaturen*, Denkmäler deutscher Kunst III. Sektion 1. Abteilung (Berlin, 1916), Taf. 50b); and Paris, Bibliothèque Nationale, Ms. lat. 9427, fol. 223 (P. Salmon, *Le Lectionnaire de Luxeuil (Paris, Ms. lat, 9427)* (Città del Vaticano, 1944, 1953), II, pl. XVIII). For a detailed study with further comparative material see Koch, *Auszeichnungsschrift und Epigraphik*, a study which has confirmed Bauer's views of more than 70 years ago ('Mainzer Epigraphik', 19).

10   L. Schiaparelli, *Influenze straniere nella scrittura dei secoli VII e IX*, Studi e testi 47 (1927), 15ff.; P. Collura, *La precarolina e la carolina a Bobbio* (Milan, 1943; reprinted Florence, 1965); A. R. Natale, *Arte e imitazione della scrittura insulare in codici Bobbiensi* (Milan, 1950).

11   A. Silvagni, *Monumenta epigraphica Christiana saeculo XIII antiquiora quae in*

the studies of Gray,[13] Panazza,[14] Kloos[15] and Petrucci.[16] From Bobbio itself there remains little from the relevant time,[17] apart from one small fragment, the tomb-slab of c. 736 of a bishop named Cummian, who, as the grave eulogy of 35 lines tells us, came from far away Ireland and preserved the teaching of the 'venerable Columbanus'. The very imposing monument[18] shows nothing in its lettering that is necessarily due to Insular influence. It belongs rather with the regional tradition and in particular with those monuments we attribute to the Lombard court style,[19] which is not very surprising, as King Liutprand is named in the monument itself as the man who commissioned it. As far as our enquiry is concerned, one might note the evident tendency of the letter S in this slender, compressed script to approach the form of a closed figure-of-eight. This feature is even more marked in the mid-seventh-century tomb inscription of Bishop Agrippinus of Como, composed of 14 distichs, from the Baptistery of Sant'Eufemia on the Isola Comacina (pl. 37).[20] An example from a later period, the second half of the eighth century, is the inscription from the baptistery of Callixtus in Cividale.[21] The form of S is conspicuous. We know it from Insular writing, both in half-uncial book script and in inscriptions. Whether such a feature is enough to speak of Insular influence cannot be decided here. Similarly the opinion of Roberto Sóriga, that Irish

Italiae finibus adhuc exstant, 4 vols (Città del Vaticano, 1943). Vol. 2 contains three parts with selected inscriptions from Milan, Como and Pavia.

[12] P. Rugo, *Le iscrizioni dei sec. VI–VII–VIII esistenti in Italia*, 5 vols (Cittadella, 1974–80). Vols 1 and 5 deal with northern Italy.

[13] N. Gray, 'The Paleography of Latin Inscriptions in the Eighth, Ninth and Tenth Centuries in Italy', *Papers of the British School at Rome* 16, n.s. 3 (1948), 38–167.

[14] G. Panazza, *Lapidi e sculture paleocristiane e pre-romaniche di Pavia* (Turin, 1953).

[15] R. M. Kloos, 'Zum Stil der langobardischen Steininschriften des achten Jahrhunderts', in *Atti del sesto congresso internazionale di studi sull'alto medioevo, Milano 21–25 ottobre 1978* (Spoleto, 1980), 169–82.

[16] A. Petrucci, 'Mille anni di forme grafiche nell'area milanese' in *Il millennio ambrosiano: La nuova città dal Comune alla Signoria*, ed. C. Bertelli (Milan, 1989), 140–63. See also R. Cassanelli, 'Materiali lapidei a Milano in età longobarda', in *Il millennio ambrosiano*, 238–57.

[17] Rugo, *Le iscrizioni*, V, nos. 137 and 138.

[18] For the best illustration see Silvagni, *Monumenta*, II/3, pl. IV 8. See also N. Gray, *A History of Lettering: Creative Experiment and Letter Identity* (Oxford, 1986), pl. 44. This inscription is further discussed by Nick Everett in his contribution to this volume (pp. 178–9).

[19] See especially Kloos, 'Langobardische Steininschriften', 178, for the tomb-stone of Cummian.

[20] The best illustration is in Silvagni, *Monumenta*, II/2, pl. VIII 1. For a transcription of the text: *I Longobardi*, ed. G. C. Menis [catalogue of the exhibition in the Villa Manin in Passariano and in Cividale, 2 June–11 November] (Milan, 1990), 162–3 (IV.10), plate on p. 163.

[21] Rugo, *Le iscrizioni*, I, no. 1.

calligraphy and scribal discipline contributed a great deal to the formation of the noble Lombard lapidary script is a very tempting supposition, but not one easy to prove.[22]

Whenever the question of Insular influence on the Continent is raised, *one* monument is named, and it is by the way the only one which in my opinion clearly shows these tendencies. It is the relatively small (45 × 30 cm) tombstone of Aldualuhus from an Early Christian graveyard near the Bergkloster in Worms and now housed in the Mittelrheinisches Landesmuseum in Mainz (pl. 38). Bauer drew attention to this many years ago.[23] In the most recent publication of this monument (in the series *Die Deutschen Inschriften*), Rüdiger Fuchs confirmed and justified this interpretation of the inscription, which probably dates from the eighth century.[24] This judgement is based on the general impression as well as on the observation of a number of individual forms. The general impression is of a calligraphic or at least orderly form of writing for its period. One characteristic is the use of angular, or 'broken', versions of round letter-forms, alongside very 'round' letters. Equally remarkable is the number of uncial and half-uncial characters, and in general the use of more than one form for one and the same character.[25] In the Aldualuhus inscription the capital form of A

[22]   R. Sóriga, *Le lapidi longobarde del monasterio pavese di Sant'Agata al Monte*, Biblioteca della Società storica subalpina 130 (1932), ix. See also Kloos, 'Die frühmittelalterliche lateinische Epigraphik'.

[23]   Bauer, 'Mainzer Epigraphik', 19–20.

[24]   R. Fuchs, *Die Inschriften der Stadt Worms*, Die Deutschen Inschriften 29 (Wiesbaden, 1991), no. 4, pl. 1 (with references to earlier literature).

[25]   Insular manuscripts with their display script and decorative pages offer an inexhaustible source of comparative material. On the one hand there is a tendency towards a hierarchical treatment of different display scripts and a combination of half-uncial and uncial forms blown up into rounded forms, angular versions of this script in which the original forms can be hard to recognize, and capriciously varied Anglo-Saxon capitals all in the same line. See the illustrations in Zimmermann, *Vorkarolingische Miniaturen*, III and IV; and in C. Nordenfalk, *Celtic and Anglo-Saxon Painting: Book Illumination in the British Isles 600–800* (London, 1977). We see an immense variety of forms, above all the co-existence of rounded and angular forms. It is not our purpose to show the interconnections in this rich Insular material between display script and inscriptions. See J. Higgitt, 'The Stone-Cutter and the Scriptorium: Early Medieval Inscriptions in Britain and Ireland', in *Epigraphik 1988. Fachtagung für mittelalterliche und neuzeitliche Epigraphik. Graz, 10.–14. Mai 1988. Referate und Round-table-Gespräche*, ed. W. Koch, Denkschriften der Österreichischen Akademie der Wissenschaften, Phil.-hist. Klasse 213 = Veröffentlichungen der Kommission für die Herausgabe der Inschriften des deutschen Mittelalters 2 (Vienna, 1990), 149–62; J. Higgitt, 'The Dedication Inscription at Jarrow and its Context', *Antiquaries Journal* 59 (1979), 343–74; J. Higgitt, 'The Display Script of the Book of Kells and the Tradition of Insular Decorative Capitals', in *The Book of*

always has a broken cross-bar which nearly reaches the bottom of the letter. The top of the letter varies: sometimes the two diagonals simply meet; in two cases the apex is formed as a triangular spur; once the apex carries a substantial cross-bar. Alongside these is a round A with a tendency to elongation, which probably derives from the uncial letter, but varies in form in accordance with the available space. C appears in its round and square forms; D with the bowl open at the top or closed; E only in the uncial form; G with an inward-curving tail; half-uncial H in its basic and angular forms. Half-uncial L appears with a triangular spur at its top, with a horizontal leading stroke, but also in a form with angular breaks at the top and base, nearly forming a Z. M is in a symmetrical and open uncial form with an elongated central stem, O comes in round and lozenge forms, the latter with decorative spurs on all four corners; P has a large, open bowl that descends a long way downwards; U appears both in V-shaped and half-uncial forms. The Insular appearance of the lettering is underlined by the particular forms of certain letters: uncial D in both cases – regardless of the differing bowls, once open, once closed – with horizontal or nearly horizontal leading stroke; N with a very low-set diagonal stroke, as well as a curved, nearly closed, figure-of-eight S. These are particularly clear Insular forms. They belong to the basic stock of Insular half-uncial. They gained entry into display scripts and also into epigraphic lettering.

The Aldualuhus stone is a unique piece within the region of the Middle Rhine, and, in my opinion, on the Continent as a whole. What we find elsewhere is, on the one hand, the descendants of the Early Christian capital-based tradition (e.g. pl. 39),[26] on many occasions of mediocre quality, sometimes with round or cursive forms, and, on the other hand, those modifications of Early Christian inscribed lettering which are ascribed to Germanic influence. Typical are the elongation of shafts and the use of angular forms characteristic of unskilled writing (e.g. pl. 40).[27] Walburga Boppert, who questions the Insular connexions of the Aldualuhus stone and argues that all the letter forms can also be found in Gallic inscriptions, is in my opinion fundamentally wrong.[28] The whole ensemble of forms and the

---

Kells: Proceedings of a Conference at Trinity College Dublin, 6–9 September 1992 (Dublin, 1994), 209–33. See also N. Gray, *A History of Lettering* (Oxford, 1986), 55–64.

[26] See, for example, the grave of the subdeacon Ursinianus from Trier: N. Gauthier, *Recueil des inscriptions chrétiennes de la Gaule antérieures à la Renaissance carolingienne, I, Première Belgique* (Paris, 1975), no. I, 170. The author dates the stone to the eighth century (or no earlier than the seventh century). See pl. 39.

[27] E.g. the stone of the priest Badegisel from St Alban in Mainz (seventh or early eighth century): Bauer, 'Mainzer Epigraphik', Abb. 40; W. Boppert, *Die frühchristlichen Inschriften des Mittelrheingebietes* (Mainz, 1971), 24–6. See pl. 40 .

[28] Boppert, *Frühchristliche Inschriften*, 156.

way they are set out, as well as the extremely Insular appearance of some individual letters, as shown above, are in combination decisive. It is true that uncial forms may appear in some places in Early Christian inscriptions, as a sign of lax standards in writing. Similarly we find square C or lozenge-shaped O in some inscriptions of Merovingian times. But we are dealing with something different here. In our inscription from Worms these features plainly derive from Insular intervention or influence. It would certainly be worth considering the sources on which Insular book script and epigraphic script themselves drew in the development of their rich diversity, as well as the phases of this development, questions which we cannot deal with in this context.

The Trier gospel-book (Domschatz Ms. 61/olim 134), written in part by an Echternach scribe-illuminator in about 730 and already compared to this inscription by Bauer, is useful for many reasons. The page in question is fol. 10r.[29] It shows the incipit of the gospel according to St Matthew carried by two archangels, obviously based on an Italian model of the sixth or seventh centuries (pl. 41). The incipit is written in an inscribed plaque set on a column. The letter-forms are similar to those on the stone from Worms in the combination of round and angular letters, and of capital, uncial and half-uncial forms, as well as in proportions and in some individual forms. On both the text has been arranged in the same way in a framed grid. We are shown an *inscription* which is deliberately distinguished from the tituli in display script on the same page. Perhaps this Insular scribe working on the Continent wanted to show, or at least suggest, an inscription with the graphic repertoire at his disposal, a simplified display script. What we may learn from this example is that we have to look for the models of the Aldualuhus inscription primarily in manuscript display script, rather than in Insular inscriptions. The former were familiar and available, the latter not.

What we do not find on the Continent, nor would we expect to, is the complete, or at least partial, adoption of the broad and stocky Insular half-uncial (or majuscule) into epigraphic script. One has only to look at Elisabeth Okasha's *Hand-list*[30] or Macalister's *Corpus*,[31] or at Huebner's old

[29]   Nordenfalk, *Celtic and Anglo-Saxon Painting*, pl. 30; N. Netzer, *Cultural Interplay in the Eighth Century: The Trier Gospels and the Making of a Scriptorium at Echternach* (Cambridge, 1994), 84–9, pl. 15.

[30]   E. Okasha, *Hand-list of Anglo-Saxon Non-runic Inscriptions* (Cambridge, 1971); E. Okasha, 'A Supplement to *Hand-list of Anglo-Saxon Non-runic Inscriptions*', *Anglo-Saxon England*, 11 (1983), 83–118. Okasha calls this script 'Insular Majuscule'. See also her essay: 'The Non-runic Scripts of Anglo-Saxon Inscriptions', *Transactions of the Cambridge Bibliographical Society* 4 (1968), 321–38.

[31]   R. A. S. Macalister, *Corpus Inscriptionum Insularum Celticarum*, 2 vols (Dublin, 1945–9).

plates[32] to recognize how common this type of lettering was in the very different cultural setting of Insular inscriptions (e.g. pl. 42).[33] This did not happen on the Continent, although there would have been enough models in the text and display scripts of scriptoria. As a manuscript text script it would not have been considered for epigraphic use. It would take some centuries for book scripts and vernacular languages to find their way into Continental inscriptions. The much studied whalebone casket from Auzon (the 'Franks Casket') of c.700 with its inscriptions in runes and Insular half-uncial is from an English, probably Northumbrian, workshop and cannot be used as an example of Continental epigraphy.[34] The presence of Insular half-uncial forms on the Adualuhus stone in Worms marks its unique position, but even on this monument their proportions have been adapted to those of the other majuscules.

When we look for further signs of Insular influence in Continental monuments – perhaps it is better to speak of traces – we are no longer on firm ground. There is one possible way forward, that is the growing use of the striking forms of capitals (Anglo-Saxon capitals), to be found in Insular writing of the eighth century.[35] I am thinking here of the following: the distinct triangular form where diagonal shafts meet, as in A or V; an A with or without a bar across the top, but with a broken cross-bar which reaches a long way down, sometimes as far as the base-line; angular S in the form of a reversed Z; rectangular U and O; lozenge-shaped O, with or without a bar at top and bottom; angular C and G. These forms can be found quite early in display script. They are used more often where a more monumental appearance is aimed at; and they also appear in more modest lines of display script. We can find them both in manuscripts (e.g. pl. 43)[36] and in Insular

[32] A. Huebner, *Inscriptiones Britanniae Christianae* (Berlin and London, 1876).
[33] See, for example, Okasha, *Hand-list*, no. 30 (Dewsbury, eighth/ninth century) (see pl. 42). Excellent examples are to be found in the lapidarium of Clonmacnois in Ireland; see the guide to the museum by C. Manning (Dublin, 1994), 44–5.
[34] A. Becker, *Franks Casket: Zu Bildern und Schriften des Runenkästchens von Auzon*, Sprache und Literatur. Regensburger Arbeiten zur Anglistik und Amerikanistik 5 (Regensburg, 1973), which includes many illustrations.
[35] For what follows see Koch, 'Auszeichnungsschrift und Epigraphik', 32–4.
[36] Nordenfalk, *Celtic and Anglo-Saxon Painting*, pls 16 and 17 (Lindisfarne Gospels, fol. 14v and 25v); E. Kessler, *Die Auszeichnungsschriften in den Freisinger Codices von den Anfängen bis zur karolingischen Erneuerung*, Denkschriften der Österreichischen Akademie der Wissenschaften, Phil.-hist. Klasse 188 = Veröffentlichungen der Kommission für Schrift- und Buchwesen des Mittelalters IV/1 (Vienna, 1986), pl. 18 (Lindisfarne Gospels, fol. 258r); *The Palaeographical Society, Facsimiles of Manuscripts and Inscriptions*, ed. E. A. Bond et al. (London, 1973–94), ser. I, no. 141 (London, British Library, Ms. Cotton Tiberius C.II); E. A. Lowe, *Codices Latini Antiquiores* (= CLA), 12 vols (Oxford, 1934–72), II, no. 217 (London, British Library, Ms. Royal 7 C. XII, fol. 3); Zimmermann,

inscriptions (e.g. pls 44–5).[37] Angular forms like these only found limited acceptance on the Continent, appearing here and there. They had nothing in common with ordinary handwriting; sometimes they seemed even more austere, more capital-like than the basic round forms of Roman capitals. In addition, forms such as angular C and G, and lozenge-shaped O were not unknown, since they appear in Merovingian inscriptions. The examples that I have in mind appear instead in disciplined inscriptions and in refined and purified texts – some of them in the years leading up to the Carolingian revival, before it became a classical renaissance. Sometimes they even appear in early Carolingian inscriptions. One might ask how far Insular influences contributed to this improvement in quality.[38] Among the few monuments that show these features clearly is the tomb-slab of Ludubertus (41 × 36.5 cm.) (pl. 46), which comes from the necropolis of St Matthias in Trier[39] – a disciplined pre-Carolingian text of the eighth century which has been purged of barbarisms. It is characterized by angular forms, especially the exclusive use of angular S, and by prominent triangular serifs. We are already in the early Carolingian period with the stone of Chrotrudis in Saint-Germain-des-Prés, preserved for us by the illustration in Guilhermy's collection (pl. 47),[40] or the stone with the so-called 'donation' of Palaiseau by Pepin, also from

---

Vorkarolingische Miniaturen, pl. 220 (Universitätsbibliothek Würzburg, Mp. theol. fol. 69, fol. 35b (= CLA, IX, no. 1424)) (see pl. 43). The presence of an angular S in the display script of a Würzburg manuscript of the early ninth century is in my opinion quite instructive. This manuscript marks the change from Insular cursive minuscule to Carolingian minuscule. See B. Bischoff and J. Hofmann, *Libri S. Kiliani: Die Würzburger Schreibschule und Dombibliothek im VIII. und IX. Jahrhundert*, Quellen und Forschungen zur Geschichte des Bistums und Hochstifts Würzburg 6 (Würzburg, 1952), 199 and pl. 3. See also CLA, VIII, 1150 (Cologne, Dombibliothek Ms. 51, fol. 1r) and the display script still in use in an Anglo-Saxon codex of the end of the ninth century (H. Fichtenau, *Mensch und Schrift im Mittelalter*, Veröffentlichungen des Instituts für Österreichische Geschichtsforschung 5 (Vienna, 1946), pl. 9).

[37] Huebner, *Inscriptiones*, no. 182 (Hackness, Yorkshire, early eighth century) (see pl. 44); Okasha, *Handlist*, nos. 116 (Thornhill, Yorkshire, eighth/ninth century) and 105 (Ruthwell Cross, Dumfriesshire, early eighth century); Okasha, 'Supplement', no. 159 (Brandon, Suffolk (eighth/ninth century) (see pl. 45); G. Henderson, *From Durrow to Kells: The Insular Gospel-Books 650–800* (London, 1987) ill. 136 (Durham, portable altar of St Cuthbert). For the survival of these forms into later centuries in England see, for example, Okasha, *Handlist*, nos. 15 (Breamore, Hampshire, tenth/eleventh century) and 85 (Little Billing, Northamptonshire, eleventh century).

[38] See the speculations on this question in Berges, *Hildesheimer Inschriften*, 31.

[39] Gauthier, *Recueil des inscriptions*, I, no. 29A.

[40] See the illustration in M. F. de Guilhermy, *Inscriptions de la France du Ve siècle au XVIIe*, I (Paris, 1873), no. CCVI.

Saint-Germain-des-Prés.[41] In the field of metalwork, the inscription on the crest of the reliquary of St Mary in Hildesheim (c.800),[42] and last but not least the chalice of Tassilo (after 768-9) in Kremsmünster in Upper Austria (pl. 48) come to mind. The chalice was probably made by a monastic workshop in Bavaria under Insular influence, perhaps in Salzburg, as is generally thought today.[43] In this artistic context it is entirely reasonable to think of Insular influences in the field of lettering. I am thinking in particular of A with angular cross-bar reaching down towards the base-line and a strong triangular terminal at the top (also found at the bottom of V), as well as angular C and lozenge-shaped O with small bars at top and bottom.[44]

Some speculation is inevitable in the search for Insular influence in Continental inscriptions. The study of lettering gives few definite results. It is certain, however, that the stimulus provided by Insular culture in the development of the Carolingian revival should not be underestimated.

[41] See the illustration in F. Cabrol and H. Leclerq, *Dictionnaire d'archéologie chrétienne et de liturgie*, VI/1, col. 1120. For another comparable inscription from Saint-Germain-des-Prés: E. Le Blant, *Inscriptions chrétiennes de la Gaule antérieures au VIIIe siècle*, I, no. 207, pl. 142.

[42] Berges, *Hildesheimer Inschriften*, no. 1, pl. 2. 1-2. See also the addenda, *ibid.*, 167-70. In this context it is worth considering Berges's view that, in monuments of this sort in which a measure of Insular influence is arguable, one can see an early, mainly western or localized form of Carolingian 'correctio', which then gave way before the dominant form based on antique models. In this context one could also ask whether this might not also explain the establishment of angular alternative forms of C and sometimes also G in the script of the Carolingian renaissance and beyond.

[43] See the recent discussion in V. Bierbrauer, 'Liturgische Gerätschaften aus Baiern und seinen Nachbarregionen in Spätantike und frühem Mittelalter liturgie- und kunstgeschichtliche Aspekte', in *Die Bajuwaren von Severin bis Tassilo 488-788*, ed. H. Dannheimer and H. Dopsch, exhibition catalogue (1988), 330-3.

[44] See also W. Koch, 'Vom Wert der Inschriften. Die Sammlung und Edition der mittelalterlichen und frühneuzeitlichen Inschriften Oberösterreichs', *Jahrbuch des Oberösterreichischen Musealvereins* 140/1 (1995), 349-50.

Script about the Cross:
The Tombstones of San Vincenzo al Volturno

JOHN MITCHELL

Carved epitaphs were ubiquitous in Antiquity and were among the salient monuments of the Roman world. However, after the sixth century, the practice of recording the name of the deceased in lapidary fashion was generally abandoned, and where funerary inscriptions were set up in the immediately post-Roman period, as often as not, it would appear that they were intended as conscious evocations of Roman practice – in idea if not always in formal design. Antique traditions of literate activity seem to have persisted more enduringly in the Italian peninsula than in other parts of western Europe, and two of the most extensive surviving bodies of epigraphic material from the earliest medieval centuries are from two of the great monastic foundations in southern-central Italy, where the skills of literacy were cultivated and exploited to particular effect: Monte Cassino and San Vincenzo al Volturno.[1] However, it is by no means certain that these two monasteries lay at the centre of this development. It is perhaps more likely that they represented peripheral manifestations of cultural initiatives which had evolved in the orbits of secular centres of governance, where strategies of this kind would have supported the ambitions and the political and social agenda of forces intent on establishing new structures of power and authority.

[1]   A. Pantoni, *Gli iscrizioni medievali dell'abbazia di Montecassino* (Monte Cassino, forthcoming); A. Pantoni, *Le chiese e gli edifici del monastero di San Vincenzo al Volturno* (Monte Cassino, 1980), 157–82; J. Mitchell, 'The medieval inscriptions', in *San Vincenzo al Volturno 3. The Finds from the 1980–86 excavations*, ed. J. Mitchell and I. L. Hansen (Spoleto, forthcoming), chap. 2. The cultivation of the arts of writing and the deployment of script at these two monasteries are discussed by J. Mitchell, 'Literacy Displayed: The Use of Inscriptions at the Monastery of San Vincenzo al Volturno in the Early Ninth Century', in *The Uses of Literacy in Early Medieval Europe*, ed. R. McKitterick (Cambridge, 1990), 186–225; J. Mitchell, 'The Display of Script and the Uses of Painting in Longobard Italy', in *Testo e immagine nell'alto medioevo*, Settimane di studio del Centro italiano di studi sull'alto medioevo 41 (Spoleto, 1994), 887–954, at 901–25; F. de Rubeis, 'La scrittura a San Vincenzo al Volturno fra manoscritti ed epigrafi', in *San Vincenzo al Volturno: Cultura, istituzioni, economia*, ed. F. Marazzi (Abbazia di Montecassino and Monteroduni, 1996), 21–40.

This process of cultural diffusion affected widely disparate regions and is evident in the adoption of particular types and designs in distant parts of Dark Age Europe. This paper is concerned with one instance of this, in which a type developed in the evolving Langobard polity in northern Italy, one particularly associated with Milan and its hinterland, travelled not only south to the two monasteries in the sphere of the southern Langobard duchy of Benevento, but also north across the Alps as far as the recently founded monastic houses in the kingdom of Northumbria in northern England. This is one instance of a characteristic phenomenon of the early medieval West, in which ideas emanating from one of the new centres of political and cultural power gave rise to vital peripheral initiatives on the frontiers of Europe.

Over the past forty years some two hundred funerary inscriptions have been recovered from the site of San Vincenzo al Volturno. A handful of these are complete, the rest mere fragments.[2] The great majority are carved into prepared stone slabs, but a few are incised into fired clay floor-tiles and there are three graves with inscriptions which form part of their painted decoration. Among these commemorative monuments there is one type which appears to have been peculiarly favoured by the community. In this the text of the epitaph is inscribed about a large cross, the arms of which span the full height and width of the stone. So far three complete and twelve fragmentary epitaphs of this kind have been found. All of these date from the last years of the eighth or the ninth century, the period in which the monastery developed into a major centre of monastic life and of cultural production.[3] Whoever embarks on a study of a particular aspect of the archaeology, architecture or visual culture of the monastery of San Vincenzo al Volturno or its neighbour, Monte Cassino, is liable to discover that the great architect, archaeologist, art historian, epigrapher and antiquary of Monte Cassino, Don Angelo Pantoni, has been there before. This is the case with these cross-inscribed epitaphs, which, thirty years ago, Pantoni described and set in their historical context in half a dozen lapidary pages.[4]

The most splendid and best preserved of the carved stone monuments with this scheme of decoration, at San Vincenzo, is a large complete

[2] On the possible phenomenon of wilful destruction of inscribed grave-markers at San Vincenzo in October 881, when the monastery was sacked by a Saracen raiding-party: J. Mitchell, 'The Early medieval Monastery as a Site of Commemoration and Place of Oblivion', in *Memory and Oblivion*, Proceedings of the XXIXth International Congress of the History of Art held in Amsterdam, 1–7 September 1996, ed. W. Reinink and J. Stumpel (Dordrecht, 1999), 455–65.

[3] The early medieval inscriptions from San Vincenzo and their dating is discussed in Mitchell , 'The medieval inscriptions'. For the early history of the monastery: R. Hodges, *Light in the Dark Ages: The Rise and Fall of San Vincenzo al Volturno* (London, 1997).

[4] A. Pantoni, 'Epigrafi tombali di San Vincenzo al Volturno', *Samnium* 36 (1963), 14–33, at 15–23.

grave-marker bearing the epitaph of one Teudelas, outstanding for the clarity and elegance of its design and execution (pl. 49).[5] The epitaph is laid out with one line above the horizontal arms of the cross and three below: HIC : || REQVI|ESCI||T : TEV|DELA||S : IN | PAC||EM. The outline of the cross is deeply incised into the smoothly worked surface of the slab; its arms are broad and straight-sided and splay out at their ends to merge into wide terminal bars. Cross and inscription are laid out on a lightly incised grid of vertical and horizontal guide-lines. The cross spans almost the full surface of the stone and the inscription similarly runs from one margin to the other. This marker was found lying in a mid-eleventh-century destruction layer in a garden-court in the part of the monastery designed for the accommodation of distinguished guests and may have come from the main monastic cemetery in the atrium of the abbey church of San Vincenzo Maggiore.[6]

A fragment of a second similar grave-marker was found nearby in one of the undercrofts of the early ninth-century guest *palatium*, again in an eleventh-century destruction level (pl. 50).[7] On this the terminal bars were evidently extremely long and swelled out dramatically towards their ends. Of the inscription only the terminal of one letter is preserved. On a third fragment from another stone, from a non-stratified context, only the tip of the swelling right-hand arm of the lower terminal bar and the adjacent letters –ONA[C]– (from the word *monachi?*) are preserved (pl. 51).[8]

Another epitaph, also from an unstratified context, three-quarters of which was recovered in four adjoining fragments, is a smaller and less

[5] First half of ninth century (= SV 1984 Context D 8107, SF. 2878). Mitchell, 'The Display of Script', fig. 31; De Rubeis, 'La scrittura' fig. 8; Mitchell 'The medieval inscriptions', cat. no. 37.

[6] The garden court: R. Hodges (ed.), *San Vincenzo al Volturno 1. The 1980–86 Excavations, Part I* (London, 1993), chap. 10. The monks' cemetery in the atrium of the basilica of San Vincenzo Maggiore: R. Hodges and J. Mitchell, *The Basilica of Abbot Joshua at San Vincenzo al Volturno* (Abbazia di Montecassino and Monteroduni, 1996), 46–7, figs 1:4, 3:4 and 3:16; R. Hodges, J. Mitchell and L. Watson, 'The Discovery of Abbot Talaricus' (817 – 3 October 823) Tomb at San Vincenzo al Volturno', *Antiquity* 71 (June 1997), 453–6; J. Mitchell, L. Wason, F. de Rubeis, R. Hodges and I. Wood, 'Cult, Relics and Privileged Burial at San Vincenzo al Volturno in the Age of Charlemagne: The Discovery of the Tomb of Abbot Talaricus (817–3 October 823)', in *Atti del 1 Congresso nazionale di archeologia medievale, Pisa, 1997* (Florence, 1997), 315–21; R. Hodges, S. Gibson and J. Mitchell, 'The Making of a Monastic City: The Architecture of San Vincenzo al Volturno in the Ninth Century', *Papers of the British School at Rome* 65 (1997), 233–86, at p. 248.

[7] First half of the ninth century (= Context G 711, SF. 0065). Mitchell, 'The medieval inscriptions', cat. no. 38. The *palatium* is discussed in Hodges (ed.), *San Vincenzo al Volturno 1*, chap. 9.

[8] First half of ninth century (collected by Pantoni before 1980). Mitchell, 'The medieval inscriptions', cat. no. 61.

accomplished version of the tombstone of Teudelas, with the epitaph, + HIC RE|QVI||ESCIT | [–]||ERT|[–]||ELLA|–, running about a cross of similar form, but with the arms of the terminal bars somewhat more harshly defined (pl. 52).[9] Again the cross fills most of the space of the slab.

A further small piece from a tombstone, found in an eleventh-century rubble layer adjacent to the main abbey church of San Vincenzo Maggiore, is incised with part of the lower stem and left arm of a similar cross (pl. 53).[10] Here the long terminal bars with their curvilinear inner profiles were simply appended to the straight sides of the cross arms. Only part of one word from the inscription, the first half of the first line below the left arm of the cross, is preserved: –PECCA– (presumably some inflection of the word *peccator*).

Another marker, an irregularly shaped stone with a tapering foot, smaller and less elegant than the previous examples, was found in a modern field wall at the southern edge of the site of the early medieval monastery (pl. 54).[11] Only the lower half is preserved, with the names of Christ in the genitive, *IHV || XPI*, inscribed on either side of the stem of a cross. The letters are somewhat irregular in formation and the cross is executed in a summary manner, with wandering contours. Its foot is a wide linear bar expanding towards the ends into rounded versions of wedged serifs which project inwards.

A larger monument is the fragmentary tombstone of the two priests, and probably brothers, Gundelaich and Liutprand, from an unstratified context (pl. 55).[12] Here the cross has simple straight-sided arms, which issue from a central disc and flare at their terminals into curling hairline serifs. The inscription was in four lines of tall well-formed capitals, of which the first one and a half lines are lost: – || DVORVM | [G]VNDEL[AI]CH || ET LIVTPRANDI | PRESBY||TERORVM. Unlike the majority of the grave-markers from San Vincenzo which are of upright format, this stone was a little wider than it was tall, and the composition of the epitaph had a horizontal rather than a vertical emphasis.

Another unstratified gravestone of similar type but with rather roughly cut and poorly formed characters is partially preserved in two fragments (pls

---

[9] First half of ninth century (collected by Pantoni before 1980). Pantoni, 'Epigrafi tombali', cat. 5, at 17, pl. I; Pantoni, *Le chiese*, 160–1, fig. 107; Mitchell, 'The medieval inscriptions', cat. no. 60.

[10] Ninth century (SV 1995, SVM 16, Context 3038, SF. 3053).

[11] Late eighth to early ninth century (context: HH 4201, SF. 0059). J. Mitchell, 'The Painted Decoration of the Early Medieval Monastery', in *San Vincenzo al Volturno: The Archaeology, Art and Territory of an Early medieval Monastery*, ed. R. Hodges and J. Mitchell, British Archaeological Reports International Series 252 (Oxford, 1985), 125–76, fig. 6:36; De Rubeis, 'La scrittura', fig. 14; Mitchell, 'The medieval inscriptions', cat. no. 40.

[12] First quarter of the ninth century (collected by Pantoni before 1980). Pantoni, 'Epigrafi tombali', cat. 4, at 15–16, pl. I; Pantoni, *Le chiese*, 158–60, fig. 106; Mitchell, 'The medieval inscriptions', cat. no. 59.

56a and 56b).[13] The cross appears to have been a spindly affair with straight-sided arms which flared slightly at the ends where they terminated in small bars with thin wedge-shaped projections. What remains of the epitaph runs: –||PVLC[–]|[–]||ETA[–] and –||BIN–.

Far grander and more ambitious is a fragmentary stone spanned by a large cross with dramatically splayed bar-terminals, which incorporates figural imagery in sunken relief as well as an epitaph (pl. 57).[14] This was found in an eleventh-century demolition deposit over the western end of the south aisle of the abbey church of San Vincenzo Maggiore. At the mid-point of the cross is the Right Hand of God, shown raised with the fingers and thumb extended upwards, in a fashion typical of monuments from the Langobard areas of Italy in the eighth and ninth centuries.[15] Each of the arms carries a three-stranded ribbon-twist. In the one preserved upper quadrant is a lamb facing in towards the cross, with a six-petalled rosette above its back; and an identical composition in mirror reversal undoubtedly filled the opposite, left-hand, upper quadrant. The two lower quadrants below the horizontal arm of the

[13]   Late eighth to early ninth century (collected by Pantoni before 1980). Pantoni, 'Epigrafi tombali', cats. 10–11, at 20, 22; Mitchell, 'The medieval inscriptions', cat. nos 58a and 58b.

[14]   Late eighth to early ninth century (SV 1994, SVM South, context 2206, SF. 1604).

[15]   At San Vincenzo itself, the Right Hand of God figures prominently in the painted decoration of a subterranean funerary oratory constructed in the 830s (H. Belting, *Studien zur beneventanischen Malerei* (Wiesbaden, 1968), ill. 18; J. Mitchell, 'The Crypt Reappraised', in Hodges, *San Vincenzo al Volturno 1*, 75–114, at 80–1, fig. 7:29). In the north of Italy this feature is quite common, for instance on a fragment of carved stone frieze from Santa Maria di Aurona in Milan, where it is set within a wreath and is adored by two lambs (C. Leonardi and R. Cassanelli (eds), *Paolo Diacono, Storia dei Longobardi* (Milan, 1985), fig. 286), in painted tombs of the eighth to ninth century in Verona (C. Fiorio Tedone, 'Tombe dipinte altomedievali rinvenute a Verona', *Archeologia Veneta* 7 (1985), 251–88, fig. 20) and in Pavia (the tomb of an abbess, Ariperga, in the disused church of San Felice: see note 24 below). The *Dextera Domini* also features in a painting of the eighth to ninth century in a subsidiary room in the hypogeum of Santa Maria in Stelle at Valpanena near Verona (B. Forlati Tamaro, 'L'ipogeo di S.Maria in Stelle (Verona), in *Stucchi e mosaici altomedievali. Atti dell'VIII convegno di studi sull'arte dell'altomedioevo* (Milano, 1962) I, 245–59, fig.4; Fiorio Tedone, 'Tombe dipinte', fig. 22); S. Lusuardi Siena (ed.), 'Le tracce materiali del Cristianesimo del tardo antico al Mille', in *Il Veneto nel Medioevo. Dalla 'Veneta' alla Marca Veronese* (Verona, 1989), 87–328, fig. 51. On the *velum* of Classe, a silk embroidered stole of late eighth-century date the Hand is depicted inverted, descending on the ranked bishops of Classe (Fiorio Tedone, *ibid.*, fig. 21; Lusuardi Siena, 'Le tracce materiali', fig. 2). On a fragmentary marble transenna recently excavated at Müstair, probably of the ninth century, the Right Hand of God is represented reaching up, issuing from a cylindrical feature and flanked on the left by an angel. (Francesca dell'Acqua kindly drew my attention to this newly discovered relief).

cross contained the memorial inscription, in neatly cut small capitals with the prominent wedged bars and frequent use of *litterae inscriptae*, typical of epigraphic practice at San Vincenzo in the ninth century. A stylized foliate scroll runs along immediately above the column of script on the right; the equivalent area of the stone on the left has been lost. Parts of the first two lines of the inscription are preserved: –RE||QVIES[–] | [–]$\widehat{DE}$||$\widehat{MARI}$:[EO]–. The design of this slab appears to have been inspired by fashions in the northern Langobard Kingdom. This derivation is apparent not only in the raised Right Hand of God, but also in the flanking lamb, ultimately derived from a Late Antique Byzantine idiom, abundantly available in Ravenna, which lay behind the sculptural achievements of eighth-century northern Langobard sculptors.

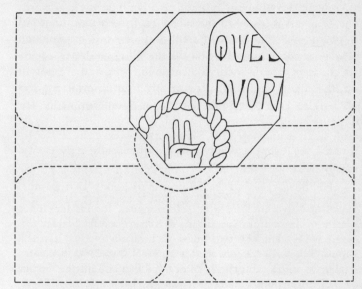

Fig. 40: Lost inscription set about a cross with the *dextera Domini*, San Vincenzo al Volturno. Regular octagon measuring 16 cm. between opposite sides (Angelo Pantoni).

A cross centred on the *Dextera Domini* featured on another ninth-century tombstone from San Vincenzo. This is a regular octagonal fragment, cut down for re-use in a pavement, which was found and published by Angelo Pantoni, but which subsequently has gone missing (fig. 40).[16] At the centre of the composition was the Right Hand of God, with the third finger bent to touch the thumb in the so-called 'Greek' gesture of benediction or address, contained within a wreath. From this issued the arms of a cross with simple expanding terminals. Only a few letters of the inscription, from the upper

[16]   First half-mid ninth century (collected by Pantoni before 1980 and now lost). Pantoni, 'Epigrafi tombali', cat. 6, at 17–18, 22; Mitchell, 'The medieval inscriptions', cat. no. 97.

right-hand quadrant, were preserved: –||QVIE͡[S–] | [–]||DVOR͡[V]–. Pantoni tentatively proposed the reconstruction: '*Hic requiescunt corpora duorum monachorum –*'.

Two fragments from ninth-century grave-markers of the same broad category, with an inscription set about a cross, were recovered from a range of buildings immediately to the south of the main abbey church. One of these was found in a context which can be associated with the destruction of San Vincenzo by a Saracen war-party in 881 (pl. 58).[17] The cross is outlined with deeply cut angular grooves. The sides of the stem curved outwards at the base and the horizontal arms seem to have had peculiar triangular serifs at their ends. Only the lower left quadrant is preserved with the letters: –CEG||[–] | PEB||–, in an exuberant interpretation of the San Vincenzo house-style, with wildly exaggerated wedged bars and tails.[18]

The other stone, which was found in the subsoil, is from a monument of the same general type (pl. 59).[19] But here the stem of the cross is ornamented with a sequence of angular configurations, and the surviving characters, again from the lower left quadrant, are decidedly eccentric in form, and are not all recognizably from the Latin alphabet. Presumably the inscription was designed to be intelligible. This text raises interesting questions about the extent to which the masons were in command of the skills of literate communication.

A further fragment of an inscription in a mid-ninth-century script, from an unstratified context, may be from another composition of this type (pl. 60).[20] The letters –AELES*TIS*[–] | [–]LA are preserved above two parallel horizontal grooves which could represent the arms of a cross. However, it is also possible that these formed part of a frame incised round an inscription which ended perhaps with the words *caelestis aula*.

A complete monument with an inscription about a cross was found *in situ*, in its original upright position, at the head of a mid- to late ninth-century grave in the floor of the Vestibule, a room at the northern end of the site, situated in the guests' quarters, just outside the limit of the monks' *clausura* (pl 61).[21] Here the cross and its surrounding inscription were cut into a re-used floor-tile rather than into a stone slab. The cross has thin arms with splaying

---

[17] Ninth century (SV 1995, SVM 16, context 3069, SF 3183). De Rubeis, 'La scrittura', fig. 11.

[18] The types of script employed at San Vincenzo al Volturno in the ninth century are discussed in Mitchell and Hansen (ed.), *San Vincenzo al Volturno 3*, chaps. 2 and 6, and by De Rubeis, 'La scrittura'.

[19] Ninth century (SV 1995, SVM 16, context 3074, SF 3107).

[20] First half of ninth century (collected by Pantoni before 1980). Pantoni, 'Epigrafi tombali', cat. 7, at 18, 22; Mitchell, 'The medieval inscriptions', cat. no. 64.

[21] R. Hodges (ed.), *San Vincenzo al Volturno 2. The 1980–86 Excavations, Part II* (London, 1995), 15–16, fig. 1:15; Mitchell, 'The medieval inscriptions', cat. no. 39.

ends, and the inscription is the common apotropaic formula: CRVX || X̄P̄Ī :
| CONF||VSIO : | DIABOLI || EST.

The same protective formula was painted in irregular black letters about
an angular pink cross on the head-end of a mid- to late ninth-century
block-built tomb, at the northern end of the site (pl. 62).[22] The tomb is set
within an arcosolium in a passage running beneath the distinguished guests'
palatium. The cross has wedged angular versions of the wide terminal bars
employed on many of the stone grave-markers.

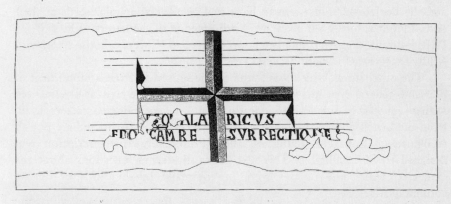

Fig. 41: Inscription from tomb of Abbot Talaricus (817–23), S. Vincenzo Maggiore,
San Vincenzo al Volturno (drawing by Lucy Watson).

Another remarkable instance of a painted cross flanked by a text, in a
funerary context, formed the principal imagery in the tomb of the abbot
Talaricus (817 – 3 October 823). This was a plastered and painted block-built
sarcophagus, situated beneath the pavement in the porch in front of the main
abbey church of San Vincenzo Maggiore, immediately to the right of the main
door of the basilica (fig. 41).[23] The inscription identifying the occupant reads:
[EG]O [T]ALA||RICVS | –[E]DO [.]CAM RE||SVRRECTIO[N]E[.] (*ego
Talaricus credo s(an)c(t)am resurrectione(m)*). The arms of the cross are
parti-coloured lengthwise, red and pink, and terminate in huge bar-terminals,
flat on their outer sides, but on their inner surfaces bulging out in graceful
curves. Crosses of this kind, parti-coloured and with the same long curvilinear
wedge-bars, were widely used in northern Italy in the later eighth and ninth
centuries, particularly in painted tombs in the major centres of the northern
Langobard duchies, like Milan, Monza, and Pavia.[24]

22 Hodges (ed.), *San Vincenzo al Volturno 1*, 147–50, pls 9:6–7, figs 9:28–30; Mitchell,
   'The Display of Script', fig. 30.
23 Hodges *et al.*, 'The Discovery of Abbot Talaricus' (817–3 October 823) Tomb';
   Mitchell *et al.*, 'Cult, Relics and Privileged Burial'.
24 A. de Capitani D'Arzago, *La 'Chiesa Maggiore' di Milano Santa Tecla* (Milan, 1952),

Slightly different from this category of tombstone are two fragments from a stone on which the epitaph was inscribed within the contours of a cross, rather than flanking its arms (pls 63a and 63b).[25]

Apart from one instance at the neighbouring monastery of Monte Cassino, a fragment of another small grave-marker of the ninth century (pl. 64),[26] the only other concentrations of monuments of this kind in early medieval Italy are to be found in the Langobard north, especially in the area around Milan and in Brescia. As we have just noted, the form of cross which was commonly employed on these funerary monuments at San Vincenzo – with arms terminating in wide bars, which expand to form pronounced curvilinear or rectilinear projections on their inner sides – was a northern type. This design must have been introduced into the southern monastery sometime in the late eighth or early ninth century.

From Milan there are a number of large and imposing grave-markers inscribed with epitaphs disposed about crosses. Perhaps the earliest is the epitaph of Manifrit from San Vincenzo in Galliano, usually dated to the seventh century.[27] Here a large cross surrounded by an inscription in capitals stands over a little lamb holding its own cross. Even larger and more elaborate is a late seventh-century tombstone, from San Giovanni in Conca in Milan (fig. 42).[28] This is almost two metres in height and carries a long and elaborate

135-8, pl. XI. figs 43-9; C. Fiorio Tedone, 'Dati e riflessioni sulle tombe altomedievali internamente intonacate e dipinte rinvenute a Milano e in Italia settentrionale', in *Atti del 10° Congresso internazionale di studi sull'alto medioevo, Milano 26-30 settembre 1983* (Spoleto, 1986), 403-28, at 411-19, figs 13-15, 19-29. Monza: R. Cassanelli, 'Sepolture altomedievali dipinte', in *Il Duomo di Monza. La storia e l'arte*, ed. R. Conti (Milan, 1989), 71-4, figs 29, 31, 32. Pavia: tombs excavated in 1996 in the atrium of the ninth-century monastery church at San Felice. Professor Saverio Lomartire kindly told me about this discovery and provided photographs of the tombs. See also Hodges *et al.*, 'The Discovery', and Mitchell *et al.*, 'Cult, Relics and Privileged Burial'. A similar cross is painted in a niche in the chapel of Anspert at San Satiro in Milan (G. Chierici, *La chiesa di S. Satiro a Milano* (Milan, 1942); J. Hubert, P. Porcher and W. F. Volbach, *Carolingian Art* (London, 1970), ill. 9).

25   Ninth century (both collected by Pantoni before 1980). Pantoni, 'Epigrafi tombali', cats. 8 and 9, at 18-20, 22, pl. I; Mitchell, 'The medieval inscriptions', cat. nos 66 and 67.

26   Pantoni, *Gli iscrizioni medievali dell'abbazia di Montecassino*, cat. no. 393.

27   (Castello Sforzesco, Museo d'arte antica.) U. Monneret de Villard (ed.), *Catalogo delle iscrizioni cristiane anteriori al secolo XI, Castello Sforzesco in Milano* (Milan, 1915), no. 37; R. Cassanelli, 'Materiali lapidei a Milano in età longobarda', in *Il millennio ambrosiano. Milano, una capitale da Ambrogio ai Carolingi*, ed. C. Bertelli (Milan, 1987), 238-55, fig. 243; S. Lusuardi Siena, '" ...PIUM [SU]PER AM[NEM] ITER ...": riflessioni sull'epigrafe di Aldo da S. Giovanni in Conca a Milano', *Arte medievale*, 2nd ser., 4 (1990), 1-12, fig. 10.

28   (Castello Sforzesco, Museo d'arte antica.) Monneret de Villard, *Catalogo*, no. 29;

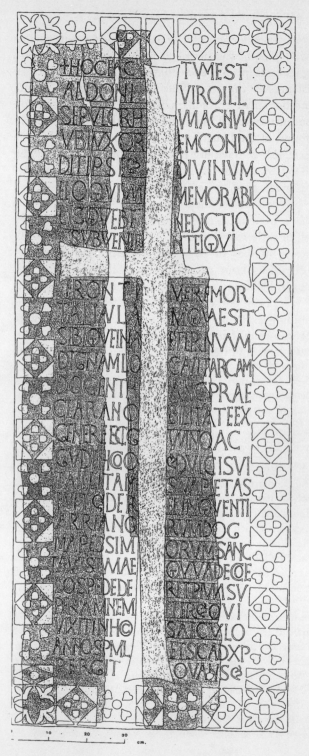

Fig. 42: Commemorative inscription of Aldo, from San Giovanni in Conca, Milan. Dimensions (when complete): height *c.*190 cm; width *c.*74 cm; depth 9 cm (after R. Rachini in Lusuardi Siena, *Arte Medievale*, 2nd ser., 4.1 (1990), fig. 2).

inscription recording the conversion, from the Arian to the Roman faith, of Aldo, who has been tentatively identified as a descendent of the Langobard queen Theodolinda.[29] A third epitaph, rather similar to that of Aldo, but somewhat later in date, is the tombstone of Benedict, abbot of the monastery of Sant'Ambrogio in Milan (d. 806).[30] Here a long and elaborate text is inscribed in close lines of capitals all round a tall cross. The cross is decorated with a running pattern of inverted heart-shaped motifs and its arms have terminal bars consisting of simple projecting triangular wedges. These bars are closely paralleled in the crosses painted on the walls of the arcosolium-grave beneath the distinguished guests' *palatium* at San Vincenzo al Volturno (fig. 41). A later instance of this kind of commemorative monument from Milan is the large intact grave-stone of the priest Dominicus, found in 1870, during the excavation of the fourth-century baptistery attached to the old cathedral, Santa Tecla.[31] This dates from the 920s – the archbishop Lampertus (922–31?) is mentioned in the inscription.

A related composition, in paint, is to be found in the lower chamber of the great tower at Torba, to the north of Milan, on the Olona, just under Castelseprio.[32] There, a large parti-coloured cross with flaring terminal bars, surrounded by an elaborate and lengthy inscription, is painted on the embrasure of an arcosolium in close proximity to a tomb. This is probably the grave of one of the abbesses of the female monastic community at Torba in the late eighth or early ninth century. The overall conception of the design is the same as that of the epitaphs of Aldo, from San Giovanni in Conca, and of Abbot Benedict, from Sant'Ambrogio in Milan. The grander sort of block-built cross-girt graves in north Italian centres of the eighth and ninth centuries, referred to above, also frequently have inscriptions of one or more lines flanking the crosses on their interior walls – on exactly the same pattern as the tomb of Abbot Talaricus at San Vincenzo al Volturno (fig. 41). A number of these were excavated immediately to the east of the southern transept of Santa Tecla, in Milan, in the late 1940s,[33] and another in Sant'Ambrogio (fig. 43).[34]

Leonardi and Cassanelli, *Paolo Diacono*, fig. 22; Cassanelli, 'Materiali lapidei', 246, fig. 285; Lusuardi Siena, '... PIUM [SU]PER AM[NEM] ITER ...'.

29 Lusuardi Siena, '... PIUM [SU]PER AM[NEM] ITER ...', 9.

30 Fiorio Tedone, 'Dati e riflessioni', 417–18, fig. 31; Cassanelli, 'Materiali lapidei', 246, fig. 287.

31 (Castello Sforzesco, Museo d'arte antica.) Monneret de Villard, *Catalogo*, no. 14.

32 C. Bertelli, *Gli affreschi nella torre di Torba* (Milan, 1988), figs 31–2.

33 de Capitani d'Arzago, *La 'Chiesa Maggiore' di Milano Santa Tecla*, 135–8, pl. XI, figs 43–9; Fiorio Tedone, 'Dati e riflessioni', 403–28, 413–19, figs 17–29. The painted plaster from one of these tombs is preserved in the Castello Sforzesco in Milan.

34 Fiorio Tedone, 'Dati e riflessioni', 411–12, figs 11–15. One painted composition of this kind is known from the Carolingian realms, north of the Alps. A

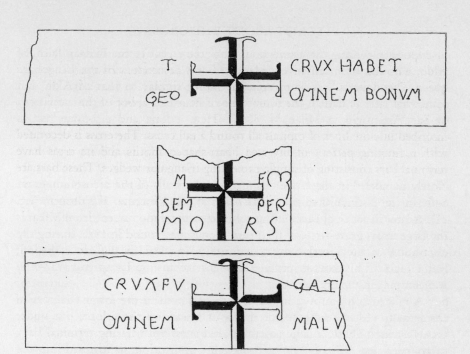

Fig. 43: Inscriptions from painted tomb in S. Ambrogio, Milan
(after Fiorio Tedone).

Fragments of two other large commemorative stones of abbesses, one of them named Ermingarda, each inscribed with an epitaph about a large cross, have been found during excavations at San Salvatore in Brescia (pl. 65).[35] Both must date from the later eighth or ninth century.

parti-coloured cross with large swelling terminal bars of a strikingly Italianate appearance, flanked by an inscription in lines of magnificent red capital letters, has recently been assembled by Matthias Preissler from wall-plaster excavated from a late eighth-century context in the area of the Carolingian royal palace at Paderborn. The painting probably dates from the last decades of the eighth century; its original context is not known but it would appear to have been funerary. Fragments of the inscription, but not the attendant cross, were published by W. Winkelmann, 'Capitalis Quadrata', *Westfalen* 48 (1970), 171–6, reprinted in his *Beiträge zur Frühgeschichte Westfalens. Gesammelte Aufsätze* (Münster, 1984), 106–9, pls 63–4. The material has recently been published in a more comprehensive form by M. Preissler, in *799 – Kunst und Kultur der Karolingerzeit, I, Katalog der Ausstellung Paderborn 1999*, ed. C. Stiegmann and M. Wemhoff (Mainz, 1999), 133–6, cat. III.17–21, and in his 'Fragmente einer verlorenen Kunst: Die Paderborner Wandmalerei', in *799 - Kunst und Kultur der Karolingerzeit, Beiträge zum Katalog der Ausstellung Paderborn 1999*, ed. C. Stiegmann and M. Wemhoff (Mainz, 1999), 197–206. This is one instance of the pervasive influence which Italian visual culture exerted on the Carolingian north in the late eighth and ninth centuries.

[35] One of these is described and illustrated in G. Panazza and A. Tagliaferri, *Corpus*

An instance of a composition of this kind on a tile is the tombstone of the priest Adelbertus, from Portadore, near Lodi, which has been assigned to the late seventh or early eighth century.[36] Here the epitaph has been incised into the clay free-hand about a cross carved in relief, which spans the full surface of the tile (57 cm. x 47 cm.).

The only other part of western Europe in which grave-markers with a text inscribed around a cross appear to be found in any numbers is the British Isles, in particular, in the late seventh and eighth centuries, the kingdom of Northumbria.[37] Monuments of this kind have been found on a number of monastic sites, Monkwearmouth and Jarrow, Lindisfarne, Hartlepool, and also from York Minster. From Monkwearmouth there is the early eighth-century tombstone of Herebericht, on which the epitaph is expertly inscribed in a capital script around a large cross carved in high relief (pl. 66) and a fragment of another rectangular slab with an inscription in both runic and Roman characters set about a cross with square terminals;[38] and from Jarrow, the other site of this double-monastery, there are fragments of two monuments with inscriptions in large capitals flanking crosses carved in relief, both from around 700, a remarkable tall stone with the inscription: *In hoc singular(i sig)no vita redditur mundo*, and a more straightforward grave-marker.[39] From Lindisfarne there is a group of eleven round-headed grave-markers with epitaphs set about crosses, dating between the later seventh and the mid-eighth centuries;[40] and from Hartlepool another group of ten such commemorative stones of seventh- or eighth-century date, all but one of

della scultura altomedievale, III, Le diocesi de Brescia (Spoleto, 1966), nos 60–1.

[36] A. Caretta, 'Note sulle epigrafi longobarde di Laus Pompeia e del Cremasco', *Archivio storico lombardo* 90 (1966), 175–95, at 190–3.

[37] J. Lang, *York and Eastern Yorkshire*, British Academy Corpus of Anglo-Saxon Stone Sculpture 3 (Oxford, 1991), 44; I. Henderson and E. Okasha, 'The Early Christian inscribed and carved stones of Tullylease, Co. Cork', *Cambridge Medieval Celtic Studies* 24 (1992), 1–36, at 25–6; R. N. Bailey, *England's Earliest Sculptors* (Toronto, 1996), 40. There is one instance of a cross surrounded by the letters of an inscription in a funerary context from Carolingian Francia. This is the cross drawn in the centre of the orchard cemetery on the St Gall Plan, with the accompanying verses: *Inter ligna soli haec semp(er) s(an)c(t)issima crux; In qua p(er)petuae poma salutis olent* ('Among the trees of the soil, always the most sacred is the cross On which the fruits of eternal health are fagrant'): W. Horn and E. Born, *The Plan of St Gall* (Berkeley, Los Angeles and London, 1979), II, 210–12; L. Price, *The Plan of St Gall in Brief* (Berkeley, Los Angeles and London, 1982), 67.

[38] R. Cramp, *County Durham and Northumberland*, British Academy Corpus of Anglo-Saxon Stone Sculpture (Oxford, 1984), I, 124 and 123–4; II, pl. 110, ills. 604 and 600.

[39] Cramp, *Durham and Northumberland*, I, 110, and 112–13, II, pl. 94, ill. 506, and pl. 96, ill. 520.

[40] Cramp, *Durham and Northumberland*, I, 202–5, II, pls 199–201, ills. 1111–27 and 1129.

which are cut on small rectangular slabs (pl. 67).[41] Fragments of three related, more or less rectangular, monuments, perhaps steles rather than simple slabs, have been found on the site of York Minster (pl. 68).[42]

Outside Northumbria, a small triangular grave-marker, carrying the epitaph NE||ITANO | SACER||DOS inscribed about a cross, preserved at Peebles, has tentatively been dated to the late seventh or early eighth century;[43] and the more or less contemporary memorial stone of Ioruert and Ruallaun, from Llanlleonfel, in Breconshire, bears a magnificent epitaph composed around a small cross.[44]

Furthermore, there is a widespread tradition of early medieval Irish grave-markers on which a commemorative inscription is set about a cross. There is one complete monument and a number of fragmentary ones from Tullylease, Co. Cork, of uncertain date, the earliest perhaps of the eighth or ninth centuries;[45] and other grave-slabs with epitaphs variously positioned in relation to inscribed crosses are known from many other sites in Ireland, with a particular concentration at Clonmacnois, Co. Offaly.[46] None of these is securely dated, but all are likely to be later than the Northumbrian tombstones.

The grave-markers with epitaphs centred on a cross from San Vincenzo al Volturno and those from the Langobard north are clearly related phenomena. The ones from San Vincenzo al Volturno are all from the ninth century and so are over a century later in date than the early examples of this type from the Langobard north. Given the close relations between the southern duchy of Benevento and the northern Kingdom in the eighth century and the many artistic and cultural contacts which existed between the two areas, it seems almost certain that the masons at San Vincenzo derived the idea for this type of monument ultimately from northern Italian practice and models.[47] This

[41] Cramp, *Durham and Northumberland*, I, 97–101, II, pls 84–5, ills. 429–49; E. Okasha, 'A Second Supplement to *Handlist of Anglo-Saxon Non-runic Inscriptions*', *Anglo-Saxon England* 21 (1992), 37–85, at 47.

[42] Lang, *York and Eastern Yorkshire*, 62–6, ills. 80, 81, 86–94.

[43] K. A. Steer, 'Two Unrecorded Early Christian Stones', *Proceedings of the Society of Antiquaries of Scotland* 101 (1968-9), 127–9, pl. 9a.

[44] C. Thomas, *And Shall these Mute Stones Speak? Post-Roman Inscriptions in Western Britain* (Cardiff, 1994), 322–3, fig. 18.9. I am exceedingly grateful to Professor Charles Thomas for drawing my attention to these two monuments and for providing me with photocopies of the relevant publications.

[45] Henderson and Okasha, 'The Early Christian inscribed and carved stones of Tullylease', nos 1, 12 and 14, and possibly 11 and 13, pls I and II.

[46] P. Lionard, 'Early Irish grave-slabs', *Proceedings of the Royal Irish Academy* 61, C (1961), 95–169, *passim*. I am most grateful to John Higgitt for drawing these Irish grave-slabs to my attention and for directing me to the relevant literature.

[47] Various aspects of the cultural connections between northern and southern Langobard regions in the peninsula are discussed by: A. Pantoni, 'La basilica di

must have occurred in the closing years of the eighth century, at the time at which the monastery was being redesigned and enormously enlarged and when the community was embarking on an ambitious programme of artistic and craft production.[48] It is less clear whether the formally related grave-markers from Northumbria were also inspired by this north Italian fashion. A major difficulty here is the uncertain dating of the earliest Italian and English monuments. However, on balance, it seems probable that the form of the English monuments was determined by knowledge of Italian practice.[49]

The many contacts which are known to have existed between England and Italy in the seventh and eighth centuries lend weight to the thesis that the idea for this type of cross-centred commemorative inscription was transmitted from the one region to the other. There was considerable individual contact between the two areas in the upper reaches of society, both in the ecclesiastical and the secular spheres. Laymen and clerics from the British Isles were constantly travelling to and from Rome, principally on pilgrimage to the resting places of Saints Peter and Paul, but also on diplomatic business to the papal court.[50] On their way many would have visited and spent time in the Langobard centres in northern Italy. The extent and significance of the cultural debt of Anglo-Saxon England to Rome and Italy in this period is immense and is well known. It ranged from the ideas and models behind the production of de luxe illuminated Gospel Books for the altars of the cathedrals and monastic churches of England, down to the forms of the bronze pins which women, in settlements throughout the country, used to

Gisulfo e tracce di onomastica longobarda a Montecassino', in *Atti del 1 Congresso internazionale di studi longobardi, Spoleto, 27-30 settembre, 1951* (Spoleto, 1952), 433–42; H. Belting, 'Probleme der Kunstgeschichte Italiens im Frühmittelalter', *Frühmittelalterliche Studien* 1 (1967), 94–143; G. Cavallo, 'La trasmissione dei testi nell'area beneventano-cassinese', in *La cultura antica nell'occidente latino dal VII all'XI secolo*, Settimane di studio del centro italiano di studi sull'alto medioevo 22 (Spoleto, 1975), 357–424, Mitchell, 'The Display of Script', 925–35; J. Mitchell, 'Arichis und die Künste', in *Für irdischen Ruhm und himmlischen Lohn. Stifter und Auftraggeber in der mittelalterichen Kunst*, ed. H.-R. Meier, C. Jäggi and P. Büttner (Berlin, 1995), 47–64.

48 Hodges, *Light in the Dark Ages*, chapter 5; Hodges *et al.*, 'The making of a monastic city'.

49 As suggested by J. Higgitt in Lang, *York and Eastern Yorkshire*, 44.

50 W. Levison, *England and the Continent in the Eighth Century* (Oxford, 1946), esp. 36–41; B. Colgrave, 'Pilgrimages to Rome in the Seventh and Eighth Centuries', in *Studies in Language, Literature and Culture of the Middle Ages and Later*, ed. E. Bagby Atwood and A. A. Hill (Austin, Texas, 1969), 156–72; R. Cramp, 'The Anglo-Saxons and Rome', *Transactions of the Durham and Northumberland Archaeological Society* 3 (1974), 27–37; É. Ó Carragáin, *The City of Rome and the World of Bede*, Jarrow Lecture 1994 ([St Paul's Church, Jarrow]); J. L. Nelson, 'Viaggiatori, pellegrini e vie commerciali', in *Il Futuro dei Longobardi – l'Italia e la costruzione dell'Europa di Carlo Magno: Saggi* (Milan, 2000), 163–71..

fasten their clothing.[51] The extent of English contacts with Italy in this period, at all levels of society, is nowhere more evident than in a famous letter of St Boniface to Cuthbert, Archbishop of Canterbury: '... it would be well and favourable for the honour and purity of your Church and a sure protection against vice if your synod and your princes would forbid matrons and nuns to make their frequent journeys back and forth to Rome. A great part of them perish and few keep their virtue. There are many towns in Lombardy and Gaul where there is not a courtesan or a harlot but is of English stock. It is a scandal and a disgrace to your whole Church.'[52] Anglo-Saxons travelling in northern Italy in the seventh century must have become aware of these striking Langobard grave-stones and conceived of the notion of commissioning similar monuments for themselves from masons back in the British Isles.

Compositions dominated by large crosses surrounded by lines of script are occasionally met with in manuscripts in the seventh, eighth and ninth centuries,[53] but what made them so appropriate for grave-markers was the powerful protective virtues associated with the cross in early medieval Europe. This preoccupation with the powers of the cross was particularly evident in the duchies of Langobard Italy and in the British Isles during this period. In Italy, not only were they commonly painted on the inside walls of tombs, but small intricately stamped crosses of gold-foil were sewn to the shrouded body, evidently to protect the individual from the powers of evil which were believed to threaten the deceased during the particularly vulnerable first months and years following death.[54] In Anglo-Saxon England, there appears to have been an even more pervasive and deeply rooted

[51] For the Italian antecedents of Insular gospel-book production in the seventh and eighth centuries, see D. Wright, 'The Italian Stimulus on English Art around 700', *Stil und Überlieferung in der Kunst des Abendlandes. Akten des 21. internationalen Kongress für Kunstgeschichte, Bonn, 1964* (Berlin, 1967), I, 81–92; R. L. S. Bruce-Mitford, 'The Reception by the Anglo-Saxons of Mediterranean Art following their Conversion from Ireland and Rome', Settimane di studio del centro italiano di studi sull'alto medioevo 14 (Spoleto, 1967), 797–825. For Anglo-Saxon and Italian dress-pins, see Seamus Ross, 'Dress Pins from Anglo-Saxon England: Their Production and Typo-Chronological Development', unpublished Ph.D. thesis, University of Oxford (1992), 365–83.

[52] C. H. Talbot (ed.), *The Anglo-Saxon Missionaries in Germany* (London and New York, 1954), 133. The letter dates from 747. John Higgitt thoughtfully drew my attention to this passage.

[53] B. Bischoff, 'Kreuz und Buch im Frühmittelalter und in den ersten Jahrhunderten der spanischen Reconquista', in his *Mittelalterliche Studien: ausgewählte Aufsätze zur Schriftkunde und Literaturgeschichte* (Stuttgart, 1967), II, 284–303.

[54] G. C. Menis (ed.), *I Longobardi* (Milan, 1990), cat. nos. II.9, 11, 18 and 19l; III.5 and 6; IV.58c and d, 100–2; V.1, 8–14; X.47a, 70, 75a, 76a, 77a, 78a, 79, 80a, 81a, 83v, 84a, 99, 172, 175, 191b.

fascination with the cross in its many forms and uses. This interest found expression in many ways, in pectoral amulets, in disc brooches with cruciform compositions on their display faces, in the remarkable so-called 'carpet pages' in Gospel Books, which usually incorporate one or more crosses in their design, and in the standing crosses which are one of the most characteristic and idiosyncratic categories of monument in the British Isles in the early medieval period.[55] It must have been their particular respect for the cross and its powers which led patrons in Langobard Italy and in Northumbria to commission memorial stones on which epitaph and cross were so effectively combined.

[55] For pectoral crosses, disc brooches and 'carpet pages': R. B. K. Stevenson, 'Aspects of Ambiguity in Crosses and Interlace', *Ulster Journal of Archaeology* 44/45 (1981–2), 1–27; L. Webster and J. Backhouse, *The Making of England. Anglo-Saxon Art and Culture AD 600–900* (London, 1991). For high crosses: G. Baldwin Brown, *The Ruthwell and Bewcastle Crosses ...*, The Arts in Early England 5 (London, 1921); W. O. Stevens, 'The Cross in the Life and Literature of the Anglo-Saxons', in W. O. Stevens and A. S. Cook, *The Anglo-Saxon Cross* (Hamden, Conn., 1977), 1–109, at 43–65; N. Edwards, 'The Origins of the Free-standing Stone Cross in Ireland: Imitation or Innovation?', *The Bulletin of the Board of Celtic Studies* 32 (1985), 393–410; Bailey, *England's Earliest Sculptors*.

Liutprandic Letters amongst the Lombards

NICK EVERETT

Sometime a little after 729, King Liutprand (712–44) founded a palace with an adjoining basilica and monastery dedicated to St Anastasius at Corteolona, around 20 km south of the Lombard capital, Pavia, along the Olona river.[1] Very little of the construction remains, yet two dedicatory inscriptions, positioned somewhere in the Corteolona complex, have come down to us through the anonymously written *Sylloge Laureshamensis*, a collection of dedicatory inscriptions recorded by a visitor to Italy in the late eighth or early ninth century.[2] In one of the inscriptions, Liutprand compares himself to King Solomon the temple-builder, and describes how he initially wished to construct baths. A visit to Rome, however, and a subsequent bout of religious fervour after kissing the head of St Anastasius, inspired the king instead to

---

[1]   First mentioned by Paul the Deacon in his *Historia Langobardorum*, ed. L. Bethmann and G. Waitz, VI. 58, in Monumenta Germaniae Historica (henceforth MGH), *Scriptores Rerum Langobardicarum et Italicarum saec.* VI-IX (Hanover, 1878), 12–187, at 185–6. On the geography and history of the area, see A. Riccardi, *Le vicende, l'area, e gli avanzi, del Regium Palatium e della cappella e monastero di S. Anastasio dei Re Longobardi, Carolingi e Re d'Italia nella corte regia ed imperiale di Corte Olona, provincia di Pavia* (Milan, 1889). C. Calderini, 'Il palazzo di Liutprando a Corteolona', *Contributi dell'Istituto di Archeologia* 5 (1975), 174–225.

[2]   Rome, Biblioteca Apostolica Vaticana, Ms. Vat. Lat. Pal. 833. Edited by I. B.[G. B.] De Rossi in his *Inscriptiones Christianae Urbis Romae Septimo Saeculo Antiquiores* (Rome, 1857–88), II, *sylloge prima, secunda, tertia, quarta*, 142–53, 124–30, 159–73 ('*circumpadana et subalpina*'), 95–118, respectively. De Rossi's separate sections do not make for clarity: his perception of different hands for different 'sections' of the sylloge is arguably mistaken. I discuss this, and the issue of sylloge collections, more fully elsewhere: 'Literacy in Lombard Italy, 568–774 AD', unpublished Ph.D. thesis, University of Cambridge (1997), 276–9. For the Lombard inscriptions under discussion here, unless otherwise noted, I have generally used the text found in K. Strecker (ed.), *Poetae Latini Aevi Carolini*, MGH (Berlin, 1923), IV, 718–31 ('Rhythmi Langobardici'), and G. Panazza, 'Lapidi e sculture paleocristiane e pre-romaniche di Pavia', in *Arte del primo millenio. Atti del II° convegno per lo studio dell'arte dell'alto medioevo tenuto presso l'Università di Pavia nel Settembre 1950* (Turin, 1953), 211–302. The text of inscriptions surviving in lapidary form is cited in capitals.

construct a church dedicated to the saint. Liutprand further contrasts himself favourably with his enemy the Byzantine emperor, Leo who, 'persuaded by a wretched philosopher, has fallen into the pit of schism'.

The above-mentioned inscription has much to tell us about the cultural ambience of Liutprand's royal court at a time when the Lombards were asserting their burgeoning dominance over the Italian peninsula. The other inscription pertaining to the Corteolona complex provides us with a further glimpse into Liutprand's political and religious policies more germane to the theme of this volume. The eight-line inscription runs as follows:

> Behold the house of the Lord, most beautifully constructed, it shines forth and glistens, decorated with various materials. Rome, which is the capital of the faith and which is made illustrious by the lights of the world [Peter and Paul], enriched it with her precious marble, mosaics and columns. Hooray for Prince Liutprand, the author of this holy work! Your deeds will proclaim you fortunate throughout time, you, who desiring to decorate the triumphs of your people, have stamped the whole country with these inscriptions (*proprie gentis cupiens ornare triumphos / His titulis patriam signasti denique totum [totam]*).[3]

The interpretation of '*his titulis*' as meaning 'with these inscriptions' is not free of problems. In late antique parlance, *titulus* could refer to a number of things, including a parish church. The context of the poem, however, tends to deny other interpretations.[4]

[3] I have used the text De Rossi, *Inscriptiones Christianae*, II, 168–9, which is more faithful to the manuscript than the MGH version, E. Duemmler, *Poetae Latini Aevi Carolini*, MGH (Berlin, 1881), I, 105–6, or that of Calderini, 'Il palazzo', 179.

[4] See Du Cange, *Glossarium Mediae et Infimae Latinitatis* (Niort, 1883–7), VIII, 114–16 (*s.v.* 'titulus'), and the comments of R. Davis in the glossary to his translation of the *Liber Pontificalis: The Lives of the Eighth-Century Popes (Liber Pontificalis)*, Translated Texts for Historians 13 (Liverpool, 1992), 242. J. F. Niermeyer *Mediae Latinitatis Lexicon Minus* (Leiden, New York and Cologne, 1976), 1029–31, lists no fewer than 22 definitions that range from tombstones to choirs: the *Liber Pontificalis* frequently used *titulus* as 'monument', its use for 'parish church' being rare after the fifth century. In the loquacious works of Ennodius of Pavia and Cassiodorus the word can refer to an inscription, title, church office, honour, tax, or a document: see, for example, Ennodius, *Opera*, ed. F. Vogel, MGH Auctores Antiquissimi (Berlin, 1885), VII, 2, 7, 22, 40, 61, 67, 101, 103; Cassiodorus, *Variae*, ed. T. Mommsen, MGH Auctores Antiquissimi, (Berlin, 1894), XII, 120, 147, 283, 90, and esp. 51, 49, 180. Note also Pope Gregory I's use of the term, *Epistulae*, I–II, ed. P. Ewald and L. M. Hartmann, MGH (Berlin, 1891), I, 85, 325, 364, II, 35, especially editors' comments, I, 54 n. 2. The use of '*signare*', to 'seal', 'sign' or 'stamp' is more suggestive of literate communication via inscriptions: C. T. Lewis and C. Short, *A Latin Dictionary* (Oxford, 1984), 1697; J. F. Niermeyer, *Lexicon*, 970; Du Cange, *Glossarium*, VII, 480.

Scholars have long recognized the existence of a small but significant epigraphic renewal in mid-eighth-century Lombard Italy, a 'sudden flowering' of inscriptions sophisticated in both form and content.[5] The palaeography of the surviving inscriptions, accompanied by an identifiable 'Lombard style' of border decoration, appears to be part of a larger movement of renewed interest in sculptured stone. The causes, however, of this indubitable 'flowering', remain obscure. The reference to Liutprand 'stamping' his kingdom with inscriptions provides us with a possible starting point, or at least invites comment. The remarkable evidence from mid-eighth-century Lombard Italy appears to derive from a deliberate use of inscriptions by Lombard-Pavian élites as a means of promoting the ideology of their rule. Indeed, it has been suggested that the artistic achievements of the eighth century were in part a result of fierce competition, or 'inter-polity rivalry', for prestige and power amongst Italy's élites, as they deployed 'painting and script as symbols of cultural authority and as vehicles of cultural control'.[6] I should like to suggest in this chapter that Liutprand's involvement with epigraphic activity for political purposes provided something of the impetus for this 'sudden flowering' of inscriptions. This is not to say that Liutprand and his court were solely responsible for the renewed interest in epigraphy as a means of communication. There is evidence to suggest that the ecclesiastical élites of the late seventh-century Pavian church continued to use epigraphy for the commemoration of its members, a matter to which I shall return

[5]   See the appreciative comments of N. Gray, 'The Paleography of Latin Inscriptions in the Eighth, Ninth and Tenth Centuries in Italy', *Papers of the British School at Rome* 16 (1948), 38–167, esp. 154–7, 'flowering' at 156. See also R. M. Kloos, 'Zum Stil der langobardischen Steininschriften des achten Jahrhunderts', in *Atti del 6° congresso internazionale di studi sull'alto medioevo, Milano 21–25 ottobre 1978* (Spoleto, 1980), 169–82; R. M. Kloos, 'Die frühmittelalterliche lateinische Epigraphik', in *La cultura in Italia fra tardo antico e alto medioevo, Atti del Convegno tenuto a Roma, Consiglio Nazionale delle Ricerche, dal 12 al 16 novembre 1979* (Rome, 1981), II, 893–901. The starting point for discussion of 'Lombard' sculptural style is G. De Francovich, 'Il problema delle origini della scultura cosiddetta "Longobarda"', *Atti del I° congresso internazionale di studi longobardi* (Spoleto, 1952), 255–76; see also A. Peroni, 'Pavia capitale longobarda. Testimonianze archeologiche e manufatti artistici', in *I Longobardi e la Lombardia. Saggi* (Milan, 1978), 73–81: A. M. Romanini, 'Committenza reggia e pluralismo culturale nella "Longobardia major"', in *Committenti e produzione artistico-letteraria nell'alto medioevo occidentale*, Settimane di studio del Centro italiano di studi sull'alto medioevo 39 (Spoleto, 1992), 57–92: see also in the same volume, the comments of S. Casartelli Novelli, 'Committenza e produzione scultorea "bassa"', 531–67.

[6]   See the stimulating discussion of J. Mitchell, 'The Display of Script and the Uses of Painting in Longobard Italy', in *Testo e immagine nell'alto medioevo*, Settimane di studio del centro italiano di studi sull'alto medioevo 41 (Spoleto, 1994), 887–954, at 951.

below. Yet Liutprand appears to have seized the opportunity offered by the medium for promoting the idea of a unified and Christian Italy under his rule.

The implications of the Corteolona inscription, that Liutprand was behind a programme of inscriptions to be set up throughout the Italy of his kingdom, may be a slight exaggeration, but there is evidence of his strong involvement with epigraphic production. We have over ten surviving inscriptions that record his name, albeit sometimes in a form that is no more than a dating clause (*tempore regis Liutprandi* and so on), yet previous or later kings do not appear very often, if at all, in inscriptions.[7] A few examples give us something of the flavour of Liutprand's commissions.

The tombstone of Cumianus (or Cummian) of Bobbio (d. *c.*736) provides an example of Liutprand's patronage of epigraphic production. The 19-line text, in neatly cut 3.8 cm. high capitals, tells how Cumianus left Ireland apparently at the sprightly age of 74 to live at Bobbio, *dogma Columbani servando*, for another 21 years before he died aged 95. The invocation at the end of the inscription testifies to Liutprand's involvement:

> but excellent father, be a powerful intercessor on behalf of the most glorious King Liutprand, who in his devotion has decorated your tomb with beautiful stone-work so that it might be known where your sweet corpse lies covered.[8]

---

[7] Liutprand: Gray, 'Paleography of Latin Inscriptions', nos 25, 28, 29, 30, 33, 34, 48, and Panazza, 'Lapidi e sculture', nos 62, 63. The exceptions amongst other kings are: Agilulf, on the plaques found in Val di Nievole, see R. Elze, 'Die Agilulfkrone des Schatzes von Monza', in *Historische Forschungen für W. Schlesinger*, ed. H. Beumann (Cologne and Vienna, 1974), 167–84; Agilulf and his son Adoald, on the stamped tile at San Simpliciano, see Mitchell, 'The Display of Script', 893; and Cunincpert, on Cunincperga's epitaph (see below) and his own, if it is not a fake. See Gray, 'Paleography of Latin Inscriptions', no. 23, p. 64. One inscription from the *Sylloge Laureshamensis* refers to King Desiderius: De Rossi, *Inscriptiones Christianae*, II, 167 (no. 17).

[8] The tombstone of Cummian is also discussed above in the chapter by Walter Koch (p. 151). See also Gray, 'Paleography of Latin Inscriptions', no. 33. Good plates are provided in G. C. Menis (ed.), *I Longobardi* (Milan, 1990), 350 (IX.18), and in N. Gray, *A History of Lettering: Creative Experiment and Letter Identity* (Oxford, 1986), fig. 44. Complete text given in Strecker, *Poetae*, IV, 723. The 180 cm. × 90 cm. tombstone was originally part of a sarcophagus for which another ornamental slab survives. The double-border decoration that surrounds the text is suggestive of both earlier and later models; see the comments of Kloos, 'Zum Stil', 178. The language used to provide the dates is of a rhetorical, even poetic nature, and has therefore caused some confusion. For example, Gray, 'Paleography of Latin Inscriptions', 70, takes '*olimpias*' (... OLIMPIADIS QUATTUOR | UNIUSQUE CIRCOLO ANNI | SIC VIXIT FELICITER ...) as referring to the Greek four-year period, but in the Latin West amongst post-Augustan poets it sometimes became synonymous with the Latin *lustrum*, a five-year period: Lewis and Short, *Latin Dictionary*, 1263. Moreover, Gray calculated Cumianus' death at 90 years of age, which misreads the phrase 'HUIC [Cumiano] AETATIS ANNI

The Cumianus tombstone is a reminder of the strong links between the Lombard royal court and Bobbio, which was founded with the support and patronage of King Agilulf and Queen Theudelinda in the early seventh century. The earliest surviving copy of Lombard law, the 'Edictus Rothari' (St Gallen, Stiftsbibliothek, Ms. 730), was most probably penned in the monastery's famous scriptorium. Bobbio's foundation charter is our earliest surviving royal charter (613), and royal privileges and immunities were continually granted throughout the seventh century. We have no contemporary charters from Liutprand that testify to his patronage of this monastery. Instead we have this inscription, and a mere fragment of another.[9]

The craftsman who executed the work was proud enough to include his name in the last line of Cumianus' epitaph: '*fecit Iohannes magister*'. Unfortunately we have no way of knowing whether this *magister* was attached to the monastery or to the Pavian court as a royally appointed artisan, or indeed worked freelance for commissions: his name does not recur in any other of the inscriptions of similar style. Liutprand's interest in the affairs of *magistri*, including *magistri marmorari*, can be seen in his legislative attempts to regulate prices and wages. Indeed, the *magistri* of Lombard inscriptions, all sporting Roman names, provide great scope for speculations upon the 'industry' of epigraphy in this period, but very little that is conclusive. The references to *magistri* and *discipuli* on some works, rare in the

---

FUERUNT | NOVIES DENI | LUSTRUN [sic] QUOQUE UNUM MENSES|QUE QUATTUOR SIMUL', which is clearly 'nine decades and one term of five years and four months'. The use of *lustrum* suggests that it may have been interchangeable with *olimpias* to mean a five-year period. For further use of *lustrum* as a five-year period, see the inscriptions of Santa Mustiola (see n. 13, below).

9   G. C. Mor, 'S. Columbano e la politica ecclesiastica di Agilulfo', *Bollettino storico piacentino* 28 (1933), 49–63; V. Polonia, *Il monastero di S. Columbano di Bobbio dalla fondazione all'epoca carolingia* (Genova, 1962). For St Gallen, Stiftsbibliotek, Ms. 730 see E. A. Lowe, *Codices Latini Antiquiores*, VII (Oxford, 1956), no. 949. See also A. Dold, *Zur ältesten Handschrift des Edictus Rothari* (Stuttgart, 1955); A. Dold, 'Zum Langobardengesetz. Neue Bruchstücke der ältesten Handschrift des Edictus Rothari', *Deutsches Archiv für Geschichte des Mittelalters* 4 (1940), 1–52. A diploma of Emperor Louis II in 860, however, refers to '*praeceptiones et privilegia regum Langobardorum*' for Bobbio and lists all Lombard kings, including Liutprand. It also mentions Liutprand's concession allowing the monastery to fish at his *curtis* at lake Garda for 10 solidi a year. See C. Brühl, *Codice diplomatico longobardo*, Fonti per la storia d'Italia 64 (Rome, 1973), III, 272; C. Cipolla and G. Buzzi, *Codice diplomatico del monastero di S. Columbano di Bobbio*, I, Fonti per la storia d'Italia 52 (Roma, 1918), 181–2. Gray, 'Paleography of Latin Inscriptions', no. 34. The fragmentary inscription, '+ D LIUTPRAND REX V–', carved in fine capitals around 5 cm. high, was discovered during restoration of the crypt of the abbey church in 1910. See Gray, 'Paleography of Latin Inscriptions', no. 34, and Cipolla, *Codice diplomatico*, 135.

ancient world, demonstrate pride in a profession with a hierarchy of instruction. We even have the sculptured portrait of a *magister*, Ursus, complete with *scalprum* and mallet in hand on the marble panel at the abbey San Pietro di Ferentillo. He is probably the same Ursus who executed 'with his disciples Iuventinus and Iuvianus' the ciborium at San Giorgio di Valpolicella, though we cannot be certain. Perhaps the best evidence for identifying the two Ursi as one and the same is the presence of Liutprand: the king is specifically referred to in the Valpolicella inscription (*'nostro lioprande rege'*) and may be linked with the Ferentillo piece by his investiture of a Hildericus as duke of Spoleto in 739, again as part of the king's centralizing policies towards the recalcitrant duchy. The exclusive use of Roman names for *magistri* is puzzling in light of other evidence which suggests that the use of Roman or Germanic names did not correspond to any divisions in Italo-Lombard society in terms of a person's status, occupation or function. We can only speculate as to whether the use of Roman names for the *magistri marmorari* in Italy is indicative of some elusive aspect of the industry that escapes us, or is merely a false impression due to the capricious nature of surviving evidence.[10]

The Corteolona inscription and Cumianus' epitaph are two examples of how Liutprand was using epigraphy as a means of royal propaganda, advertising his benevolence and piety for all to see. This raises the question of audience, for the two examples belong to an ecclesiastical context, perhaps suggesting a more restricted, monastic reception – the Corteolona inscriptions may have been situated in the adjoining monastery rather than the palatial basilica. The inscription was prominent enough, however, to be copied down by one of the many visitors to Italy in the eighth century. As with the Cumianus epitaph, these inscriptions advertising royal favour were intended to impress and reaffirm the links between the secular and ecclesiastical hierarchy. Unfortunately, none of our inscriptions survives *in situ*, so we cannot determine how widely they were intended to communicate their

---

[10] '*Memoratio de mercedes commacinorum*', in *Le leggi dei longobardi. Storia, memoria e diritto di un popolo germanico*, ed. C. Azzara and S. Gasparri (Milan, 1992), chap. 7, 221–5. Could '*axis*', that is 'board' or 'plank', refer to the preparation of marble slabs to be inscribed? Nearly all surviving Lombard inscriptions are in marble. On Ursus, see E. Herzig, 'Die Langobardische Fragmente in der Abtei S. Pietro in Ferentillo', *Römische Quartalschrift für christlichen Altertumskunde und für Kirchengeschichte* 20 (1906), 49–81; more recently, Casartelli Novelli, 'Committenza e produzione', 549. Gray, 'Paleography of Latin Inscriptions', nos 30 and 31. On the *magistri marmorari* of the Lombard kingdom, see Everett, 'Literacy', 316–18. On Spoleto's relations with Pavia, see D. Bullough, 'The Writing Office of the Dukes of Spoleto in the Eighth Century', in *The Study of Medieval Records: Essays in Honour of Kathleen Major*, ed. D. Bullough and R. L. Story (Oxford, 1971), 1–21; O. Bertolini, *Roma e i Longobardi* (Rome, 1972), 33–62.

message. Petrucci has argued that the early Middle Ages constituted a rupture in the use of inscriptions as a form of literate communication. For him the ubiquitous presence of writing found in the cities of the Roman Empire was inseparable from the ancient use and appreciation of public space. In the case of Lombard inscriptions, however, we need to consider how a church could have constituted a type of 'public space' that facilitated the display of inscriptions to be read by a more attentive audience – a 'space' that was designated for meditation on the religion of a book, a quiet 'space' where more time might be spent comprehending an inscribed text than a busy street allows.[11]

Two other examples exemplify Liutprand's politico-epigraphic strategy. A damaged verse inscription, now preserved at the Museo Civico in Modena, records how Liutprand established '*securitas*' and '*pax*' in what was formerly a place of dangers. The poem stresses the unity of all people and common purpose in the 'tranquil and flourishing' reign of Liutprand, king of the highest virtue. Although the end of every line is missing, making interpretation difficult, it is usually considered as referring to the foundation of the city of Cittanova, where the inscription was found walled into the façade of the parish church in 1559.[12] Another inscription, recording the king's involvement in the restoration of the church of Santa Mustiola, Chiusi, demonstrates Liutprand's attempt to establish alliances between the duke and bishop of Chiusi and the royal court.[13]

The evidence from Liutprand's reign testifies to royal patronage of epigraphic production to promote the political and ideological concerns of the royal court. It appears as more than a coincidence, therefore, that there is an increase in the number of inscriptions surviving in lapidary form both during

[11] Paul the Deacon describes the palatial church as a '*domicilium*', that is, a place where pilgrims would stay: *Historia Langobardorum*, VI.58. Du Cange, *Glossarium*, III, 163. A. Petrucci, *Public lettering: Script, power and culture* (Chicago and London, 1993), 1–3. For considerations of audience: Everett, 'Literacy', 269–79.

[12] Gray, 'Paleography of Latin Inscriptions', no. 28. Relevant passages for the text following the edition of Strecker, *Poetae*, IV, 723: 'HIC VBI INSIDIAE PRIVS PARABANTVR P[-]| FACTA EST SECVRITAS, VT PAX SERVETV[-]| SIC VIRTUS ALTISSIMI FECIT LONGIBARDO[-]| TEMPORE TRANQUILLI ET FLORENTISSI[-]| OMNES VT VNANIMES INPLENTES PRINC-'. (Letter-height 5.5 cm.).

[13] Gray, 'Paleography of Latin Inscriptions', no. 25. Text given by A. Mai, *Scriptorum Veterum Nova Collectio*, V (Rome, 1831), 144. It is possible that the 'Duke Gregory' mentioned in the inscription was Liutprand's nephew, whom Liutprand later installed as duke of Benevento (732) to stave off possible rebellions, according to Paul the Deacon, *Historia Langobardorum*, VI.55-6. See the comments of S. Gasparri, *I duchi longobardi*, Studi storici, fasc. 109 (Istituto storico italiano per il medio evo, Rome, 1978), 93.

and after his reign. Many more inscriptions of mid-eighth-century date survive, including a group of inscriptions representative of the distinctive 'Lombard' style, those which Gray dubbed the 'Theodota group', after the particularly striking verse epitaph of Theodota.[14] Before turning to the question of sources for Liutprand's involvement with epigraphy, I should like to discuss briefly two examples of the distinctive 'Lombard' style that emerges in Pavia immediately after Liutprand's rule.

The 'Theodota epitaph', inscribed on the top slab of a sarcophagus also using sculptured representations of animals and vegetation, is seen as one of the highlights of Lombard epigraphy in its style, and as the first true example of the 'Pavian school'. It contains a rhythmic inscription in two columns of straight and tall capitals (height 4.5 cm.). The subject of the inscription would appear to be the extremely long-haired Roman girl, Theodota, whom Paul the Deacon mentions as a victim of King Cunincpert's lust. A date of around 750 for the inscription seems acceptable on palaeographical and historical grounds. Theodota's Roman heritage may have been a factor in the design and decoration of the sarcophagus. The poetic epitaph seems to emphasize her *genus Romanum*, and the figurative sculpture of the sarcophagus uses classical and Byzantine pictorial symbols that match the message of Theodota's eternal life after death. The style in which the symbols are portrayed, that of 'static asymmetry', is characteristic of a mature 'Lombard' style that was to predominate in Italy in the late eighth and early ninth century and extend its influence throughout Christian Europe.[15]

The content of the inscription is as interesting as its form. The epitaph was composed by Theodota's disciple, who received her mistress' 'name, office and position' (*(nome)n, dignitatem, Cathetram*), meaning that she became a second abbess Theodota, causing some confusion with the dating. The text itself is not without literary merit. The opening line refers to the art of composition, and in the second half includes a *brevitas* topos, quite wordy in itself. The language of the poem includes some nice classicisms (such as '*caeliculae*') and rhetorical tricks, such as the homonymic play and antithesis in '*tribuendo dapes aegenis dapsiles*', or the use of anthropomorphic

[14] Gray, 'Paleography of Latin Inscriptions', 60–1, nos 43–7.

[15] Panazza, 'Lapidi e sculture', no. 66 (engraving of slab with text). Good colour plates of the sarcophagus in Menis, *I Longobardi*, 311 (VII.16, 17). Full text in Strecker, *Poetae*, IV, 724–5. Though now fragmentary, the full text was, luckily, transcribed by Bossi in 1604, for since then it has had a rough history, including being used as a doorstep for nearly two centuries. Paul the Deacon, *Historia Langobardorum*, V.37: '*puella ex nobilissimo Romanorum genere orta, eleganti corpore et flavis prolixisque capillis pene usque ad pedes decorata*'. The debates over dating are discussed by Gray, 'Paleography of Latin Inscriptions', 74–5. For the stress on Roman origins, cf. lines 12–15. On 'static asymmetry', see C. Sheppard, 'Subtleties of Lombard Marble Sculpture of the Seventh and Eighth Centuries', *Gazette des Beaux-Arts* 63 (1964), 193–206, esp. 198.

Christianisms: 'she nourished the little lambkins in her Lordly flock'. The poem reveals something of her character. The little lambs she 'taught, censured, corrected and loved', giving us the suspicion that she may have been a little harsh: she maintained a 'wrinkled brow, though she was pure of heart with them'. We are relieved to hear that her 'gentle hands refrained from using the whip'.[16]

From the two Theodotas we move to discuss another nun, Cunincperga, '*mater dei ancillarum suavis*', daughter of King Cunincpert and abbess of the monastery of Sant'Agata in Pavia, which was founded by her grandfather King Perctarit (661–2, 672–88), and whose epitaph dates to around 750–60. Her life and deeds are commemorated in an epitaph similar to that of Theodota's in style and layout. The vertical alignment of the final letter of each line, achieved by various uses of suprascript letters and creative ligatures, and near perfect layout of the text in the script-space, betrays careful consideration and planning behind this epigraphical monument prior to its execution in stone, although the smaller letters of the last line (2.5 cm. high, as opposed to 4.4 cm.) cast some doubt on its being perceived as perfectly proportioned.[17] The epitaph, consisting of a rhythmic poem in two columns of eleven lines, is of the '*siste et lege*' or '*titulus loquens*' genre that addresses the reader directly: 'Learn, you, who wish to know what this little tomb covers, and what figure is shut inside this decorative stone'. As in the Theodota epitaph, we learn something of Cunincperga's character, which stresses her likeness to her father in comportment and behaviour. Striking, however, is the description, unparalleled in this period, of her beauty and her features: 'she was of a beauty distinguished amongst other beautiful women, with her serene face, her youthful eyes, her brow innocent of gloom, her lips flowing

---

[16] (*Si ad cursus rerum et praesentis studia saecli│tendatur oratio, multa sunt que possomus dici.*) The topos sounds awkward and stilted, as it often does: see E. R. Curtius, *European Literature and the Latin Middle Ages* (New York, 1953), 487–94.

[17] Panazza, 'Lapidi e sculture', no. 75. Gray, 'Paleography of Latin Inscriptions', no. 45. Colour plate in Menis, *I Longobardi*, 162 (IV.8). Text given in Strecker, *Poetae*, IV, 727. Sant'Agata was part of the same foundation as Santa Maria di Theodota, therefore Cunincperga could have become abbess only after the death of Theodota, see Gray, *ibid*. The contents of the second column are rendered indecipherable by the loss of nearly the whole second half of the slab, leaving only one or two words. The last line of the first column, 'what is witnessed now [i.e. Cunincperga's pious character] in the sacred college of virgins' (*quod testatur modo virginum collegium sacrum*), suggests that the inscription was not originally situated in the monastery, but perhaps in a more prominent and public location. On the history of the slab, which was walled into the entry of the monastery between 1791 and 1823, see Panazza, 'Lapidi e sculture', 264. The creative use of suprascript letters and ligatures, comparable to that found in the dedicatory inscription on the font of Callixtus in Cividale, is well brought out in Gray's illustration of the letter-forms, 'Paleography of Latin Inscriptions', 63.

with honey. She was truly the offspring of her father, the excellent King Cunincpert ...'.[18]

The Theodota and Cunincperga epitaphs are examples of how those associated with the Pavia élite, and whose origins and social positions represent the link between the upper echelons of the secular and ecclesiastical hierarchy in the Lombard capital, were commemorated with the use of the inscribed word. Fragments of similar epitaphs suggest a wider use of such practices.[19] The surviving examples also serve as tangible evidence with which we can imagine the original lapidary form of the lengthy rhythmic inscriptions that come to us in manuscript copies such as those of the *Sylloge Laureshamensis*.

Although these two epitaphs pertain to the mistress and daughter of Liutprand's predecessor, King Cunincpert, they were executed a little after Liutprand's reign and share the type of decoration we see in the Cumianus epitaph. The lingering presence of Cunincpert in these inscriptions, however, serves to highlight the cultural milieu of Pavia in which Liutprand operated and the epigraphic traditions already at work. Cunincpert's reign has the trappings of a rapprochement with the Pavian church and a literary revival. A clear example of both phenomena is the *Carmen de synodo ticinensi*, an anonymously written rhythmic poem which celebrates the conclusion of the Pavian synod of 698 under Cunincpert's direction.[20] Relations between church and state from the inception of the *regnum* appear to have been strained at best, owing to the conflict over Arianism and the Three Chapters dispute. The *Carmen*, however, emphasizes the promotion of orthodoxy by Lombard kings, their responsibility for the spiritual welfare of their subjects, and the direct involvement of Cunincpert in the council. Pierre Riché proclaims the *Carmen* as evidence of 'the reemergence of the court poet'.[21] Liutprand did not convene any church councils, yet the ideology of power found in the *Carmen*, of Old Testament kingship and royal responsibility for the religious orthodoxy of his subjects, is that which we find in Liutprand's legislation and the inscriptions mentioned above, particularly those of Corteolona inscription.[22] The increasing rapprochement between church and state

[18] On descriptions of physical appearance in this period, see P. Squatriti, 'Personal Appearance and Physionomics in Early Medieval Italy', *Journal of Medieval History* 14 (1988), 191–202.

[19] Gray, 'Paleography of Latin Inscriptions', nos 41, 42; Panazza, 'Lapidi e sculture', no. 69.

[20] Bethmann and Waitz (eds), *Scriptores Rerum Langobardicarum et Italicarum*, 189–91.

[21] P. Riché, *Education and Culture in the Barbarian West Sixth through the Eighth Centuries* (Columbia, 1976), 409–10.

[22] See, for example, the prologues of years V (717) and XV and XVI (727, 728), and laws 30, 33, 34, 76, 84, 85, 100, 133, 140, 144; *Notitia de actoribus regis*, c.5. See further, V. F. Ohly, 'Halbbiblische und ausserbiblische typologie', *Settimane* 23

provided rulers such as Cunincpert and Liutprand with access to epigraphic traditions that had been kept alive by the Pavian church.

In the *Sylloge Laureshamensis*, for example, is a group of inscriptions that are associated in diverse ways with the bishop of Pavia, Damianus (d. 711). Damianus' literary skills are attested in other sources, and his own 26-line epitaph in rhythmic meter, itself testimony to the existence of a refined literary culture, praises the bishop as having been the *'gloria vatum'*.[23] Similarly, there are four lengthy inscriptions, three being epitaphs, in rhythmic verse that can be linked to a 'deacon Thomas', most probably the same deacon with clean underpants mentioned by Paul the Deacon as serving under bishop Damianus and who is also mentioned in the *Carmen de synodo ticinensi*.[24] Next to Thomas' epitaph in the manuscript is the long, 29-line epitaph of a certain Baronias, *'custos'* of the church of St Michele in Pavia: Baronias' *'germanus Thomas'* was responsible for the epitaph's composition and the construction of the tomb. The poem begins by beseeching the dead Baronias to help stave off the rustic muse so that the author may compose a poem worthy of Baronias' earned praises. It ends with a 'literary compositional' topos that laments the impossibility of the task.[25]

This Baronias, who is attested in no other source and whom Bognetti and Cattaneo would see as one of several 'Greek missionaries' battling Lombard paganism and heresy alongside bishop Damianus, was responsible for yet another literary and lyrical tomb, that of the 'twice widowed' Columba, a woman of high status in the upper echelons of Lombard society.[26] As with Baronias, we have no other documentation of this elusive 'dove', but like the Baronias epitaph, Columba's addresses the reader and refers to the act of composing verse, and what is more, setting it down on stone:

> whose [Columba's] life, reader, the stone-cutter could scarcely relate to you, jamming his steel chisel against the petty marble, nor could he even touch

(Spoleto, 1976), 429–72, esp. 464 on the use of Solomon.

23   Panazza, 'Lapidi e sculture', no. 61. Text also in Strecker, *Poetae*, IV, 719–20. Paul the Deacon, *Historia Langobardorum*, VI.58: *'liberalibus artibus sufficienter instructus'*. Damianus' anti-monothelist letter to the Sixth Oecumenical Council (680–1) survives: J. P. Migne, *Patrologia Latina*, LXXXVII (Paris, 1863), col. 1259–68. See the comments of Riché, *Education*, 410.

24   Panazza, 'Lapidi e sculture', no. 49; text also given in Strecker, *Poetae*, IV, 722. Paul the Deacon, *Historia Langobardorum*, V.38. The references to Thomas' chastity in both sources (Paul and the epitaph) help confirm the identity.

25   Panazza, 'Lapidi e sculture', no. 52.

26   See G. P. Bognetti, 'S.Maria foris portas di Castelseprio e la storia religiosa dei longobardi', in G. P. Bognetti, *L'età longobarda*, 4 vols (Milan, 1966-8), II, 12–674, at 237 ff.; E. Cattaneo, 'Missionari orientali a Milano nell'età longobarda', *Archivio storico lombardo* 3 (1966), 216–45. Columba: Panazza, 'Lapidi e sculture', no. 50.

upon how she was a mother to those in need, and how the stars shone with her strength and gay voice.

Yet another verse inscription associated with a 'Thomas', which follows on the next folio of the *Sylloge Laureshamensis*, is that written by John, presumably Thomas's nephew. Here the poem indicates its association with depictions (frescoes?) of events from the Apocalypse:

> John, successor to his uncle Thomas and guardian of this venerable church, who completed this holy and beautiful work which the minister of God, Thomas, began with a devoted heart, ordered these little verses to be inscribed. And, reader, if you wish to understand all that has been done (*gesta*), you will find the answers in the wonderful book of Holy John. There you will find indeed what is written concerning how the master revealed to his disciple that which shines forth in the holy atrium.[27]

The interesting reference to the use of text and image together cannot be discussed here.[28] Yet we might note how the inscription has combined four functions: the commemoration of the person initially responsible (Thomas) for the procuring and sponsoring of the art-work; self-advertisement by John for his continuation and completion of the initial work; proclamation of John's responsibility for the *versiculi* that commemorate the completion of the work; and the exhortation to read the scriptures in order to comprehend more deeply the artistic images the reader is viewing.

The epigraphic traditions of the Pavian church evident in the above-mentioned inscriptions continue with the epitaph of Peter, bishop of Pavia (723–37), also preserved in the *Sylloge Laureshamensis*. As with the Damianus group, the long 30-line rhythmic epitaph addresses the reader and uses high literary language (Peter himself receives the epithet '*vates domini*') to commemorate the bishop's life and deeds. More importantly, we learn from the epitaph and Paul the Deacon that Peter was a 'blood-relation' (*consanguineus*) of Liutprand, a family connection which caused Peter's ten-year exile in Spoleto during the reign of Aripert II (701–12).[29] The family connection no doubt further facilitated close relations between church and state in Pavia. Moreover, the connection between the two leaders played its part in Liutprand's awareness of the communicative power of inscriptions to promote the idea of a unified Christian Italy under his rule. Liutprand now

---

[27] Panazza, 'Lapidi e sculture', no. 51.

[28] See Everett, 'Literacy', 297–9.

[29] Panazza, 'Lapidi e sculture', no. 74. The allusion of the epitaph to '*inclitus prosapia regumque stemmata tangens*' is clarified by Paul the Deacon, *Historia Langobardorum*, VI.58: '*qui [Petrus] quia regis erat consanguineus ab Aripert quondam rege aput Spoletium exilio fuerat retrusus*'. For Aripert's treatment of other '*consanguinei*' of Ansprand see: *Historia Langobardorum*, VI.20, 21, 22. Thus Paul does not appear to use '*consanguineus*' as 'brother' with respect to Peter. But see VI.38.

had first-hand relations with the Pavian church in which epigraphic traditions survived and continued to develop under Lombard rule, primarily in the form of funerary monuments.[30]

Liutprand's first known use of the medium to commemorate a member of the laity is the epitaph he commissioned for his father, Ansprand (d. 712), who had been tutor to Cunincpert's son Liutpert (700–1), and after him, to Aripert II (701–12). The epitaph uses similar language to the inscriptions comemorating Pavian churchmen in the *Sylloge Laureshamensis*, stressing Ansprand's wisdom and rhetorical skills (*sermone facundus Adstantibus qui dulcia favi mellis ad instar singulis [–] promebat de pectore verba*).[31] Moreover, the indictional *datio* of the epitaph makes a point of stating when the '*apex regni*' and '*gubernacula gentis*' were passed on to Liutprand.

Gray's comments on the two styles of lettering in this inscription, a mixture of classical forms with the later developments of lettering seen in the Pavian school, brings us to another important consideration.[32] Despite the increase in the number of surviving inscriptions which date to the period of Liutprand's rule or immediately after, Gray's study of the lettering led her to conclude that there was no 'unified style of epigraphy' during his reign.[33] Yet the Ansprand epitaph, with its semi-classical lettering style and border decoration, and the Cumianus epitaph, were clearly tentative steps towards the more homogenous 'Pavian style' that emerged immediately after. The Corteolona and Damianus-group inscriptions that come down to us through the *Sylloge Laureshamensis* were carved within the same epigraphic milieu and doubtlessly shared similar palaeographical and decorative characteristics in their original lapidary form.

I have suggested that Liutprand was responsible for a renewed interest in inscriptions for communicating the ideology of rule in Lombard Italy. Was there also a conscious and deliberate attempt to create an identifiable 'court style' during his reign? The similarities of style amongst the surviving inscriptions, particularly those that date from immediately after Liutprand's reign, suggest a degree of uniformity was required by those who commissioned the works. Such homogeneity, of course, may stem from the patronage of a singular lapidary workshop in Pavia or its environs. The overall similarities in style – the use of poetic diction in rhythmic meters, the accomplished border decoration of vine-scrolls and *grappole*, the inventive

---

[30] Such traditions continued in Pavia under Frankish rule; see the verse epitaph of bishop Theodore (770–85), Panazza, 'Lapidi e sculture', no. 81; see also nos 95–107.

[31] Gray, 'Paleography of Latin Inscriptions', no. 24; Panazza, 'Lapidi e sculture', no. 62. The complete text was transcribed in 1699, but only a fragment of the inscription remains. Note also Paul the Deacon, *Historia Langobarorum*, VI:17.

[32] Gray, 'Paleography of Latin Inscriptions', 65.

[33] Gray, 'Paleography of Latin Inscriptions', 59.

letter-forms and the skilful use of serifs – tend to suggest something more than merely the epigraphic traditions of an artisan's workshop. Moreover, the figure of Liutprand hovers behind so many surviving examples of the 'Theodota group', though often the connection is no more than a tenuous possibility, however plausible. The mysterious 'Queen Raginthruda', who was commemorated with an accomplished epitaph of the above-mentioned style, appears to have been the wife of Hildeprand, Liutprand's nephew and associate king (735–44), though the identification is far from certain.[34] Perhaps in emulation of royal epigraphy in Pavia, the bold Audoald, duke of Liguria (d. 763), was commemorated with a Pavian-style inscription that celebrated his military prowess during the period of Liutprand's reign with Hildeprand as co-regent.[35] Further examples of the royal epigraphic influence emanating outward from the Pavian centre can be seen in Friuli. The font of Callixtus and the Ratchis altar, both furnished with accomplished inscriptions, might both be seen as a result of Liutprand's direct intervention into Friulian ecclesiastical and secular affairs: the king, who strongly supported the election of Callixtus as patriarch of Aquileia, deposed duke Pemmo in 731 for his maltreatment of the patriarch. The young Ratchis perhaps dedicated the altar to his now disgraced father Pemmo in an attempt to restore his father's, and his family's, standing with the Friulian church.[36]

Admittedly these are tenuous connections, but it could be argued that such commissions resulted in part from the appropriation of Liutprand's use of inscriptions as a symbol of power and prestige. An eloquent example of such imitation is the comparison of Duke Arechis to Solomon in the dedicatory inscription in his palace chapel at Salerno. Paul the Deacon probably had Liutprand's Corteolona inscription in mind when he penned the verses for his ducal patron.[37] What remains inexplicable, however, is the

---

[34] Panazza, 'Lapidi e sculture', no. 77. Gray, 'Paleography of Latin Inscriptions', no. 44.

[35] Panazza, 'Lapidi e sculture', no. 80. Gray, 'Paleography of Latin Inscriptions', no. 46, who provides convincing reasons for the dates. See also Everett, 'Literacy', 290–2.

[36] Font of Callixtus: Gray, 'Paleography of Latin Inscriptions', no. 32. Mitchell, 'The display of script', 891–2. Ratchis altar: Gray, no. 27. The latter includes the family name: *Ratchis Hidebohohrit*. Callixtus was made patriarch of Aquileia '*adnitente Liutprando*' (Paul the Deacon, *Historia Langobardorum*, VI.45). Liutprand's intervention in the struggle between Pemmo and Callixtus (*ibid.*, VI.51). See also Gasparri, *I duchi*, 69–71.

[37] '*Regnator tibi, summe decus, trinominis ille | Hebreae gentis Solymis construxit asylum*'. Full text given in K. Neff (ed.), *Die Gedichte des Paulus Diaconus: kritische und erklärende Ausgabe*, Quellen und Untersuchungen zur lateinischen Philologie des Mittelalters 3.4 (Munich, 1908), 18. On the fragment found at San Pietro a Corte, see Mitchell, 'The Display of Script', 895–8; and more fully, M. P. and P. Peduto and M. Romito, 'Chiesa di San Pietro a Corte', *Passeggiate Salernitane* 3

comparative dearth of surviving inscriptions under the later kings, Ratchis (744–9, 756–7), Aistulf (749–56) and Desiderius (757–74), further confirming the impression that the epigraphic revival was limited to the period of Liutprand's reign and therefore a result of a deliberate politico-cultural strategy. Liutprand's close connection with the Pavian church, in which epigraphic traditions were nourished and developed throughout the late seventh and early eighth century, was undoubtedly one source of inspiration for the élites of the royal court to follow. Another source, less immediately discernible, though equally important, was the pervading influence of Italy's ancient epigraphic heritage, the physical presence of surviving inscriptions commemorating Italy's powerful and prestigious imperial past. Italy had already been well and truly 'stamped with inscriptions' by the Romans, and it is surely this Roman precedent that lies behind the final words of Liutprand's Corteolona inscription that I cited at the beginning of this chapter. In his desire 'to decorate the triumphs of his own people' (*proprie gentis cupiens ornare triumphos*), Liutprand had to make his own epigraphic mark.

Acknowledgements
I should like to thank the British School at Rome for a grant in aid of research which enabled me to examine at first hand much of the material mentioned above, and the staff of the British School for their indispensable assistance. I thank also Ross Balzaretti, Tom Brown, John Mitchell, Chris Wickham, and (especially) Rosamond McKitterick, all of whom have heard or read the following (in one guise or another) and offered invaluable advice and criticism. I am also grateful to John Higgitt for his perceptive editorial comments and advice.

(1988), 20–7; P. Peduto, 'Insediamenti longobardi del ducato di Benevento (secc. VI–VIII)', in *Langobardia*, ed. P. Cammarosano and S. Gasparri (Udine, 1990), 307–74, especially 322–6.

Inscriptions on Late Medieval Brasses and Monuments

JEROME BERTRAM

Engraved copper-alloy plates – monumental brasses – and incised stone slabs have been studied extensively in England and by English antiquaries abroad, but remarkably little attention has been given to the wording of the inscriptions, their form, subject-matter and language. The only systematic work done recently by English scholars has been on the lettering, and very interesting results of this work are presented by Sally Badham in the next chapter in this volume.[1] Others have discussed only the information conveyed, in a rather random and anecdotal manner, looking for genealogical or historical evidence, and discussing the wide range of ranks, occupations and trades represented on brasses or incised slabs.[2]

As far as I know, no one in England has ever attempted to analyse the wording of the inscriptions, or to collect a sufficiently comprehensive corpus of material to work from. The only such systematic study I know for the later Middle Ages is on Italian material, and in German, Walter Koch's introductory chapter to a catalogue of all the incised memorial slabs – there are no brasses – in Rome and its surrounding region.[3] For England less material has been systematically published, so I have had to compile my own corpora of medieval memorial inscriptions, for my own native county of Sussex, and my adopted City of Oxford.[4] For both places we have an exceptional amount of information from antiquarian sources on lost

---

[1] See below, pp. 202ff.

[2] See, for instance, A. C. Bouquet, *Church Brasses* (London, 1956), 151–98.

[3] W. Koch, 'Zur Epigraphik der Stadt Rom im späteren Mittelalter', in *Die Mittelalterlichen Grabmäler in Rom and Latium vom 13. bis zum 15. Jahrhundert*, ed. J. Garms, R. Juffinger and B. Ward-Perkins (Rome and Vienna, 1981), I, 25–40.

[4] For brasses in Sussex see C. E. D. Davidson-Houston, 'Sussex Monumental Brasses', *Sussex Archaeological Collections*, 76–80 (Lewes, 1935–9). Incised slabs were recorded by the present writer in *Monumental Brass Society Transactions* 13, pt. 5 (1984), 387–96; other monuments in H. R. Mosse, *The Monumental Effigies of Sussex* (Hove, 1928); Oxford inscriptions in A. Wood, *The City of Oxford*, ed. A. Clark (Oxford, 1881–99) and A. Wood, *The History of the University of Oxford*, ed. J. Gutch (Oxford, 1786). In both areas I have added items from my own observation.

inscriptions, 21 per cent of the recorded Sussex examples and 64 per cent of the Oxford ones being now lost or illegible. Incorporating these data gives us a much more reliable picture of what actually existed, though of course many brasses and slabs have been destroyed without record. The total of known inscriptions is almost the same, 147 in Sussex, and 149 in Oxford, nearly all of them being or having been in brass.

We begin first by looking at the language of these inscriptions. As one might expect, the great majority of those before 1500 are in Latin, with a rather higher preponderance of Latin in Oxford than in Sussex. This is the pattern over most of Europe as far as I can see. Of the inscriptions in Rome and Latium virtually all are in Latin, with only two in French and three in Italian. In Germany, Poland and Central Europe again nearly all are in Latin, although Low German is found on a number of mural tablets in eastern and northern Germany. Only in France is there widespread use of the vernacular from the thirteenth century onwards, and French is also found on the earlier monuments in England as well as Flanders, though English and Flemish also rapidly emerge as common languages for inscriptions.

In Sussex out of a total of 147, 15 inscriptions are in French, dating from the late thirteenth century to 1402. English appears first on an undated inscription of about 1430, and on only three more examples before 1500, after which it rapidly moves to become the majority tongue. There is only one inscription in Flemish in Sussex, on an imported slab at Playden. In Oxford there are only eight French inscriptions, dating from 1273 to 1361, and English does not appear before 1496, only appearing on ten brasses to the end of Queen Mary's reign (1558). Latin is naturally supreme in the academic city, yet of the few English inscriptions as many are on brasses of academics as of townsfolk. Elsewhere in England the pattern seems to be similar to that observed in Sussex.

When we come secondly to look at the wording of these monumental inscriptions, it is immediately clear that the great majority are very simple, giving the minimum of information, and incorporating stock opening and closing formulae. It is in these formulae that we find curiously that English inscriptions differ markedly from those in the rest of Europe, as if there were some European convention on funerary inscriptions to which England was not a signatory.

Walter Koch discovered in Rome three common types: the first beginning *Hic iacet*, the second beginning with the date of death, *Anno Domini ...* and the third with *Hoc est sepulchrum*, but all ending with much the same formula, *cuius anima requiescat in pace*. These three types of opening appear all over Europe, with greater or lesser preponderance. In France nearly all seem to begin *Hic iacet* or in the vernacular *Ici gist*, whereas in Central Europe most of the ones I have seen begin with the date. The Spanish seem to prefer the *Hoc est sepulchrum* variation. The ending *cuius anima in pace requiescat* is common throughout the Continent, though a popular alternative in Germany and Scandanavia is *orate pro anima eius* or *orate pro eo*. In France vernacular inscriptions often end *priez pour l'alme de lui, dieu lui fasse pardon*, or something similar. Exactly the same formulae are found in Outremer, where most incised slabs seem to have inscriptions in French. Flemish inscriptions often end *bidt voer de ziele*.

England stands alone. There are two predominant opening formulae: the most common is the *Hic iacet* which occurs in 60 per cent of simple Latin inscriptions in Oxford, 78 per cent in Sussex. The second is *Orate pro anima*, which is not, as far as I know, ever found as the beginning of a Continental inscription (though it occasionally appears at the end). It is on the whole a later formula; although occasionally found in the early fourteenth century, it is not really popular until the beginning of the sixteenth century, when it becomes normative (figs 45 and 49). Of inscriptions in English, virtually all those in prose begin with *Of your charity pray for the souls* in slight variations (fig. 44).

The closing formula in England is also idiosyncratic, the form *cuius anime (quorum animabus) propicietur Deus* being almost universal from the late thirteenth century onwards (fig. 45 and pl. 68) – rendered in English as *on whose souls may God have mercy* (fig. 44), and in French as *Dieu de sa alme eit merci* (fig. 47). Again, I am not aware of any examples of this formula being used on the Continent, with the significant exception of the English-made brass to an English merchant in Bordeaux. (Only right at the end of the medieval period do German inscriptions adopt the cognate closing formula *der Gott gnedig sei*.) Conversely brasses and slabs of obviously foreign manufacture found in England use the Continental formulae, as at King's Lynn, or Brading; the one lost example of an Oxford inscription ending in *requiescat in pace* (Durham College, 1409) makes one suspicious that here too there may have been an imported memorial, though the solitary Sussex example is on a very early cross-slab of Purbeck marble at Durford Abbey. A very few begin simply *hic iacet* and end with no concluding prayer.

Between the opening and closing formulae the majority of inscriptions simply name the deceased, and give the date of death. Wives or husbands may be named, occasionally an office (*premier mestre de ceste college* at Arundel, 1382); in Oxford more often a degree: *decretorum doctor*, or *baccalaurius in artibus*. In fact of 131 pre-Reformation prose inscriptions in Sussex only 15 give more than the basic information, of 120 in Oxford only 17. Yet this sample seems to include examples typical of such extended inscriptions throughout England.[5]

Among extended inscriptions in Oxford we naturally find information on academic status and benefactions such as *quondam custos istius collegii et de*

---

[5]   E.g. *Eel Buttry su(m)tyme pryores of Campesse* at St Stephen, Norwich (fig. 44).

progenie fundatoris eiusdem collegii et ut fundator praecipuus benefactor ipsius collegii (Merton, 1471). Another switches into English to make sure we know that he *hath stablysyd and founded a perpetuall exhibition for eyght students of this collegge* (Magdalen, 1532). The famous series of five brasses to Ralph Hamsterley, made about 1515, gives us the reasons for the multiple commemoration, naming him in Durham College as a benefactor, and giving the day of his annual obit, on the feast of Saints Gervase and Protase, whereas at Queen's the obit is to be on the feast of St Peter ad Vincula, and in University College it is on the Monday after Trinity Sunday. In Merton he appears with a friend, elected to a fellowship there on the same day.

Among citizens we hear the proud boast of one who was *maior eiusdem villae tempore coronationis regis Richardi secundi* (St Peter le Bailey, 1430 – we must remember that the Mayor of Oxford has the peculiar privilege of presenting a cup to the King at Coronations). A later burgess tells he was *justyce of peas of the cytye of Oxford and for the shyer and eyght tymes mayor of the same cytye* (All Saints, 1545). Very occasionally we hear something of the circumstances of a death: *out of this world by pestilence I had my passage* (St Mary the Virgin, 1507).

Extended inscriptions in Sussex give us some public figures, such as John, Earl of Arundel, appointed warden of the frontiers of Britain by Henry V, and most distinguished in the wars in Gaul and Normandy (1421). Another Arundel figure, who married a Portuguese lady, was Usher of the Chamber to Henry V (1431). The Barttelot family at Stopham like to tell us about their status with the Earls of Arundel. John Barttelot was treasurer of the guesthouse to Thomas, Earl of Arundel (1420); his son was *consul prudens* to successive Earls (1453); and the grandson was described in verse as a Marshall, *hic comitis qui semel fuit aula marchal Arundell* (1462). Notoriously it was the extensive entourage of the Tudor tyrants who most often display their dubious titles: *sumtyme chefe clerke of the kechen to or sovrayn Lord kyng Henry the vijth and Cofferer to or sovrayn lord kyng henry the viijth* (Isfield, 1527 – one of the very few inscriptions which does not incorporate a prayer). A more personal touch is at Bodiam: *qui non litteratus uxorem duxit qua mortua se dedit studio litterali et sacerdocii ordinem suscepit* (1513/4).

Benefactions to churches may be mentioned from the earliest period: Sir William de Etchingham *fecit istam ecclesiam de novo reedificari* (1388). Again it is an obvious advantage to proclaim the benefactions in the vernacular: Sir John de Lewes *tut cest chauncellere fit* at Buxted (early fourteenth century) and Dame Katherine Grey of East Grinstead and her husband *have fowndyd indued and inorned this present churche of Estgrenested to the lawde and honor of God wt dyvers ornamentis and a almesshowse of iij persons* (1505).

One or two of the inscriptions already quoted are in verse: this is a category of some importance, as verse inscriptions, though not common, are usually the most interesting. There are 29 at Oxford, all in Latin, and 13 in

Sussex, in all three languages. A charming Sussex inscription of about 1430 reads:

> Here lyth graven under this stoon
> Christine Savage bothe flessh and boon.
> Robert huyre sone was person heere
> Moore than xxiiij yeere;
> Cryst godys sone born of a mayde
> to Xhristine and Robert huyre sone forsaide
> That owt of this world ben passed us fro,
> graunte thy mercy and to us also. Amen.

French inscriptions tend to be shorter and more direct: at East Lavant on a coffin-lid with cross in relief:

> Priet ki passet par ici
> Pur l'alme Luce de Mildebi.

It is the Latin ones, naturally, that go in for the most involved and fulsome wording. Occasionally they give biographical detail, entangled in the hexameters, as on two sets of verses at Arundel, where John Threel is found to have succeeded John Barttelot in his office:

> Pretulit hospicio me tunc comes ecce Willelmus
> Maryschall officio: sic vadit omnis honor

and his wife also worked at the Castle and was proud of her mistress:

> Hic ancillavi comitissis ante duabus,
> filia prima fuit regis, vocata Beatrix
> Portugallis regno ...

However, most Latin verse inscriptions moralize in general terms, and could be applied to almost anyone. In fact a number of stock verses are found on inscriptions at different dates and in different parts of the country, either used alone or as the opening of a set of specially composed verses. The most popular seems to be 'Quisquis' as follows:

> Quisquis eris qui transieris, sta, perlege, plora
> Sum quod eris, fueramque quod es, pro me, precor, ora.

This appears on brasses of dates ranging throughout the fifteenth century, and Sally Badham has found the same text on incised slabs going back to a much earlier period.[6] A vernacular equivalent in France was on an incised slab at Bonpart of 1317:

> Oes tous qui passez par chi priez diex que ait de moy merchi
> car si comme estes fu, tos seres comme ie suis.[7]

Other common couplets are:

---

[6] For this and related formulae see also R. Favreau, *Épigraphie médiévale*, L'Atelier du médiéviste, 5 (Tournhout, 1997), 158-60.

[7] Oxford, Bodleian Library, Gough Drawings, Gaignières 8, fol. 135r.

> Es testis, Christe, quod non iacet hic lapis iste
> Corpus ut ornetur, sed spiritus ut memoretur.

seen, for example, at Merton College (1420);

> Vermibus hic ponor ut sic ostendere conor
> Et sicut his ponor ponitur omnis honor.

used, for example, on the fifth Hamsterley brass at Oddington, Oxfordshire, c.1515; and

> Hinc tu qui transis, medius, magnus, puer an sis
> Pro me funde preces ut sit mihi veniae spes.

(for example, Wiston, Sussex, 1426). All of these are found with variations, but these seem to be the basic versions. There is a tendency for such inscriptions to be clustered in certain churches, and indeed sometimes more than one stock couplet is found on the same brass.

Oxford, as one might expect, has more expertise in Latin versification, as can be seen in these lines:

> Mors rapit ecce ferox reges proceres populumque,
>   Ex infelici germine progenitos.
> Nam post peccatum surgens in origine mundi
>   Corruit atque perit omnis ubique caro.
> Quum quondam fuerant nobis tunc tempora fixa,
>   Que nunquam potuit ullus abire hominum.

at Merton College, where the inscription wisely switches to prose for the name, John Parsons, and date, 1500. Nevertheless many other verse inscriptions are of poor quality, and most insist on trying to insert the date into the metre, which leads to some very strained prosody.

The date span for Latin hexameters is basically the fifteenth century: in Oxford we find them between 1415 and 1500; in Sussex most date from 1426 to 1465, but there is one very poor eccentric at 1374, and one cut in stone at Lewes to an eleventh-century hermit, though in thirteenth-century script, as well as the well-known slab to Gundrada of 1069, also in Lewes. The same pattern, again, seems to appear over much of England. Hexameter verses come into fashion about the time of Agincourt, and are virtually unknown after 1500, until we come to the Elizabethan revival.

Another important consideration in medieval funerary inscriptions is the prayer formula found in addition to the main inscription, usually on a scroll. This is a common adjunct to figure brasses from the earliest period to the Reformation, and is the exception to the general pattern of predictability. An extraordinary variety of short prayers is found on brasses and slabs, often the only feature on a monument that marks it out from the stock convention. Here my examples are drawn from all over England.

The overwhelming majority of these prayer scrolls are in Latin, and it appears that the principal source for the texts is the Book of Hours or Primer, used extensively by the laity for their daily devotions, so that the phrases would be so familiar as to be immediately available for executor or master mason to quote.[8]

Thus we find, on one brass or another, almost all the antiphons from the Office of the Dead (the *Placebo* and *Dirige* which were a standard feature of all Primers): *Credo videre Deum in terra viventium*, used as response at the end of Lauds and Vespers, and as an antiphon at Matins, at Hinxworth (Hertfordshire) and Terling (Essex). *Delicta iuventutis mee et ignorancias meas ne memineris*, used as the second antiphon of the second nocturn of Matins, at Great Haseley and Stoke Lyne (Oxfordshire), and Burton (Sussex). *Domine secundum actum meum noli me iudicare ...*, the responsory to the sixth lesson of Matins, at Northampton, Exeter, Ulcombe (Kent) and St Albans (Hertfordshire). *Libera me Domine de morte eterna in die illa tremenda*, the response to the ninth lesson of Matins, at Great Haseley. *Miseremini mei, miseremini mei, saltem vos amici miseremini mei*, from the eighth lesson of Matins, at New College and St Aldate's, Oxford. *Miserere mei, Deus, et salve me quia speravi in te*, the response to the seventh lesson of Matins, at Arundel. *Miserere mei Deus secundum magnam misericordiam tuam*, the first psalm of Lauds, at a great many places from 1408 to 1562. *Nunc Christe te petimus, miserere quaesumus*, the responsory after the ninth lesson of Matins, at Slaugham (Sussex), Thame (Oxfordshire) and St Aldate's, Oxford. *Omnis Spiritus laudat Dominum*, the fifth antiphon of Lauds, at Clapham (Sussex). *Timor mortis conturbat me*, the response to the seventh lesson of Matins, at Northleach (Gloucestershire). And the most common of all is the Job text, *Credo quod redemptor meus vivit ...*, which is nearly always found in the form used as the responsory after the first reading from Matins, not in the full scriptural form which appears as the eighth lesson. As well as these texts from the Office of the Dead which we would expect on funerary monuments, we have a selection from the very popular Office of Our Lady, such as:

> Te rogamus te laudamus mater Jesu Christi
> Ut intendas et defendas nos a nece tristi,

the delightful versicle at the end of each Hour of Our Lady, found at St Albans.

Another fruitful source of precatory scrolls is the Litany of Saints, often seen in conjunction with figures of the relevant saints or of the Trinity. Yet other scrolls are from well-known prayers also found in the Primers, such as *Passio Christi conforta me, sanguis Christi salva me*, at Broadwater (Sussex),

---

8   For this whole topic see E. Duffy, *The Stripping of the Altars: Traditional Religion in England c.1400 – c.1580* (Newhaven and London, 1992). The references to the Sarum Primer are taken from *This prymer in Englishe and Laten is newly translated after the Latin texte ...* (Rouen, N. le Roux, 1538); the Bodleian Library's copy is Gough Missals 89 (1).

from the 'Anima Christi', *Jesus, Jesus, esto michi Jesus*, from the 'Jesus Psalter' at Mereworth (Kent), and *Bone Jesu, miserere mei* from the 'Prayer of St Bernadyne' at Great Haseley (Oxfordshire). Doubtless many other such quotations from the regular prayer of the well-educated Catholic laity of late medieval England are to be found, though devotional texts in English are surprisingly rare, even in the last decades of Catholicism.

One final devotional theme in inscriptions is one that has attracted much attention from curious Protestant antiquaries, namely that of offering indulgences. The earliest brass-rubbing we know is among the papers collected for the revision of Camden's *Britannia* in the 1690s; it is of the notorious exaggerated indulgence offer at Macclesfield, Cheshire, collected to illustrate the history of Popery.[9] But nearly all indulgence offers are on the early fourteenth-century inscriptions, and nearly all in French. Thus on our earliest known London-made brass, of 1273, from St Frideswide's Priory we hear *Qui pur lalme priera dis iours de pardon avera* and the same phrase occurs, with steadily increasing numbers of days, at Ore and Winchelsea (Sussex), again in Oxford at All Saints, 1361, and finally in Sussex at Herstmonceux, 1402, where inflation has increased the offer to 120 days, and we are specifically told to pray *devostement Pater et Ave*. Several other inscriptions include the words *Pater Noster – Ave Maria* (for example, Graveney, Kent), and this is not uncommonly found on inscriptions in Normandy, though I have not seen any examples of specific offers of indulgence on the Continent. The nearest we get is an offer of blessing: *de dieu soit de benest qi por lame de li priera amen* at Beaulieu Priory in France, to the niece of King Henry III of England, 1306.[10]

The subject of the wording on European brasses and slabs is one that can lead us into areas yet unexplored, and there are many obvious loose ends. A possible line of investigation is to collate the data to see if there is any connection between the choice of formulae and the source of manufacture, whether particular schools of engraving had their own special texts. For this we need more evidence, and inscriptions in all media need to be collected from a much more representative area, and presented in an accessible form. I suspect that the differences between English and Continental conventions will be maintained, but more subtle differences between nations and regions may well appear. This may help us to allocate unprovenanced inscriptions and provide more specific dating for the many undated examples. For England, the work of collecting memorial inscriptions is comparatively straight-forward, using the comprehensive collection of rubbings of brasses and incised slabs in the library of the Society of Antiquaries of London, although publication still lags far behind the Continent.

9   Oxford, Bodleian Library, Ms. Eng. b 2042, fol. 108a v. See also E. Gibson, *Camden's Britannnia Newly Translated into English with Large Additions and Improvements* (London, 1695), col. 572.
10   Oxford, Bodleian Library, Gough Drawings, Gaignières 8, fol. 118r.

Fig. 44: Monumental brass commemorating Eel Buttry, *ob.* 1545, St Stephen, Norwich.
The figure of the lady is a re-use of a plate produced in the London D workshop *c.*1410,
combined with a Norwich 6 inscription of *c.*1545.

Fig. 45: Monumental brass commemorating William Twaytis, *ob*. 1499, Drinkstone, Suffolk. Typological analysis of the lettering style reveals that this inscription was produced *c.*1525 in the Suffolk 2 workshop in Bury St Edmunds, operational between *c.*1515 and 1534.

Main Group brass lettering *c.* 1270-1350

Basyng series incised lettering *c.* 1285-95

Ashford series incised lettering *c.* 1270-1310

Camoys style incised lettering *c.* 1305-1338

Fig. 46: Lettering styles employed by the London marblers before the Black Death, used for brasses and incised slabs.

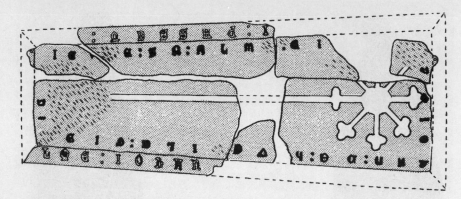

Fig. 47: Purbeck marble relief cross slab to John Havevile, *ob.* 1303–11, Clothall, Hertfordshire. The inscription on the top surface was inlaid with Main Group brass letters, while the inscription on the chamfer was incised in Ashford-style script.

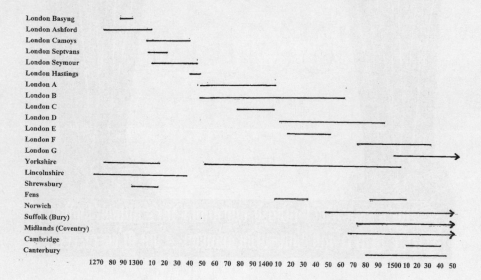

Fig. 48: Operational spans of medieval brass-engraving workshops in England.

Fig. 49: Monumental brass to Richard Howard, *ob.* 1499, with his wife Cecily, at Aylsham, Norfolk, produced in the Norwich 3 workshop. The 'split letter' style of majuscules shown on this brass (see the O, H and C) is also found on contemporary Norwich-produced painted windows and screens.

The Contribution of Epigraphy to the Typological Classification of Medieval English Brasses and Incised Slabs

SALLY BADHAM

The floors of many medieval English churches are paved with monumental slabs; some have incised or relief decoration and others brass inlay, called 'latten' in medieval times, though often the brass has been torn away, leaving only indents showing the outline of the inlays. In total in Britain there are some 7600 extant brasses from the period to 1700 and rather more incised slabs. Many of the latter, particularly cross slabs, do not carry incised inscriptions; the likelihood that they originally had painted inscriptions is suggested by slabs such as the well-preserved late fifteenth-century example at Laughton-en-le-Moor, Yorkshire, which shows a blank prayer scroll round the cross.

Many brasses and incised slabs comprise only an inscription. Wills and other evidence suggests that to those who commissioned them the inscription was probably the most important component after the tombstone itself.[1] Its purpose was to provide assistance to the dead, by soliciting prayers to shorten the time that the deceased was to spend in Purgatory, hence inscriptions such as the stock formula on the c.1400 brass to an unknown civilian in St Mary Redcliffe, Bristol, which reads in translation: 'Thou art witness, O Christ, that this stone is not here laid to adorn the body, but that the soul may be remembered. You who pass by, whether old, middle-aged or youth, make supplication for me that I may attain hope of pardon.'[2] Inscriptions invariably name the person commemorated, so that people know who to pray for, and, from the mid-fourteenth century, the precise date of death is almost always given, presumably to act as a prompt for obits, the anniversary mass when prayers were said for the soul of the person commemorated. This helps to pinpoint the likely date of manufacture, though it is not an infallible guide. Some people prepared their monument in their own lifetime, whereas in the case of others their executors delayed commissioning their monument for some years. However, there is strong evidence, including analysis of Norwich wills by Greenwood to suggest that the majority of monuments in England

[1]   S. Badham, 'Status and Salvation: The Design of Medieval English Brasses and Incised Slabs', *Transactions of the Monumental Brass Society* 15 (1996), 413–65.
[2]   *Ibid.*, 434, fig. 11.

were set up by the anniversary of death.[3] The relative precision with which brasses and incised slabs can thus be dated has proved a tremendous help in establishing typologies and their chronological placement and development.

Systematic stylistic analysis of brasses began in 1949 with Kent's study of military brasses of the period c.1360–1485, in which he identified six pattern series with a national distribution apparently centred on London and a number of other pattern series with a purely regional distribution.[4] His thesis, which has been confirmed by subsequent findings of other writers, was that each of these pattern series represented the output of an individual workshop. Whether the workshop was a single firm producing brasses to a set of stock designs, or whether a group of businesses shared patterns is unclear, but what is crucial is that each workshop had its own distinctive and exclusive patterns. Thus a London Series A knight will not be found with a lady drawn to Series B patterns, or with an inscription in Series C lettering. In the period up to the end of the fifteenth century all components of a brass were always engraved to the designs peculiar to the workshop of origin, though for sixteenth-century London-made brasses several inscription styles are found with figures of one set pattern.

Although Kent adopted a pioneering approach and his work remains the basis of our understanding of the brass-engraving industry in London after the Black Death, he nonetheless adopted what can now be seen as a somewhat narrow perspective. His study examined only the military effigies themselves, using as diagnostic features for analysis the way in which their armour was drawn. He made no attempt, beyond setting out a few general stylistic pointers, to analyse accompanying female figures or inscriptions on the brasses he classified or to look at contemporary brasses of civilians, clerics or academics; that work was largely done by Emmerson and Norris a quarter of a century later.[5] A comprehensive approach to typological classification first emerged in the 1958 examination by Page-Phillips of London-made brasses of c.1535–1612, in which inscriptions were analysed alongside effigial representation.[6] This set the pattern for future typological studies of brasses and incised slabs.

[3]   J. R. Greenwood, 'Wills and Brasses: Some Conclusions from a Norfolk Study', in *Monumental Brasses as Art and History*, ed. J. Bertram (Stroud, 1996), 82–102.

[4]   J. P. C. Kent, 'Monumental Brasses: A New Classification of Military Effigies c.1360–1485', *Journal of the British Archaeological Association* 3rd ser. 12 (1949), 70–97. For an examination of the evolution of typological analysis see M. W. Norris, 'The Analysis of Style in Monumental Brasses', in *Monumental Brasses as Art and History*, ed. Bertram, 103–31.

[5]   R. Emmerson, 'Monumental Brasses: London Design c. 1420–85', *Journal of the British Archaeological Association* 131 (1978), 50–78; M. W. Norris, *Monumental Brasses: The Craft* (London, 1978).

[6]   J. Page-Phillips, *Monumental Brasses: A Sixteenth-Century Workshop* (Monumental Brass Society, Occasional Publication No. 1, 1999).

In essence stylistic analysis is straightforward, involving the grouping of monuments that look the same. Complications arise first in the sheer volume of material to be analysed (identification of the 89 brasses attributed to the Suffolk workshop, for example, required examination of the brasses of 7 counties, well over 1000 items in total) and secondly, in the exercise of judgement as to which features are stylistically significant and which just reflect the fashion of the time. The use of lettering as the most reliable diagnostic feature eliminates the latter difficulty, for lettering on monuments is almost as distinctive as handwriting. Thus, whilst the fashion in the fifteenth century was for inscriptions to be in black letter (formal Gothic minuscule, or *textura*), no two workshops engraved individual letters in exactly the same way, thus enabling us to distinguish between their products. Although only one publication has concentrated solely on the typological analysis of lettering on brasses,[7] analysis of script styles has formed part of most typological studies published since the 1970s. Studies by Badham, Blair, Emmerson, Greenwood and Norris have all have adopted a broadly similar methodology, studying both figure and inscription style, and have reached a very large measure of agreement in their conclusions. Comprehensive typologies have been published for most known regional centres of brass engraving and the London-made brasses up to c.1370 and from c.1420 to 1485. Recently this approach has been extended to include incised slabs produced in the same workshops. Gaps nonetheless remain, notably the brass-engraving London workshops of c.1370 to 1420 and most incised slab workshops, including the important Midlands *ateliers* which produced large numbers of alabaster slabs.

Typological analysis has had a profound influence on the study of brasses and has led over the past couple of decades to important changes in our understanding of them. First, it is an invaluable tool for establishing the provenance and date of previously undated examples. An excellent example of this is Bertram's recent analysis of a tiny inscription in private possession in Oxfordshire giving only the name of the person commemorated, John Whyttyl.[8] Using typological analysis he was able to identify it as a product of Norwich series 4, thus dating between 1505 and 1521. Further work suggested that the inscription most probably came from Felmingham or Hardingham in Norfolk, where other members of the Whitewell family are buried. Secondly, typology can help distinguish brasses where part of the composition is a re-use of an earlier monument, as on Eel Buttry's 1545 brass at St Stephen, Norwich, which combines a London D style lady of c.1410 with a Norwich 6 inscription (fig. 44), and brasses laid down long after the date of death, such as

7   S. Badham, J. Blair and R. Emmerson, *Specimens of Lettering from English Monumental Brasses* (London, 1976).

8   J. Bertram, 'A Monumental Brass at Stonor Park, Oxfordshire', *Antiquaries Journal* 74 (1994), 332–4.

William Twaytis's brass at Drinkstone, Suffolk, dated 1499 but engraved in Suffolk 2 script produced c.1515–34 (fig. 45). Thirdly, and perhaps most importantly, it has thrown important new light on the organization and development of the brass-engraving industry.

Brasses were first produced in England around 1270. In the period before the Black Death brasses generally had inscriptions in Lombardic lettering (Gothic capitals or Uncial). This script, which is composed entirely of majuscule letters, is characterized by rounded forms with swellings and variations in the thickness of lines and closed letter shapes. Although incised slabs of the fourteenth century and before often combined Uncial with Roman letter-forms, this mixture of styles is rarely found on brasses, being limited to lesser workshops, particularly those based in the provinces. On most pre-1340 brasses inscriptions take the form of letters individually inlaid into the slab, usually around the perimeter, and fixed with pitch. This form of fixing was not very secure and out of 800 such slabs recorded so far only a handful have letters remaining *in situ*. Most survive only in indent form, though often the letter indents are sufficiently well-preserved to show their precise shape.

Analysis of these letter shapes by Blair showed that the vast majority of slabs throughout the country used a uniform lettering style, known as Main Group (fig. 46).[9] These letters were cast centrally, in three standard sizes, in a brazier's workshop probably based in London, and were supplied to a range of masons and marblers for assembly into memorials. Most examples of Main Group lettering are found on brasses of evident London design. The common alphabet used without significant modification over a period of some 70–80 years precludes more detailed typological analysis on the basis of the script, though stylistic analysis of other components of the monuments has enabled a series of workshop patterns to be identified. Binski's analysis of figure brasses led to the identification of the Camoys, Septvans, Seymour and Hastings pattern series.[10] Binski and Blair both believed that while some brasses were made in London in the late thirteenth century, production did not become fully established until c.1305. Badham and Norris subsequently linked brasses covered by Binski's analysis with Purbeck marble incised slabs drawn to the same patterns.[11] Some had inscriptions in Main Group brass lettering, whilst others had incised inscriptions; analysis of the latter was crucial in establishing typologies. Changes in the incised inscription style (fig. 46) corresponded with

9   J. Blair, 'English Monumental Brasses before 1350: Types, Patterns and Workshops', in *The Earliest English Brasses*, ed. J. Coales (London, 1987), 133–74.

10 P. Binski, 'The Stylistic Sequence of London Figure Brasses', in *Earliest English Brasses*, ed. Coales, 69–132.

11 S. Badham and M. W. Norris, *Early Incised Slabs and Brasses from the London Marblers*, Reports of Research Committee of the Society of Antiquaries of London, 60 (London, 1999).

changes in effigial style, enabling two additional pattern series, termed the Basyng and Ashford series, to be identified. An important example at Clothall, Hertfordshire, commemorating John de Havevile, *ob.* 1303–11, had two inscriptions, one in indents of Main Group brass lettering and the other incised in the Ashford style script, demonstrating the use of both in a single workshop (fig. 47). Reassessment in the light of the newly established typologies of London-made products led to redating of some brasses, thus providing evidence that brass engraving in the late thirteenth century took place on a larger scale than had previously been believed. It also became clear that, though in the period *c.*1273–1338, the Ashford workshop and then the Camoys workshop dominated the brass and incised slab trade in London, they never established a complete monopoly and had always to operate in competition with one other London supplier and intermittently with regional centres (fig. 48).

Provincial use of Main Group lettering can normally be detected by the unusual composition of the other brass components or the use for the slab of stones other than the Purbeck marble used by the London marblers.[12] In addition Blair identified several Lombardic scripts which differed significantly from the Main Group alphabet, pointing to other workshops which produced their own individually inlaid brass lettering.[13] The Westminster Abbey group, including examples dated between 1268 and 1274, are mainly found in London, with some outliers in Oxfordshire. Another workshop, probably based in Lincoln, produced two series of brasses with distinctive scripts: five examples are known of Lincolnshire A style, dating from 1272 to 1302, and seven examples of Lincolnshire B style, dating from 1308 to the mid-1340s. A group of six slabs and two fragments of brass lettering were probably produced in Shrewsbury in the opening years of the fourteenth century. Other contemporary workshops apparently operated at York, Newcastle, Exeter and Wells, though only a handful of examples from each survive. Overall, the number of regionally made examples is very small compared with the output of the London marblers, particularly after the first decade of the fourteenth century.

The shortcomings of individual-inlay brass lettering probably soon became apparent and from the late 1280s an alternative form of inscription engraved on fillets of brass inlaid round the perimeter of the slab was employed. Initially fillet inscriptions were relatively uncommon, but by the 1340s they largely replaced individually inlaid lettering. About the same time, the Lombardic script was superseded by black letter inscriptions, the earliest examples being on the 1337 brass to Lawrence Seymour at Higham Ferrers, Northamptonshire, and a contemporary commemorative inscription from

[12]   Blair, 'Brasses before 1350', 152–3.
[13]   *Ibid.*, 142–4 and 153–66.

Bisham Abbey preserved on the back of the 1662 brass at Denchworth, Oxfordshire. Black letter was taken from the Gothic book hand and may have been adopted for monumental inscriptions because the letters are tightly packed, thus permitting longer texts (see figs 44, 45 and 49 and pl. 69). The minuscule letters used for most of the text are composed of a series of tightly packed vertical lines or minims, with sharply angular strokes at the top and bottom, often joining the individual letters of a word together. The capital letters used for initials are again notably angular in form and much more elaborate than their Lombardic equivalents, often being decorated with patterns of lines and circles and, in the cases of brasses from the prestigious London workshops, even with faces.

It has long been thought that the Black Death had a devastating effect on the organization of the London brass-engraving industry, but ongoing epigraphic analysis by the present author of mid- and late fourteenth-century brasses has revealed continuity of production, albeit on a reduced scale. London Series A and B, previously thought to have begun c.1358 and c.1360 respectively, can actually both be traced back, mainly through a series of insignificant inscription brasses, to the early 1330s and late 1340s respectively, Series A having developed out of the pre-Black Death Seymour style. By the 1360s, however, the industry had changed its nature, for these workshops no longer produced incised slabs to the same patterns as their brasses. From the late fourteenth century the main suppliers of incised slabs were the Midlands alabasterers, rather than the London marblers, though, as was the case with the London workshops before the Black Death, they faced considerable competition from a proliferation of small regionally based suppliers.

Until the Reformation there were always at least two suppliers of brasses of broadly equal importance based in London (fig. 48). Most pattern series spanned a few decades and probably comprised the brasses produced under the guidance of a single master. Documentary evidence has enabled named masons or marblers to be linked with many of the pattern series and the date of death of these key figures and the end of the pattern series often coincide. There are exceptions to this one series–one master correlation, most notably with Series B and D, which spanned far longer than a working life and to which a succession of masters have been linked.[14] London B was the more prestigious of the two, producing late fourteenth-century brasses to members of the royal family and Richard II's close friends and servants and also engraving fillet inscriptions for cast latten tombs including those for Edward III, the Black Prince and Richard II. London pattern series were very stable and produced monuments which were standardized to an unusually high degree, varying little over the years except to reflect changing patterns of dress. Emmerson demonstrated that near identical letter-forms of majuscule

---

[14]   Emmerson, 'London Design', 65–8.

A, the single most useful diagnostic majuscule letter for fifteenth-century London brasses, can be found on London D brasses engraved fifty years apart.[15]

In the century following the Black Death the London workshops operated with few competitors. Brasses and incised slabs produced by the prestigious Tournai marblers were imported, but are generally limited to ports on the south and eastern coasts and their immediate hinterland. Brass-engraving workshops in York, a major city geographically far from London, operated continuously until the early sixteenth century.[16] A relatively short-lived but important workshop producing brasses and incised slabs operated in Boston from c.1408 to c.1435.[17] The London workshops' near stranglehold on the market continued until the mid-fifteenth century, when a succession of workshops sprang up in regional centres including Norwich,[18] Durham,[19] Coventry,[20] Bury St Edmunds,[21] Boston,[22] Cambridge[23] and Canterbury[24] (fig. 48). These regional workshops mainly had very limited marketing zones, though typological analysis of inscriptions in particular has enabled some far-flung examples to be recognized, including the 1400 Yorkshire series 1 brass to John Danby at Bole, Nottinghamshire, the Cambridge style brass of c.1530 to John and Alice Watson at Leake, North Yorkshire, and Suffolk series 2 brasses dated 1515, 1520 and 1519 at Winthorpe, Ingoldmells and Horncastle, Lincolnshire (pl. 69).

[15]   Badham, Blair and Emmerson, *Specimens*, compare particularly fig. 161 (Dodford 1422) with fig. 174 (Enfield *c.* 1470).

[16]   S. Badham, 'Monumental Brasses: The Development of the York Workshops in the Fourteenth and Fifteenth Centuries', in *Medieval Art and Architecture in the East Riding of Yorkshire*, ed. C. Wilson, British Archaeological Association Conference Transactions 9 (Leeds, 1989), 165–85.

[17]   S. Badham, 'The Fens 1 Series: An Early Fifteenth Century Group of Monumental Brasses and Incised Slabs', *Journal of the British Archaeological Association* 142 (1989), 46–62.

[18]   R. Greenwood and M. Norris, *The Brasses of Norfolk Churches* (Norwich, 1976); M. Norris, *Monumental Brasses: The Memorials* (London, 1977), I, 179–86.

[19]   S. Badham, *Brasses from the North East* (London, 1979).

[20]   Typological analysis of the Coventry workshops by J. Bayliss, based on initial analysis by R. Greenwood, 'Coventry Style Brasses', *Monumental Brass Society Bulletin* 4 (1973), 8, has yet to be published in full, though some of his findings are summarized in P. Cockerham, 'A Sixteenth Century Indent at Hungerton, Leicestershire', *Transactions of the Monumental Brass Society* 14 (1990), 360–72. See also Norris, *The Memorials*, I, 192–5.

[21]   S. Badham, 'The Suffolk School of Brasses', *Transactions of the Monumental Brass Society* 13 (1980), 41–67.

[22]   Badham, *North East*, 21–3.

[23]   R. Greenwood, 'Haines' Cambridge School of Brasses', *Transactions of the Monumental Brass Society* 11 (1971), 2–12.

[24]   Norris, *The Memorials*, I, 187–8.

Most of these regional centres of brass-engraving were of minor significance compared to the London workshops and could sustain only one workshop at any one time. There are only just over 100 known products of the York workshops in a period spanning 150 years; some 90 Bury St Edmunds brasses over an 80-year period; 60 Cambridge brasses produced over 70 years; less than 60 Coventry products in a 110-year span; 35 Boston brasses produced over a total of 50 years; just over 10 Canterbury brasses produced in 20 years; and 5 Durham brasses produced in as many years. Of course, these are not the total output figures, as what survives the theft, iconoclasm and neglect of the centuries is undoubtedly a tiny proportion of the number of brasses originally laid down. The key point is that these figures are small in comparison with the London output. Over 760 effigial brasses alone survive from the London workshops in the period 1420–85. The only regional centre of brass engraving with a very substantial output was Norwich, producing 725 effigial and inscription brasses over a 90-year period. Accordingly, it comes as no surprise that for some of the time there was sufficient demand for two workshops to have operated from Norwich.

All of these regional workshops produced brasses with distinctive styles of lettering and all detailed typological studies of their products have included analysis of the inscription style associated with each pattern series. For most of these, analysis has been limited to an identification of the most diagnostically useful letters and illustration of their forms on successive series from each centre. More detailed analysis to show how the script style developed over time is not possible for most regional workshops, partly because of the relatively small numbers of their products surviving, but also because significantly fewer remain with their inscriptions intact. Many were lost during the Reformation, particularly during Edward VI's reign, when Parliamentary Visitors were appointed to oversee the demolition of superstitious pictures and ornaments in churches. The images of the deceased on brasses often survived because they did not offend Protestant sensibilities, but inscriptions were removed because of their exhortations to pray for the dead, often accompanied by indulgences and other 'Popish practices'. Thus, for example, only 33 of the 59 known Cambridge style brasses and 52 out of 89 known Suffolk style brasses retain their inscriptions.

The Norwich workshops present a different picture. Their large output has already been noted; luckily over 650 of the 725 known examples are in Norfolk, a county where an unusually high proportion of brasses retain their inscriptions. As Greenwood and Norris noted in their authoritative study of Norfolk brasses, it is the abundance of inscriptions that allows Norwich school brasses to be assessed with such precision. Inscriptions from the two most prolific series, Norwich 3, of which 147 examples are known dating between c.1485 and 1507 (fig. 49), and Norwich 6, of which 289 examples are known dating between c.1506 and 1551 (fig. 44), were each divided into four distinct phases of development, permitting even closer dating of previously undated examples.[25]

Finally, the study of epigraphy is also helping to provide an insight into design influences for brasses. The inscriptions of some regionally produced brasses have features which link them to the products of other trades. One such is the Suffolk series 2 brass to Sir Lionel Dymoke, *ob.* 1519, at Horncastle, Lincolnshire (pl. 69). The first two lines of the black letter inscription both begin with a Lombardic initial against a scrollwork rectangle. Lombardic lettering for texts, as opposed to initials, is hardly ever found at this late date, the exception being inscriptions on bells which usually take the form of applied letters in Lombardic script against a decorative background. Evidence suggests that certainly Suffolk series 1 and possibly other Suffolk brasses were produced by bell-founders, thus perhaps explaining the use of Lombardic forms for the initials on the Horncastle brass.[26] Again, the Norwich 3 inscriptions are characterized by 'split-letter' majuscules, seen to advantage on the 1499 cadaver brass at Aylsham, Norfolk (fig. 49), which can also be found on Norwich-made glass, as for example the east window at East Harling painted *c.*1463–80, and locally painted screens and other woodwork such as the *c.*1480 pulpit at Horsham St Faiths. Perhaps this should not be surprising in view of the will evidence discovered by Greenwood that a brass to John Ayleward, *ob.* 1503, of East Harling was to be bought from William Heywood of Norwich, a prominent glazier probably responsible for the East Harling glass.[27] Comparative epigraphy of this sort is an almost unexplored field which, like other aspects of the epigraphy of brasses and incised slabs, would repay further study.[28]

[25] Greenwood and Norris, *The Brasses of Norfolk Churches*, 26–7.

[26] S. Badham and J. Blatchly, 'The Bellfounders Indent at Bury St Edmunds', *Proceedings of the Suffolk Institute of Archaeology and History* 36 (1988), 288–97.

[27] Greenwood and Norris, *The Brasses of Norfolk Churches*, 28.

[28] For more recent work referring to comparisons of epigraphy of brasses with that of other media, see: S. Badham, 'Monumental Brasses and the Black Death: a Reappraisal', *Antiquaries Journal* 80 (2000, forthcoming); J. Bertram, *A Catalogue of Mediæval Inscriptions in the Abbey Church of Dorchester, Oxfordshire* (Oxford, 2000).

The Uses of Masons' Marks and Construction Instructions in Medieval Buildings

JENNIFER S. ALEXANDER

Introduction

The major buildings of medieval western Europe were constructed by an illiterate labour force directed by foremen and master masons whose level of literacy remains unknown. Means of transfer from detailed plans and specifications, equivalent to those of modern building operations, to site workers had to be undertaken in the absence of written instructions.[1] A flexible but secure payment scheme also had to be developed to cope with the fluctuations of the building operation. All these processes operated through a communication system incised on the building stone of most of the major buildings of medieval Europe. The marks, which have been loosely termed 'masons' marks', have been noted for a considerable time but their meaning and purpose eluded the antiquarian writers of the nineteenth century; and it is only in the recent past that more scientific study has revealed the significance of these marks.[2]

---

[1] There is sufficient documentary evidence surviving from European and British buildings to demonstrate that concepts familiar to modern builders, such as elevation drawings, plans and projections, were available in the medieval period, as well as materials prepared for patrons' approval. See, for example, R. Branner, 'Villard de Honnecourt, Reims and the Origin of Gothic Architectural Drawing', *Gazette des Beaux-Arts*, 6th ser., 61 (1963), 129–46; F. Bucher, 'Medieval Architectural Design Methods, 800–1500', *Gesta* 11 (1972), 37–51; N. Coldstream, *Medieval Craftsmen: Masons and Sculptors* (London, 1991); R. Recht (ed.), *Les bâtisseurs des cathédrales gothiques* (Strasbourg, 1989). The question of literacy amongst medieval masons has been considered by Lon Shelby: see L. R. Shelby, 'The Education of Medieval Master Masons', *Medieval Studies* 32 (1970), 1–26; and L. R. Shelby, 'The Geometrical Knowledge of Medieval Master Masons', *Speculum* 47 (1972), 395–421.

[2] R. H. C. Davis, 'A Catalogue of Masons' Marks as an Aid to Architectural History', *Journal of the British Archaeological Association*, 3rd ser., 17 (1954), 43–76; J-L. van Belle, *Nouveau dictionnaire des signes lapidaires: Belgique et nord de la France* (Louvain-la-Neuve, 1994); H. Janse and D. J. de Vries, *Werk en Merk van de Steenhouwer* (Zwolle, 1991). For a bibliography of studies on masons' marks and related subjects see J. S. Alexander, 'Masons' Marks and Stone Bonding', in

Masons' marks can be found on stone buildings from a wide range of periods and places, in which dressed stone has been used in construction. Marks occur on the regular ashlar blocks, either used for the mass of the building, or reserved for specific parts such as windows, doorways or piers, and on moulded stone, and can be found on exterior as well as interior surfaces. Marks are rarely encountered on less finished stonework and none has been recorded on rubble. The marks were cut freehand using a punch or a narrow-edged chisel struck decisively. They normally consist of a series of lines that meet at angles or intersect in geometric patterns, with considerable variety in both the number of lines used and the complexity of their form. Curved line marks, although encountered, are less common, and circles drawn with dividers are known. The number of strokes that make up a mark seems to have been important in the thirteenth century at least, and possibly at other periods as well. Although the stonemasons were unlikely to have been literate, they were clearly numerate and analysis of the format of the marks seems to support their having a numeric basis. In some instances connections can be made between the work of free-stone masons and cutters of inscriptions.

Documentation in England from the period of use of masons' marks is only available from the end of the medieval era and is open to different interpretations, and so one is forced to work backwards from the marks themselves and determine by observation what processes were at work. It can be shown by examination of the marks in their setting that they were used in a number of different ways: to allow correct assembly of complex sections of stonework; or to identify the quarry source, or size of a block; to identify an individual mason's work within the context of a single building project.

There are a number of assumptions, made by certain earlier writers, that still underpin some studies today about the 'meaning' and 'purpose' of the marks. It was thought in the nineteenth century, for example, that marks were specific to individuals and that by compiling inventories of marks from medieval buildings it would be possible to trace the progress of itinerant masons from one building project to another across Europe. This thinking lay behind the antiquarian collecting of masons' marks that was initiated by a number of learned societies and it is an attitude still found today.[3] This theory is very attractive and, if proven, would be a great asset to architectural historians, but there is a fundamental problem. Examination of marks from different sites and dates clearly demonstrates that masons' marks of very similar form occur at all periods. Bronze Age marks from Knossos and thirteenth-century marks from Southwell share the same vocabulary of saltire

The Archaeology of Cathedrals, ed. T. Tatton-Brown and J. Munby, Oxford University Committee for Archaeology Monograph 42 (Oxford, 1996), 219–36.

[3]   For example in A. Erlande-Brandenburg, The Cathedral Builders of the Middle Ages (London, 1995), 99.

crosses, triangle-based shapes and intersecting lines. The simpler marks, and even some of the more complex ones, recur at sites of distinctly different periods and were clearly not unique to specific masons (fig. 50 (e)–(f)).

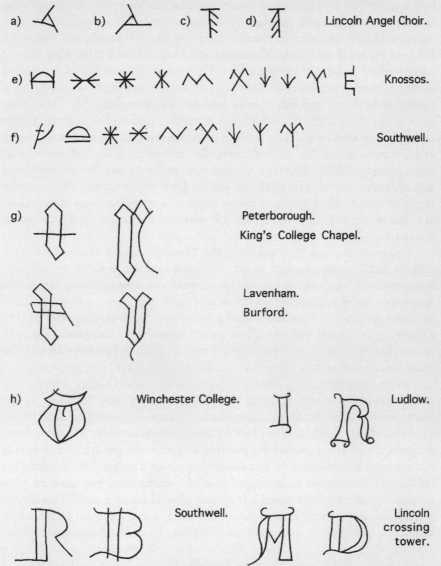

Fig. 50: Masons' marks. Not to scale. (a)–(d) Lincoln Angel Choir, mid 13th century. (e) Knossos, Bronze Age (after Sir Arthur Evans). (f) Southwell Choir, early 13th century. (g) Peterborough, *c.*1496–1509 (after Davis); Cambridge, King's College Chapel, *c.*1447–9; Lavenham, *c.*1523 and Burford, mid 15th century (after Davis). (h) Winchester College, *c.*1437; Ludlow, *c.*1471 (after Davis); Lincoln Cathedral, crossing tower, mid 13th century; Southwell Choir, early 13th century.

The reasons for the repetitions of marks are apparent when their cultural context is established. Masons' marks are a form of non-phonetic writing that stands outside literacy, although the marks clearly have a numeric component, and they belong to the group of signs based on triangles, loops, spirals, comb-forms, zig-zag lines and so on that have acted as property marks throughout the non-literate world.[4] Masons' marks acted as a form of communication accessible to others within a limited context, but they may be compared with the use of symbols to convey more complex ideas, as for example in mathematics. In both the signs are universal, not tied to a particular language, and share the advantage that the repertory of signs need only be quite small.[5] The technology of stone building has remained little changed over time, with only the nineteenth and twentieth centuries seeing important developments in machinery for winning and lifting stone. The manual work of finishing stone, either as ashlar blocks or as sculptured mouldings, capitals and decorative work has always been carried out in a very similar manner. Given this situation it does not require any direct links between stone building projects in different periods or places for the same systems to have evolved in answer to similar practical problems. It would be more surprising if this had not occurred. Masons' marks merely provided a simple and practical solution to a number of problems in building construction. That is not to say that the marks have been used in precisely the same way in the construction of buildings in different regions or from different periods. Each works department would have its preferred way of organizing its labour force and one would expect to find variations in the running of different sites, since they were working independently of each other.

Assembly Marks

Marks were needed when critical sections of stonework were constructed to ensure correct installation of specific stones without the use of written instructions. This scheme used a numbering system that was basically simple but was capable of imparting complex instructions. These assembly marks are similar in both form and function to the carpenters' marks found on roof-trusses and timber-framed buildings and to the marks seen on sectional metalwork, alabaster retables made up of separate panels, stained glass, and on many other objects constructed from separate parts.[6] These marks occur

---

4   A. Gaur, *A History of Writing* (London, 1984), 23–5.

5   This subject is developed in W. C. Brice, 'The Principles of Non-Phonetic Writing', in *Writing without Letters*, ed. W. Haas (Manchester, 1976), 29–44. A twentieth-century example of precisely this use of symbols is the set of a triangle, square, lozenge and circle used on road signs to indicate by-pass routes to lorry drivers.

6   Assembly marks on building timbers are usually found associated with joint beds

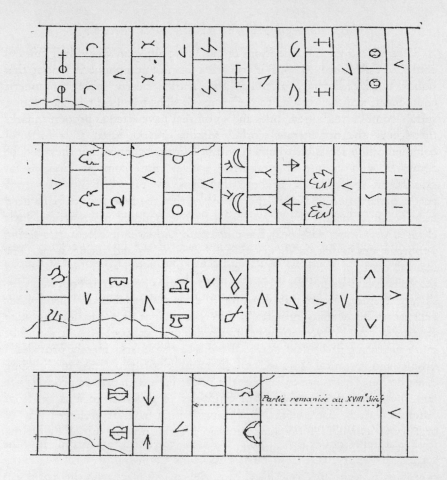

Fig. 51: Assembly marks on the underside of the arches of the bell tower of Saint-Jacques, Reims (after Deneux).

and considerable ingenuity was employed to ensure that prefabricated timbers with similar joints at each end were erected correctly. The marks occur on buildings dated between the twelfth and eighteenth centuries, and were perhaps also used outside this period, and show little variation in form across the period of use. Most of these marks are straight-line marks based on Roman numerals, with some curved marks found. Lettering-derived marks have also been found, used for example in the octagon at Ely as positioning marks. C. A. Hewett, *English Cathedral and Monastic Carpentry* (Chichester, 1985), 117; P. Hoffsummer, 'Les marques de charpentiers dans les toitures de Belgique et du nord de la France. L'apport de la dendrochronologie', *Actes du IXe Colloque International de Glyptographie de Belley* (Braine-le-Château, 1995), 197–234. For details of assembly marks in medieval alabaster retables and stained glass see F. Cheetham, *English Medieval Alabasters* (Oxford, 1984), 24, and H. Wayment, *The Stained Glass of the Church of St. Mary, Fairford, Gloucestershire*, The Society of Antiquaries of London Occasional Papers n.s. 5 (London, 1984), 46–7.

frequently on the moulded stonework of arches, doorways and windows. Restoration work on the tower of the church of St-Jacques in Reims following the First World War revealed a sequence of marks on the underside of the fourteenth-century tower arches where those voussoirs that were made of two stones had the same mark cut into each stone to enable the pairs to be matched up in the construction of the arch (fig. 51). Duplication of marks was encountered on some of the single voussoirs but each pair of stones shared a unique mark.[7]

A commonly found system is one based on a loose version of the Roman numeral system, chosen partly because of the ease of cutting, with adaptations made for particular situations. This can be seen on numerous doorways and windows in parish churches from the medieval period. At St Laurence's church, Ludlow, for example, the inner face of the fifteenth-century west doorway has the voussoirs of its quadrant arch numbered with the Roman numerals I, II, III, IV from the springing of the arch on each side, culminating in V at the keystone and with the addition of 'L' after the numeral for the left side. The door jambs continue the sequence, numbered down from the arch springing, with 'L' used again to denote the left side.[8]

Sections of the main fan-vault at King's College Chapel, Cambridge, are also marked in this way, suggesting that the individual pieces that made up each of the conoids were dry-assembled before installation. A complex system was used which marked the exact location (indicating joints and quadrant of the bay) in which each piece was to be erected. The numbering scheme was based on Roman numerals, with Arabic numerals and symbols employed for the spandrel sections.[9] A similar system was also employed for the thirteenth-century west front portals at Reims Cathedral, to ensure that the portal figure sculptures were installed in the correct places and the marks can still be seen on the plain walling behind the individual figures.[10] Assembly marks were also used on the rib spurs of roof bosses that had to be inserted in a particular orientation for iconographic or sequential reasons and these are sited on the jointing faces. These can be found on dismantled bosses, for example a boss from Thurgarton Priory, Nottinghamshire, with five rib sections emerging has marks surviving on two rib spurs.

---

[7]   H. Deneux, 'Signes lapidaires et épures du XIIIe siècle à la Cathédrale de Reims', *Bulletin Monumental* 84 (1925), 99–130, at 102.

[8]   J. W. Jackson and E. F. Northway, *St Laurence's Church, Ludlow* (Ludlow, 1976).

[9]   W. C. Leedy, *Fan Vaulting: A Study of Form, Technology and Meaning* (London, 1980), 143 and pls 90–1.

[10] Visible, for example, behind the angel's wing in plate 86 of H. Focillon, *The Art of the West*, volume II, Gothic Art (Oxford, 1963). The scheme, which was also used for the sculptures of the archivolt, was deciphered by Deneux in the 1920s: Deneux, 'Signes', 112–19.

A type of assembly mark may be found cut at the edge of one stone and continued across the joint to a second stone. These marks, usually consisting of numbers of straight lines, were made before the stone was used in the structure and ensure precise alignment of critical blocks within courses.[11]

Banker Marks

The majority of marks found are those made by the banker masons working in the lodge who prepared the stone ready for the building masons to use. Marks were needed when a piece-work system was operated to identify an individual mason's work for the paymaster. Evidence for this system can be found in some of the building accounts, such as the contract of 1306 for work at Lincoln, which specified different pay schemes for plain walling and carved stone. The carved work was to be paid for by day and the plain walling by measure. One would therefore expect to find masons' marks on the plain walling built under this contract, the upper parts of the crossing tower, and that is indeed the case. Masons on regular wages would not need to mark the stone and this is what is found at Exeter where very few marks can be seen on the work carried out in the period covered by the fabric accounts that list weekly wages for the masons. Usually it will be seen that not all stones in a given section of walling are marked. This may be due to the use of different systems of payment with some masons on task work. In some cases, for example at Ely in the twelfth century, marks were also placed on the jointing faces of the stones and are therefore not visible.[12]

The Allocation of Masons' Marks

There is no direct evidence from England for the way that marks were allocated to specific masons. It is often assumed that the masons themselves chose their mark and, if it was duplicated, changed it slightly. An alternative explanation is that marks were site-specific and were allocated by the foreman mason at the start of a building project.

There is no evidence for a registration system by which individual masons in England entered their personal marks on a central register, similar to those maintained by heralds for coats of arms, or by civic authorities for merchants' marks.[13] There are also no references to such registers in any of the masons'

---

[11]   Alexander, 'Masons' Marks', 221. Further marks on a stone, that were made before it was dressed to ashlar blocks, could record the quarry source and the size of the whole block, *ibid.*, 221–2.

[12]   *Ibid.*, 219.

[13]   Merchants' marks, which bear a formal resemblance to masons' marks fulfilled a single and very specific function, that is to identify produce once it had left the merchant's warehouse. The marks were widely displayed on tombs, brasses and other monuments, often in a quasi-heraldic form as on the wool-merchants' brasses in Northleach church in the Cotswolds; and seals with these marks are

ordinances which survive from the later medieval period, although they are very specific in other matters and, more importantly, these ordinances do not refer to masons' marks at all.[14] In the absence of a registration system it is not possible to provide direct evidence for the work of specific named masons in England on the basis of the masons' marks.

Scotland on the other hand provides an apparent example of a registration system in the Schaw Statutes of 1598. Amongst other requirements for masons entering a 'lodge' on a building site was that they record their mark in a register held in that lodge. Although the writer of the Statutes, William Schaw, was a practising stonemason, and was at that time principal Master of the Works to the king, the purpose of the Statutes has recently been re-examined and a very different interpretation placed upon them. Stevenson has shown that, while the Statutes may represent a statement of existing practices and, as such, refer directly to medieval site practice in Scotland, they also allowed the masons to achieve independence from burgh authorities and changed the form of the masons' lodge from a purely practical site building into what would later be recognized as the meeting place of the Freemasons. Stevenson has claimed that the Schaw Statutes represent the origins of Freemasonry in Scotland, opening up membership of a trade organization to non-practising individuals of merit.[15] In the light of this, and in the absence of pre Schaw-period registers, the requirement for registration of marks must be seen as a purely symbolic act. This is supported by the evidence of the enactment of the Statutes. Within two years the Edinburgh lodge meeting of 1600, with William Schaw present, admitted Laird John Boswell of Auchinleck who signed his name together with a mark granted to him as a non-functioning 'stone'-mason.[16]

---

known. There is also sufficient documentary evidence from ports in England and Europe to establish that these marks were routinely recorded and merchants can therefore be identified by their marks. Their period of use seems to have been shorter, with most examples dated to between c.1400 and c.1700. F. A. Girling, *English Merchants' Marks* (London, 1964).

[14] It has long been recognized that stonemasons worked outside the guild system, with their training and working practices regulated by other means for the period of the eleventh to the fifteenth centuries, when most of the major building projects were undertaken. These later ordinances may suggest that sufficient masons had become settled in the larger cities by the later medieval period for them to be organized on a guild system but this may not reflect the earlier era. D. Knoop and G. P. Jones, *The Medieval Mason* (Manchester, 1967), 142.

[15] D. Stevenson, *The Origins of Freemasonry: Scotland's Century 1590–1710* (Cambridge, 1988), 26–51.

[16] *Ibid.*, 49. The well-documented Torgau statutes of 1462 and 1563, which regulated stonemasons' activities in Germany and which dealt with the allocation of marks in a practical context, are part of a system that has no parallels in either England or France in this period. For a discussion of this see Alexander, 'Masons' Marks',

The Design of Marks

A certain amount can be inferred about the reasons behind the masons' choice of marks. The number of strokes used to create a mark will help to determine its uniqueness, which can be achieved more easily with a larger rather than a smaller number, but such marks take longer to cut. In order to assess the priority of the medieval masons the banker marks from two thirteenth-century buildings, the choir of Southwell Minster and the Lincoln Cathedral Angel Choir were analysed (fig. 52). In both cases by far the largest number of marks was created from three or four strokes (over twice as many as the next largest category), with two strokes and five also common at Southwell but not at Lincoln. Six-stroke marks were commoner than seven-stroke ones and higher numbers, although encountered, were rare. Southwell produced several high number marks, including one fourteen-stroke mark, but it is clear that speed of execution was of greater importance at both these sites.[17]

The degree of difference between marks that is significant is not completely clear but there are one or two points that emerge, for example the handedness of a mark is not always important. In the case of marks (a) and (b) on fig. 50 the only difference between them is the direction of rotation. When they are plotted in the building, Lincoln Cathedral's Angel Choir, (a) is found more frequently than (b), but they are only ever found close together (on the same window or pier course). The likelihood of two masons with such similar marks preparing stones that were used so closely together in separate parts of the structure seems very remote and it has to be concluded that it is the same mark. Exactly the same situation occurs with marks (c) and (d), where the difference is again one of handedness (fig. 50). Similarly, inverted or reversed versions of marks are commonly found within the same structure, confirming their non-literate basis.

Script-based Marks

Marks resembling script have been recorded at a number of sites from the late medieval period, mostly on buildings constructed in the Perpendicular style, such as the New Work at Peterborough from c.1496 to 1509, or King's College Chapel in Cambridge from c.1447 to 1449. These marks seem to be derived from the Gothic *textura* script and have a strongly angular form with

---

223.

[17] For a detailed analysis of the masons' marks at Lincoln and Southwell, see J. S. Alexander, 'Early Decorated Architecture in the East Midlands c.1250–1300: An Analysis of the Major Building Campaigns', unpublished Ph.D. thesis, Department of Archaeology, Nottingham University (1994); and J. S. Alexander, 'Southwell Minster Choir: The Evidence of the Masons' Marks', in *Southwell and Nottinghamshire: Medieval Art, Architecture and Industry*, ed. J. S. Alexander, British Archaeological Association Conference Transactions 21 (Leeds, 1998), 44-59.

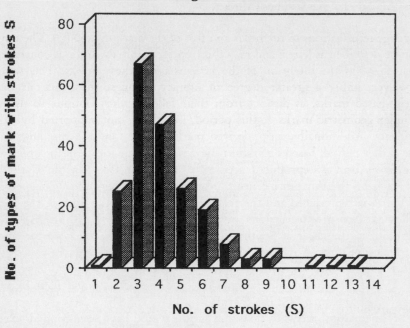

Lincoln Angel Choir masons' marks

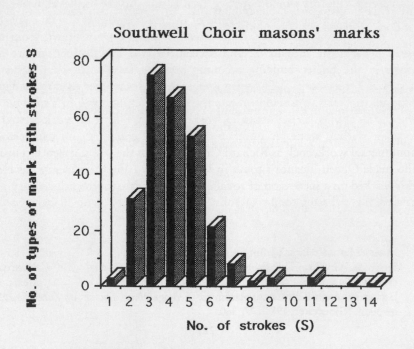

Southwell Choir masons' marks

lozenge terminations to the heads and feet of the mark (fig. 50 (g)). The marks can be described as letters and may thus represent initials; and it is conceivable that this was the intention of the masons using these marks. This would, however, imply a greater degree of literacy amongst those masons using script-based marks, as distinct from their fellows who continue to use the simpler geometric marks at this period, but this is not supported by other evidence. Additionally, script-derived marks can be found in buildings from the earlier period, based on Lombardic script (Gothic capitals). In some cases the letter-form is reproduced accurately, as in the two Lincoln Cathedral marks from the thirteenth-century crossing tower, where the 'V'-shaped bar of the A is reproduced and the relative thicknesses of the lines of the D are followed. Less precise versions are also found, such as the R- and B-derived forms from the choir at Southwell Minster from the second quarter of the thirteenth century. This use of Lombard script continues into the fourteenth and fifteenth centuries, with the letter T found at Winchester College from *c.*1437 and at Bolton Castle from 1378, and the letters I and R at Ludlow parish church from *c.*1471 (fig. 50 (h)).[18]

Stonemasons' access to texts and scripts would have been limited, except in the case of the masons responsible for cutting inscriptions for monumental work, and it seems likely that the script-based marks evolved through contacts between freestone masons and letter-cutters. The attribution of medieval work in stone is a complex problem but the division of stone-cutters into masons and sculptors would not have been familiar in the medieval period. At Exeter Cathedral, for example, several of the masons paid at a higher rate for work on the stone altars in the fourteenth century were drawn from the works department, moving freely between the two, and distinctions are not drawn in the Exeter building accounts between the professional status of carvers and freemasons.[19] The term *imaginator* is sometimes used in medieval accounts to describe a sculptor but the more commonly used *lathomus* or *cementarius* applied to masons who worked on more intricate work as well as on plain walling stone. A number of the royal master masons undertook monumental work, such as Richard Crundale from the late thirteenth century who made Queen Eleanor's tomb in Westminster Abbey, or Henry Yeveley, who worked on a succession of royal castles in the late fourteenth century and ordered the alabaster tombs of John of Gaunt and his wife Blanche in the 1370s.[20]

[18] Davis, 'Masons' Marks'; J. Wood, pers. comm.
[19] See J. A. Givens, 'The Fabric Accounts of Exeter Cathedral as a Record of Medieval Sculptural Practice', *Gesta* 30/2 (1991), 112–18.
[20] J. Harvey, *English Mediaeval Architects: A Biographical Dictionary down to 1550*, rev. edn. (Gloucester, 1984), 77, 360.

Masons who were also letter-cutters are less easy to identify. There is the instance of the eleventh-century tub-font at Little Billing, Northamptonshire, which is inscribed '*Wigberhtus artifex atq(ue) cementarius huic fabricavit ...*' but this is a rare occurrence, or survival.[21] Several masons are known to have been involved with tomb slabs, such as Simon the Mason of York Minster whose wife sold a number of marble slabs after his death in 1322. A second York Minster mason, Robert Patrington, who was master mason at York from 1369, made a series of marble tombs for the Minster and was contracted to make a marble matrix for a brass to a priest and to set up its inscription in 'laton' in 1382. William Hyndeley, who became master mason at York in 1473, very probably was involved in cutting inscriptions since he included in his will, dated 1505, his tools for 'les gravyng in plaite', presumably for engraving brasses.[22] Whilst it would probably be an overstatement to claim that those masons using lettering-derived marks were letter-cutters, it is clearly the case that the two skills were carried out by the same group of craftsmen working in common.

Conclusion

Masons' marks represent a utilitarian form of communication universally used and simple to operate. It arose to meet the specific needs of the stone-building industry and was an essentially pragmatic system that operated outside literacy. In the absence of documentary evidence examination of marks in use in medieval buildings enables the different purposes that these marks served to be elucidated. Although the marks cannot be used to trace the progress of medieval masons from site to site, they can help to shed light on the processes involved in the construction of the major buildings of medieval Europe.

[21]   N. Pevsner, *The Buildings of England, Northamptonshire*, 2nd edn (Harmondsworth, 1973), 351; E. Okasha, *Hand-list of Anglo-Saxon Non-runic Inscriptions* (Cambridge, 1971), 97–8.

[22]   Harvey, *English Mediaeval Architects*, 274, 229, 156.

1 (Tedeschi). Caernarfon, Wales, Segontium Fort Museum, milestone (*RIB*, no. 2263). Reversed D on the third line (Carlo Tedeschi).

2 (Tedeschi). Penmachno, Caernarfonshire, Wales, Parish Church. + C/ARA/VSIVS | HIC IACIT | IN HOC C/ON|GERIES LA|PIDVM (Carlo Tedeschi).

3 (Tedeschi). Llanerfyl, Montgomeryshire, Wales, Parish Church. HIC [IN] | TVM[V]LO IA|CIT : R[V]STE|CE : F/ILIA : PA|TERNINI | ANI XIII : IN | PA(CE) (Carlo Tedeschi).

4 (Tedeschi) (far left). Llangefni, Anglesey, Wales, Parish Church. CVLIDOR | IACIT | ET ORVVITE | MVLIERI | SECVNDI (Carlo Tedeschi).

5 (Tedeschi) (centre). Llangadwaladr, Anglesey, Wales, Parish Church. + CATAMANVS | RE/X SAPIENT/ISI | MVS OPINAT/ISIM | VS OMNIVM RE/G | VM (Carlo Tedeschi).

6 (Tedeschi) (left). Llanfihangel Cwmdw, Breconshire, Wales, Parish Church. CATACVS HIC IACI/T | F/IL/IVS TEGERNACVS (Carlo Tedeschi).

7 (Tedeschi) (far left).
Capel Llanilterne,
Glamorganshire, Wales,
Parish Church.
VENDVMAGLI | HIC
IAC/I/T
(Carlo Tedeschi).

8 (Tedeschi) (centre).
Wareham, Dorset,
England, St Mary's
Church. CATGVG :
C[-] | [FI]LIVS : GIDEO
(Carlo Tedeschi).

9 (Tedeschi) (left).
Llanrhos (Llandudno),
Caernarfonshire, Wales,
Parish Church.
SANC/T|INVS |
SAC/ER|[DO]S
C-T and C-E ligatures.
(Carlo Tedeschi).

10 (Tedeschi) (above). Gwytherin, Denbighshire, Wales, Churchyard. VINNEM/AGLI FILI | SENEM/AGLI Detail with M-A ligatures (Carlo Tedeschi).

11 (Tedeschi) (right). Tregony, Cornwall, Parish Church. NONNITA | ERCIL/IVI | RICATI TRIS F/IL/I | ERCIL/INGI H-shaped Ns, inverted A (first line) and V (second line); 'half-uncial' Gs; F-I and L-I ligatures (Carlo Tedeschi).

12 (Tedeschi). Margam, Glamorganshire, Wales, Margam Abbey Museum. BODVOCI HIC IACIT | F/IL/IVS CATOTIGIRNI | PRONEPVS ETERNAL/I | VEDOMALI Inverted As; horizontal Is; minuscule H; horizontal last stroke in R; F-I and L-I ligatures (Carlo Tedeschi).

13 (Tedeschi). Mathry, Pembrokeshire, Wales, Parish Church. [-] | C/VDICCL | FILIUS | C/ATIC|V/VS Greek letter sigma used instead of S for last letter (Carlo Tedeschi).

14 (Tedeschi). Henllan Amgoed, Carmarthenshire, Wales, Parc y Maen. QVENVENDANI | F/IL/I BARCVNI Minuscule Q; horizontal final Is; As with V-shaped cross-bar; B with separated loops; F-I and L-I ligatures (Carlo Tedeschi).

15 (Tedeschi) (far left). Lundy Island, churchyard. –IGERNI | [–]TIGERNI 'Uncial' E (second line); 'half-uncial' Gs; horizontal final Is (Carlo Tedeschi).

16 (Tedeschi). Whitchurch, Flintshire, Wales, Parish Church. HIC IACI/T MVL/I|ER BONA NOBIL/I A with V-shaped crossbar; trident-shaped M; L-I ligature (Carlo Tedeschi).

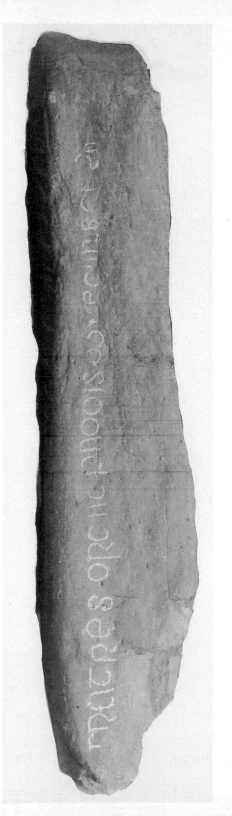

17 (Hamlin). Connor, Co. Antrim: inscribed stone now in Ulster Museum (copyright Ulster Museum).

18 (Hamlin). Kirkinriola, Co. Antrim: slab in St Patrick's Church, Ballymena
(copyright Ann Hamlin).

19 (Hamlin). Clonca, Co. Donegal: damaged stone built into west wall of church
(copyright Ann Hamlin).

20 (Hamlin). Movilla, Co. Down: slab set into wall of Augustinian abbey church
(copyright Ann Hamlin).

21 (Hamlin) (opposite, top). Aghavea, Co. Fermanagh: inscribed stone now in National Museum of Ireland, Dublin (copyright Ann Hamlin).

22 (Hamlin) (opposite, below). Devenish, Co. Fermanagh: recently-recognized fragment (Crown Copyright).

23 (Hamlin) (above). Inishmacsaint, Co. Fermanagh: broken slab with fragment of inscription (Crown Copyright).

24 (Hamlin) (right). Kilcoo I, Co. Fermanagh: slab recently moved into Fermanagh County Museum (Crown Copyright).

25 (Hamlin). Kilcoo II, Co. Fermanagh: broken stone in National Museum of Ireland, Dublin (copyright Ann Hamlin).

26 (Hamlin). White Island, Co. Fermanagh: slab photographed when first found in 1958 (Crown Copyright).

27 (Hamlin). White Island, Co. Fermanagh: slab as set on site (Crown Copyright).

28 (Higgitt). The dedication inscription from Deerhurst, Gloucestershire. Ashmolean Museum, Oxford (copyright Ashmolean Museum, Oxford).

29 (Spurkland). 'Now it's my intention to make you an offer of marriage. Provided that you don't prefer Kolbein.' The oldest concrete documentation of a Norwegian marriage proposal. Rune-stick from Lom (Oslo, Runic Archives A74).

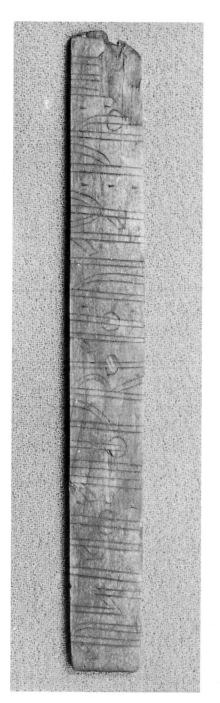 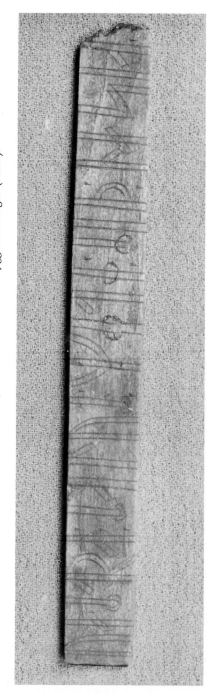

30 (a) (Spurkland). *Ducite discrete vitam, que* … 'Conduct in a sensible way a life which…' (b) *Vestra salus mete sit nescia* … 'May your health be unrestricted'. The two sides of the rune-stick from Bryggen in Bergen (N604).

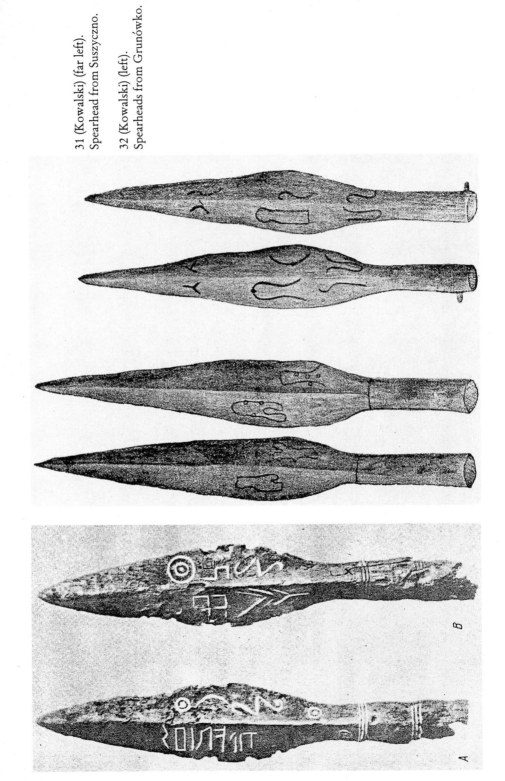

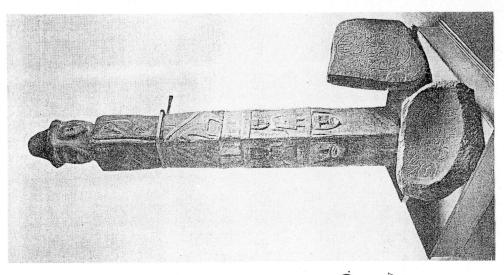

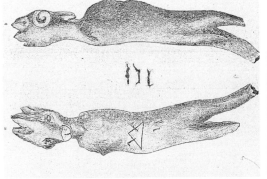

33 (Kowalski) (top left). Bracteate from Wapno.

34 (Kowalski) (left). Medal from Cracow (faces a and b).

35 (Kowalski) (centre, above). Figure from Ostrów Lednicki.

36 (Kowalski) (right). Monument of Światowit and stones from Mikorzyn.

37 (Koch). Tomb inscription of Bishop Agrippinus of Como, from the Baptistery of Sant'Eufemia, Isola Comacina. Church of Sant'Eufemia, Ossuccio, Lago di Como.

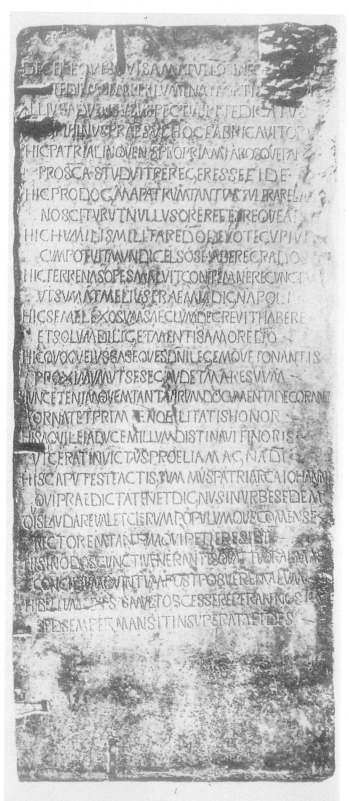

38 (Koch). Tomb-stone of Aldualuhus, Worms. Mainz, Mittelrheinschisches Landesmuseum (copyright Inschriften-Kommission Mainz).

39 (Koch). Tomb-inscription of the subdeacon Ursinianus, Trier
(copyright Rheinisches Landesmuseum).

40 (Koch). Tomb-stone of the priest Badegisel, St Alban in Mainz (after K. F. Bauer).

41 (Koch). Trier Gospels, incipit of St Matthew's gospel. Trier Cathedral, Domschatz Ms. 61, fol. 10r (copyright Prestel Verlag, Munich).

42 (Koch). Inscribed fragment of stone cross from Dewsbury (Yorkshire) now in the British Museum, London (copyright British Museum).

43 (Koch). Pauline Epistles, Würzburg, Universitätsbibliothek, M.p. theol. fol. 69, fol. 35v (after Zimmermann, *Vorkarolingische Miniaturen*).

45 (Koch). Gold plaque found at Brandon, Suffolk, now in the British Museum, London (copyright British Museum).

44 (Koch) Inscribed fragment of stone cross at Hackness, Yorkshire (after Huebner).

HIC REQVIESCIT IN
PACE VIR VENERA
BILES LVDVBERTVS
DE NOBILI GENERE QVI
VIXXIT ANNVS PIVS
MINVS LXV EVIVS DE
POSILIO EIVS EST XVI
KL IIET ONES RESSVS
SCO PETRO TRADE
DIT ET SE CLERICVFECI

VIIIe siècle.

TVMVLVS EROTRVD
EVTHARD PRORRIAGEN
VNS VIXIT RIBVS ETO
TORREAPOSTLINOVENS CAELI
TRNSITVS EROTRVDIS CELE

Pierre. — Haut. 0^m,50; larg. 0^m,73.

48 (Koch) (above). Detail of the Tassilo Chalice, Kremsmünster Abbey (copyright Praehistorisches Staatssammlung, Munich).

46 Koch) (opposite, top). Tomb-slab of Ludubertus from the necropolis of St Matthias in Trier (copyright Inschriften-Kommission Mainz).

47 (Koch) (opposite, below). Tomb-stone of Chrotrudis, Paris, Saint-Germain-des-Prés (after de Guilhermy).

49 (Mitchell). Grave-marker of Teudelas, mid-ninth century, San Vincenzo al Volturno. H. 50 cm., W. 36.5 cm., D. 4.5 cm. (Ben Taylor).

50 (Mitchell). Fragmentary grave-marker with epitaph composed about an incised cross, San Vincenzo al Volturno. H. 8.5 cm., W. 13 cm., D. 2 cm. (Ben Taylor).

51 (Mitchell). Fragment from a grave-marker of a monk with epitaph composed about a cross, San Vincenzo al Volturno. H. 8.1 cm., W. 8.6 cm. (Ben Taylor).

52 (Mitchell). Fragment of a grave-marker with epitaph about a cross, San Vincenzo al Volturno. Dimensions (when complete): H. 22 cm., W. 22.5 cm., D. 5.1 cm. (John Mitchell).

53 (Mitchell). Fragment of a grave-marker with epitaph composed about an incised cross, San Vincenzo al Volturno. H. 7.4 cm., W. 10 cm., D. 1.6 cm. (James Barclay-Brown).

54 (Mitchell). Fragment of a grave-marker with IHV XPI about a cross, San Vincenzo al Volturno. H. 12.5 cm., W. 13 cm., D. 2.5 cm. (Ben Taylor).

55 (Mitchell). Fragment of the grave-marker of Gundelaich and Liutprand, San Vincenzo al Volturno. H. 23.5 cm., W. 42.5 cm., D. 7.8 cm. (Ben Taylor).

56a and 56b (Mitchell). Two fragments of a grave-marker with epitaph about a cross, San Vincenzo al Volturno. H. 11.3 cm., W. 15.2 cm., D. 4.2 cm.; and H. 11.5 cm., W. 15.3 cm., D. 4.2 cm. (Ben Taylor).

57 (Mitchell) (left). Fragment of a grave-marker with epitaph about a cross with the *Dextera Domini* and a lamb, San Vincenzo al Volturno. H. 18 cm., W. 12.5 cm., D. 5.2 cm. (James Barclay-Brown).

58 (Mitchell) (below). Fragment of a grave-marker with epitaph about a cross, San Vincenzo al Volturno. H. 8.7 cm., W. 9.5 cm., D. 2.5 cm. (James Barclay-Brown).

59 (Mitchell). Fragment of a grave-marker with indecipherable epitaph about a cross, San Vincenzo al Volturno. Dimensions: H. 11.7 cm., W. 8 cm., D. 3 cm. (James Barclay-Brown).

60 (Mitchell). Fragment of a grave-marker, San Vincenzo al Volturno. H. 11 cm., W. 14.5 cm., D. 5 cm. (Ben Taylor).

61 (Mitchell). Grave-marker with cross surrounded by apotropaic inscription cut into a re-used floor-tile, San Vincenzo al Volturno. H. 54 cm., W. 38.5 cm., D. 4 cm. (John Mitchell).

62 (Mitchell). Painted cross flanked by an apotropaic inscription at the head of a grave located at the mid-point of the passage beneath the Distinguished Guests' Hall at San Vincenzo al Volturno. Dimensions (of painted panel): H. *c.*45 cm., W. *c.*83 cm. (John Mitchell).

63a and 63b (Mitchell). Two fragments of a grave-marker with the epitaph inscribed on a cross, San Vincenzo al Volturno. H. 21 cm., W. 29.5 cm., D. 4.5 cm.; and H. 15 cm., W. 11.5 cm., D. 4.5 cm. (Ben Taylor).

64 (Mitchell). Grave-marker from Monte Cassino, Abbazia di Montecassino. H. 19.5 cm., W. 13 cm. (James Barclay-Brown).

65 (Mitchell). Grave-marker from S.Salvatore in Brescia. Brescia, Musei Civici di Brescia. Original width: c.104 cm.

66 (Mitchell). Grave-marker of Herebericht. Monkwearmouth, St Peter's Church. H. 104 cm., W. 53 cm., D. 18 cm. (copyright Department of Archaeology, University of Durham; photographer T. Middlemass).

67 (Mitchell). Grave-marker of Hildithryth from Hartlepool. H. 27.9 cm., W. 29.2 cm., D. 14 cm. (Copyright Department of Archaeology, University of Durham; photographer T. Middlemass).

68 (Mitchell). Fragmentary grave-marker of Leobdeih from York Minster. York, Yorkshire Museum. H. 16 cm., W. 26 cm., D. 9.5 cm. (Copyright Department of Archaeology, University of Durham; photographer T. Middlemass).

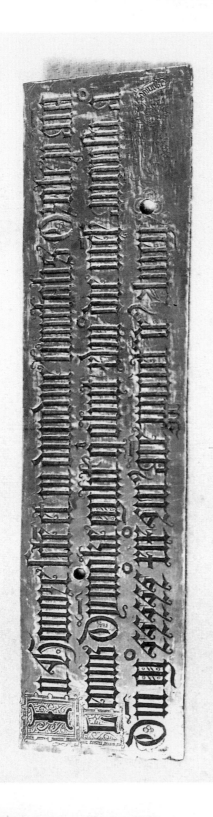

69 (Badham). Inscription from the monumental brass to Sir Lionel Dymoke, *ob.* 1519, Horncastle, Lincolnshire, produced in the Suffolk 2 workshop at Bury St Edmunds. The initials with Lombardic letter-forms at the beginning of the first two lines parallel the form of lettering used on contemporary Bury bells.